KT-502-676

THE ROUGH GUIDE TO
ETHICAL SHOPPING

BY DUNCAN CLARK

ROUGH GUIDES CREDITS

Series editor: Mark Ellingham **Text editor**: Matthew Milton
Design and layout: Duncan Clark **Production**: Julia Bovis
Proofreading: Susannah Wight

PUBLISHING INFORMATION

This first edition published October 2004 by Rough Guides Ltd,
80 Strand, London WC2R 0RL
375 Hudson Street, New York 10014
Email: mail@roughguides.co.uk

Distributed by the Penguin Group
Penguin Books Ltd, 80 Strand, London WC2R 0RL,
Penguin Putnam USA Inc., 375 Hudson Street, New York 10014,
Penguin Books Canada Ltd, 10 Alcorn Avenue, Toronto, Ontario MV4 1E4,
Penguin Books Australia Ltd, PO Box 257, Ringwood, Victoria 3134,
Penguin Books (NZ) Ltd, 182–190 Wairau Road, Auckland 10

Printed in Italy by LegoPrint S.p.A
Typeset in Minion and Trade Gothic to an original design by Duncan Clark

All photographs © Corbis except: p.21, *The Garstang Courier*; p.37,
James Patten; pp.110 and 338, Adrian Arbib; p.127 and 199, Compassion
in World Farming; pp.147 and 149, the Marine Stewardship Council;
p.155, the Fairtrade Foundation; p.158, DK Images; p.167, Day Chocolate
Company; p.182, FARMA; p.185, Abel & Cole; p.214, Ganesha; p.216,
Howies; p.235, *The Chichester Observer*; p.318, Rick Mills; p.323, Daniel
Blackburn; p.325, GoinGreen; p.327 Honda.

The publishers and author have done their best to ensure the accuracy and
currency of all information in The Rough Guide to Ethical Shopping;
however, they can accept no responsibility for any loss or inconvenience
sustained by any reader as a result of its information or advice.
No part of this book may be reproduced in any form without permission
from the publisher except for the quotation of brief passages in reviews.

© Duncan Clark, 2004
384 pages; includes index
A catalogue record for this book is available from the British Library
ISBN 1-84353-265-4

3 5 7 9 8 6 4 2

CONTENTS

PART II : PRODUCTS & COMPANIES

ACKNOWLEDGEMENTS

The author would like to thank the scores of people who have contributed the emails, interviews, information, images, books and advice that made this Rough Guide possible. These have included, in no particular order: Harriet Lamb, Abi Murray and Diana Gayle at the Fairtrade Foundation; Mike Brady at Baby Milk Action; Beverly Mirando at Nestlé; Becky Price at Genewatch; Professor Michael Wilson from Horticulture Research International; Nina Smith at RUGMARK Foundation; Anne Lally at the Fair Labor Association; Mil Niepold at Verité; Wendy Higgins at BUAV; Bernadette Clark at the Marine Conservation Society; The UK Social Investment Forum; Jon Entine; Shelley Simmons at The Body Shop; Oliver Knowles at Greenpeace; Matthew Criddle at Naturesave Insurance; Paul Garrod at Chandni Chowk; Meagan Tudge at Ethically Me; Richard Young at the Soil Association; Sam Maher from Labour Behind the Label; Frances Galvanoni from the Energy Saving Trust; Greg Valerio at CRED; Scott McAusland at EIRIS; Elanor Gordon at *Ethical Consumer*; Kat Alexander at the Ethical Company Organization; Daniel Blackburn at VegOilMotoring; Christine Miles at *The Chichester Observer*; the Garstang Courier; Rick Mills; and many more.

Many thanks also to Jonathan Buckley and Mark Ellingham for believing such an off-the-wall Rough Guide could be a runner; Andy Dickson for persuading me to write a proposal; Matt Milton for superb editorial input under pressure, as well as hours well beyond the call of duty; Joe Staines for picture research and a year of press cuttings; Andrew Lockett for useful comments and patience with last-minute delivery; Pete Buckley for Quartwork. Most of all, thanks to Francesca Panetta for incalculable patience and encouragement.

INTRODUCTION

Ethical shopping – and ethical consumerism in general – is about taking responsibility for your day-to-day impact upon the world. It doesn't mean deluding yourself that shopping can solve all the world's problems, or that the check-out is the new ballot box. And it doesn't mean following a prescriptive list of evil companies and countries that need to be boycotted. It means taking the time to learn a little about how your lifestyle affects people, planet and animals, and making your own decisions about what constitutes an ethical or unethical purchase.

The case for making the effort – laid out further in chapter one – is strong. After all, the things we buy involve us in just about all the pressing issues in the world: not only the conditions in the sweatshop that make our clothes, but everything from the funding of US presidential election campaigns to the hundreds of thousands killed or injured in workplace accidents each year; from the world's dwindling fish stocks to the increase in "natural" disasters partly blamed on the greenhouse-gas emissions of our cars and electricity suppliers; from the long-term sustainability of our farming systems to oppressive governments benefiting from foreign trade. That's not to say all these problems are our fault, of course, or that consumers are in a position to solve them. But we live in an increasingly integrated world, and the implications of our purchases reach far further than we might think.

Where do you start?

Once you start thinking about all the positive and negative implications of what you buy and use, it quickly becomes clear that there's no one-size-fits-all approach – no simple list of moral ticks and crosses. For one thing, there are always conflicting priorities. Is it better, for instance, to support the local independent café round the corner, or buy a fairly traded cup from the global chain across the road? Is it "ethical" to favour local products – doing your bit to limit environmentally harmful transportation – or does that mean harming impoverished countries that are keen to export? Should we boycott goods from countries run by oppressive regimes, or will economic isolation just cause their peoples even more suffering – perhaps even helping the regime stay in power?

It's also difficult to know whose information to trust. Facts get muddled and distorted, and views are thrown at us from such highly partisan sources as transnational companies and transnational single-issue pressure groups (which, some say, have as much interest in exaggerating stories as the big companies have in playing them down). So should we take it seriously when we hear of child slaves assembling our trainers, banks lending our money to arms exporters, or passenger planes frying the climate? Should we trust companies who tell us, "don't worry about it, we have a code of conduct". And what about the arguments that ethical shopping may do more harm than good?

All these unanswered questions are enough to make many people think that to shop ethically is just too much work, and that no choice is really "ethical" if you scrutinize it hard enough. True, we're always going to be compromised by incomplete information, conflicting priorities and the time we have available to think about it all. But an ever growing number of people *are* attempting to be more conscientious in the things they buy and use – at least that's what every new study seems to show. And that's why we've published this book.

About this book

Though it certainly won't provide all the answers, this Rough Guide should help you navigate the often confusing and contradictory world of ethical consumerism. If you're after a list of every high-street brand name with columns for the various types of bad behaviour they're up to, then you'll need to look elsewhere (such as the magazines and books listed in chapter ten). If, however, you want a balanced assessment of issues ranging from organic food to fair-trade clothes, and pointers to companies that have put moral standards at the heart of their operations, then you should find this book useful.

Part I looks at ethical consumerism as a whole: the arguments for and against it, and the various different approaches. Part II gets particular, running through specific products and services, in each case looking at the issues, the debates and the ethical (or supposedly ethical) options. Finally, Part III provides some pointers to where you can read more, and includes tips on doing your own research into a company's practices.

But before moving on to all that, a brief note about the book's title. "Shopping" is used here in the broadest sense: to mean anything you can "shop" for. So expect to find sections on holidays, financial services and electricity supplies – not just all those things you can put in a trolley.

PART I

ISSUES

ETHICAL CONSUMERISM
FIVE APPROACHES
SHOULD WE BUY FROM ...

ETHICAL
CONSUMERISM

SHOULD WE SHOP ETHICALLY?
The cases for and against

Most of this book is concerned with the social and environmental implications of specific products, companies, labels (such as organic or Fairtrade) and approaches to ethically minded shopping. But first of all it's worth asking something more fundamental: is ethical consumerism a good idea? This may sound like a silly question. But, though very few people suggest we should deliberately *ignore* ethical issues when choosing what to buy, many do claim that focusing on them too much is a waste of time – or even counterproductive. Here are the main arguments for and against ethical shopping.

ARGUMENTS FOR

The basic case for ethical shopping, "responsible consumerism", or whatever you want to call it, is very simple – that now more than ever, the things we buy and consume link us to a huge range of social, economic, political and environmental issues. We can choose to ignore this fact if we like, but there's really no denying it.

It's not that you have to be vindictive to "shop unethically". After all, it won't say on the label if an item of clothing has been made in a factory that denies workers the basic right to join a union and bargain for decent pay and conditions. Nor will it say if a piece of furniture is made from wood logged from Indonesia's swiftly disappearing rainforests. But the fact remains: if we buy such products, we support the companies in question and the way they produce their goods. Likewise, if we buy products from the firms which fund politicians – which many of them do (see p.79) – we give our vote to whichever party they're bankrolling.

However, it's not all about the *negative* impacts we make on the world. As most people in the ethical consumerism movement are keen to point out, shopping ethically can make a *positive* difference, too. By supporting progressive businesses, or products bearing labels that testify to their social and environmental credentials, we may help bring about deeper change. CRED jewellery, for example, are a small fair-trade supplier, but they've been integral to the slow ethical awakening of the whole jewellery industry. Similarly, companies specializing in renewable electricity, "green" paints or electric cars are likely to be actively involved in the research and development of eco-friendly products that may gradually enter the mainstream.

Or think of the **Fairtrade** labelling scheme, which aims to ensure that marginalized producers in poor countries – cocoa farmers in West Africa, say – get a bigger

> **❝** *We have to accept that we're born consumers, and the only rational course open to us is responsible, accountable consumerism.* **❞**
>
> Anita Roddick

proportion of the price we pay for their goods, as well as up-front payments and other benefits. The scheme is entirely consumer driven, yet many of its principles are starting to crop up in the policy ideas of parliaments, companies and radical political writers alike. This doesn't mean that ideals of equity and partnership will soon come to be embedded in all global trade (and some people doubt whether that would be a good idea

> **❝** *Buying ethical products sends support directly to progressive companies ... while at the same time depriving others that abuse for profit.* **❞**
>
> *Ethical Consumer* magazine

anyway – more on that later), but it does show that ethical consumers have influenced thinkers of all kinds.

Furthermore, buying socially or environmentally focused products can **raise the profile of issues** that might otherwise be ignored. The very availability of an "ethical" option inevitably gets people thinking, whether it's about the real costs of fossil fuels (in the case of a solar roof) or the environmental and animal-right impacts of intensive agriculture (in the case of organic food).

Finally, on a less ambitious level, considering the implications of what we buy may simply allow us to align our beliefs with our actions – a purely personal aim, but there's nothing wrong with that.

ARGUMENTS AGAINST (AND THE ARGUMENTS AGAINST THEM)

Arguments against the "moralization" of consumerism come from both the reactionary right and the radical left, as well as semantic pedants and good old-fashioned miserable conservatives (who simply grumble that it's all "political correctness gone mad"). The following few pages take a look at the most common objections. Arguments for and against approaches to ethical shopping about specific industries, or types of product, are discussed throughout this book, in the relevant sections.

Nothing's truly "ethical", so why bother?

The argument that no consumer – let alone a producer or product – can be truly, 100%, categorically "ethical" is often given as a reason for not bothering with ethically minded shopping. After all, if it's ethical to, say, choose a car with lower greenhouse emissions, it must be even more ethical to walk instead of drive, to take the stairs rather than the lift, or to only eat raw food to save wasting the energy used in cooking. The logical conclusion, sceptics sometimes revel in pointing out, would be to minimize your negative impact on the world by stopping breathing altogether.

The "e" word is without a shadow of a doubt **subjective**, morally loaded and often problematic. And it's easy to make ethical consumerism sound laughable by taking it to its apparently absurd logical conclusions. But, while you could spend hours arguing over the subjectivity of it all, semantic nit-picking is not really very good grounds for ignoring the effects we have on the rest of the world. And, while we all have our own specific ideas of what should and shouldn't count as "accepted standards", it's probably fair to say that we all aspire to some common ideals. For example: *no* to unnecessary harm to people or the environment; *yes* to the provision of safe, dignified conditions for workers; *no* to hiding the social and environmental implications of a product from the person buying it. It's surely more constructive to ask how these standards can be achieved than to argue over whether or not ethical shopping is an oxymoron.

That said, it's true that you should treat ethical claims with a certain degree of caution until you know exactly what it is they refer to – especially when someone's trying to make money out of them.

A distraction from the real problems?

Ethical consumerism has an love-hate relationship with **the radical left**. Though many dutifully buy their fairly traded bananas, others worry that it is, in its own, well-meaning way, potentially dangerous. After all, while it is usually seen as a progressive, essentially left-wing movement, ethical shopping is still all about buying things. It's a form of **consumer power** (something once described by the *Guardian*'s Larry Elliott as "one of the unintended consequences of the Thatcherite revolution") and it may act as a distraction from engagement with real politics and **the big issues** – such as national and international legislation on tax, equality, climate change and labour and environmental standards enforced by governments and international bodies such as the UN. Writer and activist George Monbiot, for example, claims that this problem has been apparent for years. The greatest failure of the green movement in the 1980s, he once wrote, was the misconception that "we could buy our way out of trouble".

But it's not as if anyone who thinks about ethical shopping is somehow using up all their intellectual energy and will give up engaging in real politics – especially when you consider that many organizations involved in ethical consumerism spend considerable effort raising awareness of broader political issues and campaigning for global, structural change. Fairtrade companies, for example, have long campaigned for a reduction in the the European farm subsidies which make it hard for developing world farmers to compete (see p.18).

> ❝ Because ethical consumerism is based *wholly* on market solutions ... it is incapable even of recognising the *root* cause of that crisis, namely the atomising nature of market society. ❞
>
> Anarchist FAQ Webpage

> ❝ 'Light' green business tends to merely perpetuate the colonisation of the mind, sapping our visions of an alternative and giving the idea that our salvation can be gained through shopping rather than through social struggle. ❞
>
> Christopher and Judith Plant, *Green Business: Hope or Hoax*

That said, some of ethical shopping's advocates do like to hint at the goal of a new "**consumer democracy**", that can deliver where the state and social activism has failed. In this model, the checkout is the new ballot box and "**commercial disobedience**" is the new *civil* disobedience. British writer Noreena Hertz, for example, has written that "In a world in which power increasingly lies in the hands of corporations rather than governments, the most effective way to be political is not to cast one's vote at the ballot box but to do so at the supermarket or at a shareholders meeting."

Such statements (which, it should be said, do not fully reflect Hertz's views), are dangerous – not just because they might discourage political engagement, but also because they're based on a skewed concept of democracy that's heavily weighted in favour of the wealthy. Political democracy is based on the principle of one person one vote, but in a consumer democracy you **vote in hard currency**.

For all this, the sensible response is not to dismiss ethical consumerism; rather, we should simply make sure that we are always aware of its limits and not let it take the place of politics. Some have put it like this: be **ethical citizens** first, and ethical consumers second.

Letting governments off the hook

Another view from the left is that, by pressuring companies rather than politicians, ethical shoppers make it easier for governments to avoid legislating for legally enforceable, across-the-board change. This doesn't apply to to fair-trade companies and other "ethical specialists", but if consumers manage to persuade big firms to introduce **voluntary codes of conduct**, for example, or join **ethical trade bodies**, then politicians can say "we don't need to introduce any new laws or regulations … the corporate sector is already dealing with the problems".

This argument is entirely valid (politicians have indeed sometimes taken this line) but it's not entirely persuasive. For one thing, it's just as logical to suppose that progressive, responsible companies will catalyze new laws and new regulations – by showing that good corporate practice is achievable – than deter them. After all, once a company has committed, say, to only selling wood from sustainable sources, then a law making this a general requirement would actually be in its interest, since the company's competitors would then be forced to play catch-up. So supporting big companies that make voluntary improvements may weaken, rather than strengthen, anti-regulation corporate lobbying.

Furthermore, in reality, **laws can often only go so far**. Much, perhaps most, of the world's labour abuse and environmental damage is already illegal, but it still goes ahead regardless. That's why an increasing number of charities and non-governmental organizations (NGOs) now agree that problems ranging from safety in diamond mines to working hours in clothes factories can only be really solved when governments, NGOs *and* companies are all genuinely committed to change. And companies will never become committed without pressure from consumers.

> ❝ *The purpose of corporate social responsibility is to avoid regulation. It permits governments and the public to believe that compulsory rules are unnecessary, as the same objectives are being met by other means. Of course, the great advantage of voluntary rules is that you can break them whenever they turn out to be inconvenient.* ❞
>
> George Monbiot

Hurting the poor

From the opposite side of the political spectrum comes the opposite criticism: not that ethical consumerism may deter new laws and regulations, but that it might in itself be almost *too much* of a regulation. This argument is based on a strong belief in the **free market** – that if you let **supply and demand** do their thing, it will be in everyone's interest, and anti-market ethical meddling, however well meaning, will simply get in the way.

For example, if coffee prices are low due to oversupply, then we must let the market do its work and force down the number of coffee growers: propping up an unsustainable system via the Fairtrade label is just dragging the problem out. Likewise, if Western consumers demand higher labour standards for workers in poor countries, this will force up the cost of producing in developing world, reducing the number of companies moving their facilities there, and denying

> 66 *The adoption of Western standards would mean that the cost of production in the developing countries increases manifold; this would take away their entire competitive edge.* 99
>
> Ranvir Nayar, *The Indian Express*

people naively described as "exploited" the very jobs they desperately want and need.

Furthermore, the argument goes, if we have patience, the "invisible hand" of the market will eventually improve working conditions: once enough sweatshops and export farms open up in a country, unemployment will drop, the workforce will get better off, and soon the employers will be competing with each other to raise standards and attract staff.

There is certainly some truth in all this but, again, it's not a wholly convincing case. For one thing, it makes little sense to criticize ethical consumerism as being "anti-market". It is, after all, about people making free choices about what they do and don't want, and using their spending power in the marketplace to implement those decisions – practically a textbook definition of how a free market should work. Second, there's quite clearly no such thing as a genuinely free market anyway: all markets exist within a framework of laws (covering everything from monopolies and the minimum wage, to slavery and toxic dumping) and ethical shopping, like voting, is a perfectly valid way of taking a stand about what these laws should be. Third, on the ground level, and especially in poor countries, "free" markets are often in practice hugely distorted, with political corruption and violent threats having far more sway than supply and demand. In many cases, ethical consumerism is helping to limit, not add to, these market distortions – by giving us the option to buy direct from producers, for example.

Despite all this theory, however, it's still a valid question to ask whether well-meaning ethical shoppers may end up doing more harm than good in relation to specific issues, such as third-world labour standards and Fairtrade coffee. These questions are dealt with in the sections on sweatshops (p.51) and Fairtrade (p.23).

WHY NOT ETHICAL THRIFT?

One argument against certain areas of ethical shopping is that they mean **spending extra money** that could be better used elsewhere. Granted, buying organic food lets us support a more responsible farming system that is better both for wildlife, soil fertility and animal welfare – undoubtedly worthy causes. But the problems they address are arguably far less acute than – to pick a random example – the lack of food and essential medicines at any number of the world's refugee camps. As such, how can we justify spending an extra £20 or so each week buying organic food "on ethical grounds", instead of hunting down bargains and giving the money saved to Oxfam or Médecins Sans Frontières? Can conventional agriculture really be so bad that we'll prioritize it over appalling human misery?

Some would say that the answer is that ethical shopping allows us to deal with the structural problems rather than just the symptoms. And that's a fair point – the world needs social and environmental justice as well as charity. But could it also be partly that conscientious consumerism gives us greater "guilt relief" than charity, as it makes us feel at ease with our comparative wealth?

FROM FRINGE TO MAINSTREAM
How big is ethical consumerism?

The impact of ethical shopping is largely down to how many people get involved, so "How many ethical shoppers are there?" is an obvious question to ask. However, this is actually something that's very hard to measure. We can keep tabs on how much people are spending on explicitly "ethical" goods, such as those carrying the Fairtrade label (more than £100 million annually at the time of writing, and rising fast). But it's not so easy to work out what people *aren't* buying on ethical grounds – through **consumer boycotts** – or whether they are favouring some mainstream shops or brands because they suspect they're more ethical than the others.

The only way to gauge it is by asking people, and, as social scientists tend to agree, people often give the answer they feel the questioner wants to hear; or one which reflects their ideals, even though they might rarely actually act on them. In one poll commissioned jointly by *The Guardian* and Toyota, for example, **two-thirds of consumers claimed to make ethical buying decisions**. Yet ethical sales simply don't bear such claims out. Countless reports have suggested that consumers are adamantly against animal-testing for cosmetics, but products bearing the Humane Cosmetics Standard (see p.228), account for less than two percent of UK market.

Even when people are buying "ethical" goods, it's easy to read too much into the figures. Consumers choosing energy-efficient washing machines, say, might be doing it to save money rather than save the planet; or favouring local stores because they're nearer (rather than because they want to take a stand against the supermarkets' oligopolistic control of the food chain). Similarly, millions have said they want to avoid GM foods, and the supermarkets' quick decision to stop selling them is often held up as an example of the power of ethical shoppers. But, arguably, most GM boycotters have done so mainly on the grounds of a perceived health risk, rather than for the wider ethical implications (see p.107).

But if there's one thing we can say for certain, it's that conscientious consumerism as a whole just keeps on growing. Though the ethical share of the total UK market is still valued at less than two percent, and occasionally something suggests a slow-down (such as Oxfam scaling back their fair-trade goods arm at the beginning of 2003), nearly every pointer suggests a clear upward trend. The best guide is the **Ethical Purchasing Index**, which attempts to keep tabs on the whole movement, from boycotts of firms to people opting for public transport

The Ethical Consumerism Report 2003

UK ETHICAL CONSUMERISM IN FIGURES

£19.9 billion ▷ the value of "ethical consumption" in the UK

£6.9 billion ▷ the total spent on "ethical goods and services"

£8.1 billion ▷ the total spent by consumers on ethical financial services

£4.2 billion ▷ the total amount invested in ethical or green funds

£3.9 billion ▷ the total value of deposits placed in banks with ethical policies

£2.6 billion ▷ the cost to companies of ethically driven boycotts

£1.77 billion ▷ the total spent on Fairtrade and organic food

£1.47 billion ▷ the total spent on eco-friendly household cleaners and goods, and energy-efficient appliances

£187 million ▷ the total spent on cosmetics and other "personal items" certified as not tested on animals (less than 2% of total)

£107 million ▷ the total spent on responsible tourism

2/3 ▷ the proportion of people who would never return to a product once they have boycotted it

52% ▷ the proportion of people who claimed to have avoided at least one product on ethical grounds in the last year

40% ▷ the proportion of eggs sold that are free range

40% ▷ the proportion of shoppers who recognise the Fairtrade Mark (see p.18)

5% ▷ the proportion of consumers in the "global watchdogs" category, according to MORI

1–2% ▷ the total market share of ethical goods and services

Sources: Co-operative Bank (Ethical Consumerism Report 2003); *MORI; EIRIS*

over their car on ethical grounds. Since its launch in 1999, the index – updated annually by The **Co-operative Bank** and the New Economics Foundation, and published in the Bank's **Ethical Consumerism Report** – has charted the steep and steady rise of the responsible shopper. According to the most recent figures, the total spending on ethical shopping rose 44 percent, and its market share 30 percent, in the period 1999–2002 (see the box on the previous page for more statistics).

Another report, *Shopping With Attitude*, commissioned by the Co-operative Group supermarkets, found that 60% of respondents were more concerned with ethical issues than they were ten years ago, and 84% are prepared to pay more for ethically produced products (up from 62% in 1994).

Like all such figures, none of these stats should be treated as concrete (the Co-operative Bank accepts that "the full extent of ethical consumerism will always be difficult to gauge, given that it is about the motivation behind a particular purchase as much as the product or service itself"). But they do provide a broad-brush impression of ethical consumer's rise.

Another observation made by just about every relevant survey and poll is that people would *like* to be more active ethical shoppers than they are, but feel held back by a lack of information. Considering that as morally minded consumerism grows more information is becoming available, this suggests a possible snowball-effect growth for ethical shopping in the not-too-distant future.

> 66 *In order to make an ethical choice, consumers wanted the full facts about the make-up of the different products on offer. But three quarters (76 per cent) said they were being kept in the dark ... they were hungry for information.* 99
>
> Co-operative Group, *Shopping With Attitude*

FIVE APPROACHES

Every consumer area has its own "ethical approaches", from investment screening in financial services to organics in the world of food. There are scores of similar examples, most of which you'll find discussed in the relevant sections of this book. However, there are also more general approaches that cut across the whole field of ethical shopping: concepts such as "fair-trade", boycotts and simply buying less. This chapter takes a look at five of the most important.

#1: FAIR-TRADE
How does it work? How "fair" is it?

There are various approaches to fair-trade, and even more various terms to describe them. For instance, "fair" is sometimes substituted with "**alternative**", "**responsible**" or "**ethical**" – perhaps on the grounds that no business arrangement between rich consumers and poor producers can ever be entirely fair. Other organizations prefer the term "community trade", to emphasize how their version of the idea aims to support local communities. And then there are are different levels of formality, from officially certified products bearing the Fairtrade Mark, to uncertified goods whose ethical credentials are based mainly on trust (more on these two systems below).

But, for all this, the basic idea remains the same: a business model that aims to **improve the livelihoods of poor and marginalized workers** in the developing world. As most consumers understand it, this simply means paying producers – whether they be farmers, plantation workers, manufacturers or craftspeople – more money for their goods. And it's true that dealing directly with suppliers and paying them a decent price for their work is a key fair-trade principle. But this isn't the end of the story. Fair-trade also aims to **empower producers** by – among other things – encouraging them to form democratically run co-operatives. And it means making **up-front payments** and **long-term trading arrangements**, to save producers relying on potentially crippling loans and to enable them to plan ahead.

In return, the suppliers are expected to produce goods of a very high **quality** and ensure that the **environment** is properly cared for. All in all, the exchange is based on partnership and co-operation, rather than straightforward buying power.

As well as making a direct difference to producers, the fair-trade movement also aims to improve things beyond its immediate sphere of influence. And this seems to work. You wonder, for example, whether without fair-trade's existence, company-specific initiatives (such as Chiquita's "Better Banana" initiative and Starbucks' "Commitment to Origins"), however imperfect they may be, would ever have happened at all.

What's wrong with "normal trade"?

The fair-trade movement aims to re-connect producers with consumers, and ensure a better deal for the former. There are a whole

FAIR-TRADE DEFINED

The closest thing to an official definition of fair-trade has come from FINE, an association of four international organizations:

F ▷ **Fairtrade Labelling Organizations International** ▷ www.fairtrade.net

I ▷ **International Federation for Alternative Trade** ▷ www.ifat.org

N ▷ **Network of European World Shops** ▷ www.worldshops.org

E ▷ **European Fair Trade Association** ▷ www.eftafairtrades.org

THE DEFINITION

"Fair-trade is a trading partnership, based on dialogue, transparency and respect, which seeks greater equity in international trade. It contributes to sustainable development by offering better trading conditions to, and securing the rights of, marginalised producers and workers – especially in the South.

Fair-trade organisations (backed by consumers) are engaged actively in supporting producers, awareness raising and in campaigning for changes in the rules and practices of conventional international trade."

THE GOALS

▷ **To improve the livelihoods** and well being of producers by improving market access, strengthening producer organisations, paying a better price and providing continuity in the trading relationship.

▷ **To promote development** opportunities for disadvantaged producers, especially women and indigenous people and to protect children from exploitation in the production process.

▷ **To raise awareness** among consumers of the negative effects on producers of international trade so that they exercise their purchasing power positively.

▷ **To set an example** of partnership in trade through dialogue, transparency and respect.

▷ **To campaign for changes** in the rules and practice of conventional international trade.

▷ **To protect human rights** by promoting social justice, sound environmental practices and economic security.

host of reasons why this is necessary, but one of them is that under current world trade rules, things often seem distinctly skewed in favour of rich countries. This is what organizations such as Oxfam (with their "Make Trade Fair" campaign) have been trying to publicize over the last years or two.

One issue is **import tariffs**. At the moment, for a poor producer to sell their goods in the UK, they often face duties that are four times higher than those paid by producers in rich countries. This is estimated by trade justice campaigners to cost poor nations around twice as much as they receive in aid: $100 billion annually. And, in the agricultural sector, the tariffs are usually higher on "processed" goods (tinned fruit, say, rather than fresh fruit), which locks poor producers into selling raw commodities while the West benefits from lucrative processing, where most of the profit is made.

A second problem is **Western farm subsidies**: the EU spends around half its total budget – tens of billions of pounds – subsidizing its own farmers to produce and export agricultural goods, making it very difficult for poor countries to compete. Take sugar: though few people realize it, we subsidize British farmers to grow sugar in Yorkshire and East Anglia, while poor African and Caribbean farmers are desperate to sell us their crops. After numerous wranglings at the World Trade Organization, Western farm subsidies are now due to be phased out, but at the time of writing no timetable for this has been agreed.

One aim of fair-trade, then, is to help producers in the developing world overcome these kinds of barriers.

THE FAIRTRADE MARK

Though the concept of fair-trade has been around much longer than the formal **labelling and certification system** – which first emerged in Holland in the 1980s, in response to plummeting international coffee prices – this "official" system now dominates the fair-trade world.

So how does it work? Basically, any product bearing the label, or "Mark", has been traded according to a set of **internationally agreed** standards (more on these below) and the supply chain has been **audited** to make sure that the rules are being stuck to. It's important to note that Fairtrade is **not a brand or a company**, but a certification system.

Almost uniquely among comparable schemes, the Fairtrade system isn't funded by the producers. Other than a small percentage of grants and donations, the price of administration and certification are passed on to the licensee of the Mark – the specific coffee brand, for instance – which ultimately passes it on to the consumer or absorbs it in reduced profits. This system allows the economically marginalized to get involved without requiring up-front capital, which can be a problem

The Fairtrade Mark, administered in the UK by the Fairtrade Foundation, was changed in 2003 from a large "F" to the yin-yang-esque symbol shown above. Though people often see one or the other, the symbol shows both a man holding up his arm in solidarity, and a landscape with a road going forward.

with other ethically driven schemes – organic food being one example.

From its niche origins, the Fairtrade Mark has undeniably become part of mainstream British culture, with two in five adults now familiar with the label. Since the first product bearing the Mark was launched in the UK – Green & Black's Maya Gold organic chocolate, in 1994 – sales of Fairtrade-labelled retail products have climbed to £100 million a year, and continue to rise steeply. In the case of roast and ground **coffee**, they account for around 15% of the total market.

At the other end of the chain, nearly a million producers and their dependants, in more than 40 countries, are benefiting from the system, and (though food and drink is still the focus) there is an ever-growing range of products available. There are now even "**Fairtrade towns**" proudly being declared all over the UK (see p.21).

The standards

Unlike with organic foods, say, where the "rules" are very general, each new product certified under the Fairtrade system gets its own specific criteria, since each raises a different mix of problems and priorities. But there are certain core ideas that apply to all products. Fairtrade traders must:

▷ Pay a price to producers that covers the costs of **sustainable production and living**

▷ Pay a "premium" that producers can invest in **development**

▷ Make partial **advance payments** when requested by producers

▷ Sign **contracts** that allow for long-term planning and sustainable production practices

Behind these core ideas there are two underlying sets of standards. One covers crops such as coffee and cocoa, mostly grown by **small-scale independent producers**, and is primarily concerned with ensuring that farmers in "democratic and participative" co-operatives receive a decent and stable minimum price for their crops, rather than being left to ruthless middlemen and the fluctuating prices of the world commodity markets. The other set of standards is for crops such as tea, which are largely produced on estates; it focuses mainly on issues such as the **pay and conditions** of the workers, the right to form unions, health and safety, child labour, and so on.

> ❝ *Proper economic prices should be fixed not at the lowest possible level, but at a level sufficient to provide producers with proper nutritional and other standards.* ❞
>
> John Maynard Keynes, 1944

As well as these minimum trading requirements, Fairtrade bodies also have a set of not-quite-mandatory "**process requirements**". These encourage producer organizations to invest continuously in improving environmental sustainability, working conditions and product quality.

FAIRTRADE TOWNS

The small town of **Garstang**, near Lancaster, may not be a familiar name. But in 2000, it created a place for itself in the history books by becoming the world's first Fairtrade town. Right back in 1995, just a year after the Fairtrade Mark was launched in the UK, the tireless Garstang Oxfam Group were out on the streets doing their own version of the Pepsi Challenge – the Cafédirect challenge – showing punters that Fairtrade coffee was good for the tastebuds as well as social justice. Five years of campaigning later, the town was Fairtrade crazy, and the council, the government and the Fairtrade Foundation all agreed that it should become "the world's first Fairtrade town".

Soon after, the Fairtrade Foundation drew up a set of goals for anyone wanting to achieve **Fairtrade status** for their local town, city or zone. These include the local council committing itself to promoting awareness of the Fairtrade Mark, and a range of Fairtrade products being readily available in local shops and cafés. Scores of regions, towns and zones are now on the list, which takes in major cities such as Liverpool (London is in the process of getting there) as well as an island (the aptly named Fair Isle). The Archbishop of Wales is even involved in a campaign to try and create the first Fairtrade country. And a similar scheme has also been established for Fairtrade **schools**, **universities** and **churches**. But no one can match the tireless folks of Garstang, who are now twinned with a cocoa-producing town in Ghana, and organize regular exchanges for adults and children.

Picture supplied by *The Garstang Courier*

If you fancy trying to convert your own town or zone, download the *Fairtrade Town Goals and Action Guide* from: www.farirtrade.org.uk

BETTER LEFT TO THE MARKET?

Few people argue against the aims of fair-trade, but some free-marketeers have made a case against one aspect of the system. They claim that, by offering a minimum-price guarantee to, say, coffee and cocoa farmers, fair-traders are interfering with the market, and this, they claim, may do more harm than good. So is this true?

As touched on in chapter one, the idea that fair-trade is anti-market is on one level quite odd: no one is forcing the consumers, traders or suppliers to play by these rules; no one is manipulating fair-trade supply and demand. Indeed, in many ways you could see this as less of a distorted free market than the equivalent non-fair-trade goods: there is almost no fair-trade **advertising**, after all, and the direct links with producers aims to cut out middlemen who can genuinely distort the operation of a fair market by exploiting a monopoly over delivery equipment – or even the straightforward use of force. What the people who make this case are promoting, then, is not exactly a free market, but a specific (and rather "unfree") version of it in which low price is the only consideration consumers are allowed to consider important.

That said, the argument does raise a legitimate question: if people buy a "fairly traded" product, might this not reduce the demand for the non-fair-trade alternative, depressing prices and forcing uncertified producers to plumb even lower depths of bad working conditions to stay afloat?

In a market where supply and demand are pretty much balanced, this argument simply doesn't stand up: if half the shoppers start purchasing fairly traded mangoes, and half the producers start producing them, then the remaining half of the market still has the same balance of supply and demand as before, and hence the price they receive shouldn't be affected. However, things are different for products where supply *does* exceed demand, such as the market for coffee. As discussed on p.159, the most serious problem currently faced by coffee farmers is low price caused by massive **oversupply**. Ultimately, if there is oversupply, the free-marketeers argue, there must be too many producers. So, unless consumers start altruistically doubling their caffeine intake, the problem will only really be resolved when some coffee farmers stop producing and start diversifying into other crops. Fair-trade, they claim, can only get in the way of this essential market mechanism by propping up the inefficient producers.

As usual, the issues are not quite as simple as the free-market fundamentalists make out. True, it's essential that more coffee farmers diversify into other crops to reduce oversupply. But which farmers are best equipped to do this? According to the Harriet Lamb of the Fairtrade Foundation, diversification is often easier for those currently supplying Fairtrade coffee than for those who aren't: after all, they are likely to have access to more **capital, advice and support**. Furthermore, for as long as farmers are getting paid very low amounts for their products, the only response open to them will be to try and produce even more than before – hence fanning the flames of oversupply – until their reserves of money and energy are exhausted, at which point diversification may be less likely than starvation. And, indeed, many thousands of farmers and their children have died as a result of being left to the free market.

There are ways, of course, to support marginalized farmers and encourage diversification without "interfering with the market" namely through financial and other types of **support from governments** and individuals. But all these things require people to be aware of the issues, and there can be little doubt that the Fairtrade scheme has done a pretty amazing job at getting Western consumers thinking about something as far removed from their lives as the plight of equatorial coffee farmers.

But even if this were not the case, there would be a more fundamental question: if some farmers are going to have to go out of business, which of them should we do our best to save from this unfortunate fate? Or, put another way, which trade model do we want to survive? The first one (non-fair-trade) offers the potential for the lowest price and cheapest production, but might mean poor wages and substandard health and safety for farmers and farm workers; child labour and even slave labour (such as the 1000 enslaved coffee farmers set free in Brazil in 2003); environmental and therefore also economic sustainability sacrificed to short-term crop maximization; and large companies winning over smaller players as their deep pockets allow them to support their operations through the economic winter. The other option is a system in which the market is allowed to play out but within a set of minimum standards: small farmers paid a minimum price upfront, allowing them to invest without relying on debt; importers audited to ensure no bullying or malpractice is going on; transparency and redistribution ensured; and the environment cared for. Fair-trade provides consumers with a free-market-style choice between these two options.

Who's in charge?

After having grown independently in different countries, the Fairtrade system become internationally unified in the late 1990s, with the establishment of the **Fairtrade Labelling Organizations International** (FLO). This body is now ultimately responsible for defining the standards and for certifying that accredited products really are produced in accordance with them. To do this, it works "with a network of independent inspectors that regularly visit all producer organisations", and implements a trade auditing system which "checks that every Fairtrade-labelled product sold to a consumer has indeed been produced by a certified producer organisation".

Based in Bonn (Germany is very much at the heart of ethical consumerism), the FLO comprises a membership of so-called National Initiatives – eighteen at the time of writing – which implement the FLO system on the country level. The UK's body is the London-based **Fairtrade Foundation**, originally set up by CAFOD, Christian Aid, Oxfam, Traidcraft Exchange and the World Development Movement – with a little help later on from the Women's Institute.

For more info on the organizations, standards and so on, see:

FLO International www.fairtrade.net
Fairtrade Foundation www.fairtrade.org.uk

Beyond food

Though "unofficial" fair-trade covers a wide range of goods, you'll currently find the official Fairtrade label only on foods (see p.167 to get an idea of the range of products available) plus one or two other products such as, bizarrely enough, **footballs** and **roses**. The reason for the focus on food and drinks is partly historical – as already mentioned, the labelling scheme was set up as a response to the coffee crisis – but it's also practical. While it's relatively easy to define a set of clear criteria for a specific crop, the same isn't true of many other goods. The supply chain for an item of clothing, for example, is highly convoluted, taking in cotton or wool farmers, synthetic fabric and thread factories, weavers, dyers, various levels of subcontracted cutters and garment-workers, and a whole host of people distributing between these groups.

Despite all this, we can expect to see the Fairtrade Mark on many more non-food goods in the not-too-distant future. Work is already underway to agree Fairtrade standards for **cotton products**, and from there the sky's the limit. Handicrafts and precious metals and stones are all possibilities. Considering the problems that exist in the rubber industry, the head of the Fairtrade Foundation told Rough Guides, at some stage we might even see **Fairtrade condoms**.

Beyond the third world?

Despite the fact that the Fairtrade label is appearing on an ever-wider selection of goods, one parameter likely to remain is the focus on products from the developing world. The organizers recognize that some small-scale producers and farmers in **rich countries** suffer many of the same problems as those in the third world, but they have decided – after consultation with Fairtrade consumers – that the system should focus on "absolute poverty" rather than the "relative poverty" found in countries in the West. This was the reason why the idea – floated back in 2003 – to market Fairtrade **organic food** grown in the UK never finally took off. But now the UK organics movement has decided to set up it's own "ethically traded" label (see p.157).

FAIR-TRADE WITHOUT THE MARK

Unlike those bearing the Mark, these goods are not necessarily certified or traded according to any single set standards. So anyone can theoretically slap "fairly traded" on their products without adhering to any specific international code. As such, it sometimes all seems to be entirely based on trust. The VeganLine website, for example, at the time of writing describes its T-shirts as "said to be made in fair working conditions by the Nepalese exporter". Such statements, though admirably honest, don't wholeheartedly inspire confidence in the integrity of unlabelled fair-trade. Indeed, they seem oddly similar to the ethical assertions of most transnational companies such as Nike – which, though never calling itself a fair-trade company, claims to ensure all its workers receive a "fair wage". So can we trust a self-declared "fairly trade" item to be what it says it is?

IFAT & BAFTS

Speak to those in the fair-trade movement, and they'll tell you that we shouldn't worry too much about people trying to pull the organic wool over our eyes. For one thing, the majority of unlabelled fair-trade goods are produced, imported and sold by groups who are members of respected fair-trade organizations, the most important being **IFAT**: the **International Federation for Alternative Trade**.

To join IFAT, producer groups have to undertake an extensive self-assessment programme according to the core IFAT principles, and be open to random spot-checks to ensure they are sticking to their plan. Importers have to undergo a similar process and have to have fair-trade as their primary focus. Similarly, shops specializing in fair-trade goods are usually members of the **BAFTS – British Association for Fairtrade Shops** – which keeps a carefully vetted directory of approved importers and is itself a member of IFAT (for a list of BAFTS shops, see p.349).

In any case, much of the importing and selling is done by trusted groups who have been around for longer than the Fairtrade Mark and were, in fact, central to its establishment. Perhaps the best-known example is **Traidcraft**, a faith-based (Christian) organization set up in 1979 with the sole aim of combating poverty through trade.

Unfortunately, however, there's still no way for shoppers to tell what is and what isn't produced by an IFAT member. The Association recently launched the **FTO (Fair Trade Organizations) logo**, which member groups can use on their promotional material. But there's nothing that appears on the actual products. Discussion is now underway about the introduction of a product label, but it remains to be seen whether this will happen and, if it does, whether it will be a completely separate one from the Fairtrade Mark we're already familiar with.

Either way, it would certainly help introduce a new level of trustability to the system. In the mean time, if you do wonder about the legitimacy of a "fairly traded" product that doesn't bear the Mark, try asking the retailer whether it comes from an IFAT-approved supplier, or whether the shop is a member of BAFTS. If they can give you an informed response, then there's no need to worry. After all, fair-trade "scams" are pretty well unheard of – there are easier ways to make a fast buck than trying to con ethical consumers.

For more on IFAT or BAFTS, see:

IFAT www.ifat.org
BAFTS www.bafts.org.uk

To confuse things further, the Soil Association recently launched its own "Ethical Trade" label for English-grown organic produce (see p.157), while a number of big businesses are taking part in the Ethical Trading Initiative – a project to improve conditions among their developing world suppliers (see box on pp.68–69).

#2: BOYCOTTS
Bashing the bad guys

The idea of punitively refusing to do business with a particular person, company or country is nothing new. The term dates from the late nineteenth century (**Charles C Boycott** was a land agent in Ireland who, after ignoring calls for lower rents, found himself shunned by mailmen, servants, shopkeepers and others) and boycott organizers since then have included the likes of **Mahatma Gandhi**, whose *swadeshi* campaign encouraged the rejection of British goods in favour of local self-sufficiency. However, the idea of shoppers taking part in national or worldwide boycotts in response to problems which don't affect them directly is a more recent phenomenon. It first really took off in the 1970s and 1980s with calls for consumers to avoid companies doing business in apartheid **South Africa**, and **Nestlé** for its irresponsible promotion of baby milk products in the third world.

Today, boycotts are perhaps the most widely understood approach to ethical consumerism, aimed not just at companies and countries but also at types of products, such as prawns, mahogany and GM food (all discussed later in this book). Though it's impossible to measure accurately, it is estimated that the value of goods boycotted on ethical grounds – by UK shoppers alone – is between two and three billion pounds per year.

Do boycotts work?

People would probably still want to boycott companies, governments and products they find morally reprehensible even if they doubted they could make much of a difference. But, in theory at least, a boycott can be a powerful force for change if enough people get involved: the moment a company thinks that improving its behaviour is more profitable than not doing so, it will opt for reform. After all, directors have a legal duty to their shareholders to take the path of maximum profits, even if it means swallowing their pride. And, in an era of "brand value", companies are so keen to avoid negative publicity that they might capitulate even if a boycott isn't currently making much difference to their bottom line.

In practice, of course, it's actually very difficult to tell how effective boycotts are. For one thing, rather like the invariably wildly contrasting attendance numbers given by police and organizers after a political demonstration, the targets and practitioners of consumer boycotts tend to have very different views on their impact. A case in point is the **StopEsso** campaign (see p.318). The organizers' website claims at the time of writing that one million people don't buy Esso petrol on ethical grounds, but, as *The Observer* reported, the oil giant disagrees: "The Stop Esso campaign … has not affected our fuel sales." The company does seem to have gradually shifted its position on global warming since the boycott kicked in, though they deny this has had anything to do with the boycott.

Likewise with **Nestlé**, who for more than a quarter of a century have suffered a high-profile international boycott on the grounds of their alleged advertising of formula milk in the developing world (see p.172 for more details on this particular case). While the campaigners claim that the company has still not cleaned up its act, they acknowledge that things have improved. But the extent to which this has anything to do with the boycott is debated. Nestlé claims that any changes in its behaviour are due entirely to it proactively responding to new regulation and health research. But then they also told Rough Guides that the boycott has had no effect on their sales, which – since it's clear some people do avoid Nestlé goods cannot be true. Their evidence was simply that sales have kept rising rather than falling: not the same point at all. That said, if Nestlé thought the boycott was costing them as much in lost sales as their developing-world formula milk brings in (and that's reported to be less than 1% of their total turnover) you might think they'd stop selling formula milk in poor countries, which they haven't done.

The campaigners, for their part, claim that the boycott has hit sales, with some product lines down by 3% when the Church of England started advocating avoiding Nestlé, forcing the company to up their advertising budget. Furthermore, the negative publicity has hurt the company in other ways, making it hard for them to get stand space at graduate recruitment fairs, for instance.

Of course, boycotts are usually only one part of a wider campaign, so even when a company does capitulate, it's very difficult to work out how much of this is down to consumers withholding their custom and how much is down to the inconvenience and embarrassment of having hardcore **activists** invading and picketing their stores, offices or petrol forecourts. Activists and ethical shoppers may be two sides of the same coin, but we shouldn't credit consumers for all the hard work of committed campaigners.

However, consumers' boycotts, and the public debate they help generate, can be very effective. One case often given as an example is the international boycott of Shell in 1995 against the proposed dumping of the **Brent Spar** oil platform into the North Sea. Many people now think that the environmental arguments against the dumping were factually flawed – and hence describe the result as a mixed success – but the boycott certainly seemed to work. Sales were reported to drop below half in some stations and Shell eventually backed down (though here, too, pressure didn't only come from consumers: the issue became so high profile that German chancellor Helmut Kohl is said to have personally requested prime minister John Major to do something about it).

Another good example is the numerous companies that stopped doing business in South Africa after consumer boycotts of their product. **Barclays Bank**, for example, pulled out soon after its share of the student market starting falling. Similarly, the Burma Campaign UK (see p.32) has successfully used consumer boycotts, or the threat of them, to persuade companies to stop dealing with Burma's brutal ruling junta. Victims have included **Kappa**, **JJB Sports** and the underwear company **Triumph**, who couldn't fail but to capitulate after the success of the "support breasts not dictators" campaign. The tuna fishing industry taking measures to stop killing dolphins is another success.

Furthermore, regardless of their *direct* impact, boycotts – like fairtrade – can still be useful in simply raising the profile of important issues. Even if you believe the Nestlé line on the ineffectiveness of the boycott against them, it's difficult to deny that it has massively raised people's awareness of a problem linked to tens of thousands of unnecessary deaths each year (see p.172). The same goes for the Esso boycott and what it has revealed to people of the corporate response to global warming. And while boycotts of high-profile clothes and footwear brands have been contentious – since non-name-brand clothes are arguably at least as bad (see p.62) – the consumer debate has pushed the issue of third-world workers' rights into the public eye like never before.

Regardless of how much or little impact consumer boycotts have at the moment, one thing we can certainly say is that they are less

Greenpeace activists at Shell's Brent Spa oil platform, the subject of a high-profile consumer boycott in 1995 that forced Shell to abandon plans to sink the disused rig into the North Sea

WHO'S BOYCOTTING WHOM?

Following are some of the high-profile boycotts under way at the time of writing – some serious, some less so. Please note that inclusion of a campaign here doesn't suggest endorsement from Rough Guides.

Drugs www.huumeboikotti.org
We might rail about oil firms and trainers companies, but, according to this Finnish campaign, the illicit drugs industry is probably the least ethical of all. Cocaine, especially, has led to countless deaths in Columbia, but all drug production and distribution is "firmly in the hands of organized crime [and] goes hand in hand with corruption and money-laundering".

George W Bush donors www.boycottbush.net
You'd be amazed who bankrolls the US's simplest-ever president. See the box on pp.80–81 for a list of companies.

Nestlé www.babymilkaction.org
International Baby Food Action Network promotes the ongoing boycott of Nestlé's armada of products for allegedly irresponsible marketing of breast-milk substitutes in the developing world. For more on this issue and a list of brands, see pp.172 and 173.

Esso www.stopesso.com
A major campaign to encourage consumers to avoid the oil company doing the most to "sabotage international action on global warming". For more on the Esso boycott, see p.318.

Companies doing business in Burma www.burmacampaign.org.uk
Appeals to UK consumers to boycott all the companies who still do business in Burma, despite calls from the pro-democracy groups within the country for them to pull out (for more on the situation in Burma see p.339). A more comprehensive list, including many foreign companies you've probably never heard of, can be found at: www.global-unions.org/burma

Companies doing business in Israel www.bigcampaign.org
More controversial than most consumer campaigns are the calls – now relatively widespread – for consumers to boycott goods produced in Israel. Some of the pressure has subsided since Israel bowed to EU requests to stop labelling items which have been grown or manufactured in the Occupied Territories as "produce of", or "made in", Israel. But the bigger issues are still

driving on many consumer campaigns, such as this website and product list maintained by the Palestine Solidarity Campaign, which targets "Israel's refusal to abide by UN Resolutions, International Humanitarian law and the Fourth Geneva Convention". The controversy is heightened by the Israeli claim that if people stop importing Israeli produce, then their goods will be consumed domestically, which will ultimately hurt the Palestinian producers who rely primarily on export to the Israeli market.

Companies doing business in China www.boycottmadeinchina.org
A collection of "loose-knit groups and individuals" are behind this campaign to boycott Chinese goods. The campaign is a response to the full range of human rights abuse by the Chinese government and its refusal to recognize independent trade unions, but it focuses primarily on the occupation of Tibet. Note that not all human-rights activists think that a China boycott is a good idea, for the reasons discussed on pp.77–78.

Companies doing business in the US
Calls to boycott the US – in response to everything from the invasion of Iraq to the financing of the Turkish military – are nothing new. But George W Bush's tearing up of international initiatives on climate change and the International Criminal Court has provoked more bad feeling than ever. There are many groups suggesting US boycotts, though about the only website that provides a huge list of US companies and the brand names they own in the UK is: www.krysstal.com/democracy_whyusa_boycott.html

There are scores of other boycotts under way, from **tropical timber** (see p.292) and **tiger prawns** (see p.144) to **Janet Jackson**, for duetting with Beenie Man, a ragga deejay whose lyrics, some maintain, advocate the murder of homosexuals. Also on lists are **Gillette**, for using "spy chips" to stop shoplifters making off with their Mach 3 razorblades (see www.boycottgillette.com); **Canada**, for the mass slaughter of seals (see www.boycott-canada.com); **Gap**, for its owners' felling of old-growth forest in the US (see www.gapsucks.org); **Bacardi**, for allegedly attempting to have Fidel Castro overthrown while continuing to use Cuban imagery to promote its products (www.ratb.org.uk); and **Adidas**, for using kangaroo skin in its football boots (www.viva.org.uk).

To stay up to speed with boycott news, visit:

Ethical Consumer Boycotts List www.ethicalconsumer.org/boycotts/boycotts.htm

effective than they should be. That's because most boycotters don't take the time to tell the company that they are actually boycotting them, which in many cases renders their action ineffectual (more on this in the next section).

What about the workers?

When it comes to developing-world factories, some commentators – including many of the most vocal trade unions and campaigning groups – take the line that boycotting companies may be counterproductive. If workers are being treated badly, we should demand better treatment for them, but if we actually boycott their employer, we'll **reduce demand** for the goods they're producing, putting their jobs at risk – hurting the very people we're trying to help.

It's certainly true that an uninformed, knee-jerk reaction from the public might have a negative effect: a big Western company pulling out of a factory or region after child labour is discovered may mean catastrophic loss of jobs in a poor area. However, a few things are worth bearing in mind here. For one thing, most boycotts relating to sweatshops and child labour are called when a Western company *pulls out* of a factory rather than staying put and cleaning up its act.

Secondly, it's unlikely that a company will change its ways unless "requests" for it to reform are backed up by a credible threat of force – in this case reduced sales. Companies follow the most profitable business model they can come up with and, unless their profits are threatened, then they won't change it – even if the directors actually think, deep down, it would be morally right. Company bosses have a **fiduciary duty** to act in the interests of their shareholders. To follow their moral instincts – or moral requests from consumers – without a financial motive would be to breach the terms of their contract.

So, even if it's possible that a boycott might harm workers now, this has to be weighed up against the potential for creating long-term change. And that's not necessarily unattainable: even the commentators (such as Philippe Legrain, author of *Open World*) who write about Nike being far more ethically progressive than unbranded clothes producers admit that actual or threatened boycotts have been integral in raising Nike's standards.

Thirdly, while there's a theoretical possibility that we might be jeopardizing the jobs of the people we're trying to support, this has to be balanced against **supporting decent jobs elsewhere.** Unless boycotting a company means that you're actually going to stop buying something full stop – which usually isn't the case – then, by taking your custom somewhere else, you're probably going to be supporting the same number of jobs, only decent ones rather than bad ones. True, we each need to decide where to draw the line about what constitutes "decent" standards: boycotting any company that pays low wages by Western standards, for example, would mean boycotting all companies who produce in the developing world, which would hurt the poorest people (for more on the question of employment and exploitation of the poor world, see p.51). But boycotting sweatshops in favour of ethically sourced goods from the same countries can hardly be a bad thing overall for workers there.

As for boycotting whole countries in favour of other countries, that's a different, and rather more complex, matter (see p.72).

For a list of current boycotts, see pp.32–33.

❝ when you threaten to boycott a company that buys stock from a shady supplier, the company's immediate reaction is to cancel orders and turn to another supplier who is not necessarily any better. This attitude does not help to improve the conditions of those working for the first supplier, who are likely to be laid off, whilst other workers are faced with the same problem elsewhere. So boycotts should only be used as a last resort, but we should not rule it out entirely as an option, because we should have at least one weapon we can use to fight against those who refuse to cooperate in any way. ❞

Neil Kearney, General Secretary of the International Textile, Garment and Leather Workers' Federation

#3: SELECTIVE SHOPPING
Shop by shop, brand by brand

While products from ethical specialists and labels like Fairtrade are great when they're available, and while boycotts are fine for taking a stance against exploitative companies or countries, these approaches only cover a small proportion of what we buy, at opposite ends of the spectrum: the very good and the very bad. So what about the **high-street shops and brands** that account for the vast majority of our

BARCODES: THE FUTURE OF ETHICAL SHOPPING?

Books, magazines and websites are OK for getting the ethical lowdown on companies. But with single supermarkets stocking more than 30,000, and companies endlessly changing ownership and practices, you'd need a great deal of time to check every item you might want to buy. The future of conscientious shopping, then, will surely include some means by which we can get information about any product at any time.

Enter the **Corporate Fallout Detector** (CFD). Created by American "interaction designer" James Patten, the CFD combines a barcode scanner with the ECRA Corporate Critic database (see p.360), and another database of US polluters. When a product is swiped, the device makes a geigercounter-style clicking in proportion to the nastiness of the company in question. Just "swipe and gripe".

OK, it's early days. The CFD is a big, cumbersome box with limited information inside it – as Mr Patten is well aware. But the idea is a good one. There's no reason why, in a few years, we shouldn't have barcode scanners in our mobile phones, say, which would be able to provide all sorts of product info, including the ethical standards of the company in question. They might even be able to send an email to each company that has been scanned but not passed the test, to let them know that they've "just been boycotted".

Obviously, any system of ranking companies automatically is rife with problems of methodology and standards. But there's no reason why we couldn't each set out our own "ethical criteria".

purchasing, the companies which don't feature on boycott lists yet equally are not exactly known for being all that sound. Should we bother – where possible, or perhaps just when convenient – making ethical discriminations between high-street names such as, say, Sainsbury's and Tesco, or Philips and Samsung?

Considering that companies like these account for most of what we buy, it would be odd not to include them in our ethical-shopping efforts. Getting them to improve standards, even in a small way, would arguably have a bigger effect than anything else we might achieve. Either way, it's near-enough impossible to avoid high-street

The devil's in the barcode: James Patten armed with his Corporate Fallout Detector, ready to "swipe and gripe" in the supermarket aisle

companies, so we might as well give our money to the most responsible ones, even if very few of them are really all that conscientious. And these days it's not too difficult to get information comparing the ethical "performance" of them. Many of them are touched on in this book, and more comprehensive information can be gleaned from both online and paper sources (see p.359). In particular, the tireless *Ethical Consumer* magazine scrutinizes the ethical credentials of household-name companies according to a wide range of criteria, the details of which are given in each of their reports, which are then updated and used in a book called *The Good Shopping Guide*. The latest report on TVs, for example, encouraged us to plump for Grundig and Alba instead of Goodmans and Aiwa.

But does this kind of picking and choosing between brand A and brand B actually make any difference? As always, it's hard to measure the exact effect. But one thing that seems clear is that it won't make much difference unless you tell the shops or brands what you're doing: if you don't, there's absolutely no reason to believe they'll even realize you're shunning them.

Words speak louder than actions

In free-market theory, **supply and demand** naturally work their way towards a happy equilibrium: if people don't want something, it will stop being produced; if people want more of something, more will be supplied. This is, of course, just as true of ethical shopping: the more demand there is for ethical companies, the more ethical companies there will be.

But economists (some of them at least) understand that such elegant market mechanisms don't work when buyers and sellers don't have access to the same information: so-called "**information asymmetry**" stops supply and demand from functioning properly. And so it is with ethical shoppers: *you* might know why you're avoiding one shop and favouring another, but *they* don't. As such, it's even possible that your decision may have the opposite effect from the one you intended.

If a clothes shop, for example, notices that sales are down in a season, it will probably assume (and their assumption will probably be correct) that this is mainly because consumers were unhappy with the season's styles or prices. Unless the shop operates an unusually comprehensive market-research strategy, they will probably never realize that a small percentage of that loss might have been people going elsewhere on ethical grounds. To quote George Monbiot again: "the signal they are trying to send becomes lost in the general market noise". And if that market noise is demanding, say, lower prices, the quiet ethical shopper may be unwittingly contributing towards a price-slashing drive, in which the shop leans even more heavily on its suppliers to produce more goods for less money: not good news for workers' rights.

That's the irony about selective ethical shopping: you'll probably make a bigger difference **expressing concerns** to a shop's assistant manager as you hand over your credit card than you will by simply not going in. Indeed, for anyone who likes the idea of trying to favour the more progressive of the big brands but ultimately always caves in to the lowest price or best design, maybe a useful rule of thumb would be this: shop anywhere you like, but whenever you give custom to a business you don't trust, make up for it by writing to them pretending you just boycotted them on ethical grounds.

Of course, you'll make the *most* difference (putting aside the option of campaigning naked outside the shop) by both voting with your wallet *and* making your views known to the businesses in question. Some within the ethical shopping movement understand this well. *Ethical Consumer* magazine, for example, lists the names and addresses of each company it reviews, encouraging readers to write/email and let them know that from now on they won't – or will – be buying from them on ethical grounds. They even produce ready-made **thumbs-up and thumbs-down postcards** ready for you to add an address, tick areas of objection/praise and send off. For subscription details, see p.362.

Also check-out The Good Shopping Guide ethical shopping site:

The Good Shopping Guide www.thegoodshoppingguide.co.uk

#4: BUY LESS
... and save the planet

While trying to support ethical brands or products is all well and good, many in the environmental movement point out that it doesn't take account of a more fundamental issue: that we Westerners consume too much. A fairly traded T-shirt is laudable enough, they'd say, but the most ethical approach to shopping would involve simply **buying as little as possible**. There are many prongs of reasoning here, beyond the argument that buying too much stuff turns us all into super-materialist consumption machines.

First, there is only so much stuff in the world, and so buying more of it must somewhere down the line mean **depriving others** of their fair share. According to the UN's *Human Development Report 2003*, the richest 20% of the world's population consume 88% of the world's goods and services, while the poorest fifth consume only 3.3%. Such staggering inequality won't be solved, of course, by ethically minded consumers buying less. But for as long as the comparatively wealthy people in the world spend all their money on buying things – as opposed to giving to charity, say – it's unlikely to change.

Second, our consumption habits are ultimately **unsustainable**, and we'd do well to remedy this before the end of the oil age turns the situation into a global crisis. With easily accessible reserves quickly becoming exhausted, it seems very likely that, within a few decades, oil production will be on the decline. As the inevitable worldwide recession kicks in, we're bound to look back with dismay on our massive consumption of everything from petrol to plastic bottles at a time when cheap, abundant oil could have been used in the development of alternative energy sources.

But perhaps the most widely stated argument for buying less is that our consumption habits are a driving force behind much of the devastation that humans are wreaking on the planet. The most obvious and worrying example is **climate change**, to which pretty much

HOW BIG IS YOUR FOOTPRINT?

Everything we buy, from cars to food to electricity, contributes something towards our "ecological footprint" – a measure of our consumption levels, in terms of the total area of the average patch of earth that would be needed to support our lifestyle. This area – measured in hectares of average productivity – includes the space for growing crops, grazing animals, harvesting timber, catching fish, accommodating infrastructure and absorbing carbon dioxide emissions. The pics below give some sense of the inequity in the footprints of people around the world:

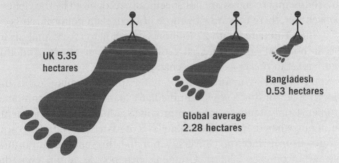

UK 5.35 hectares

Global average 2.28 hectares

Bangladesh 0.53 hectares

To calculate your own ecological footprint (and find out how many planets we'd need if everyone lived just like you) see www.myfootprint.org, or, for more on the ecological footprint system, visit: www.redefiningprogress.org

Source: World Wildlife Fund, Living Planet Report 2002

everything we buy contributes (see below). But this isn't the only problem area. In the second half of the twentieth century alone, according to *New Scientist*, "the Earth lost 300,000 species", most of them due to human activity such as **rainforest clearance** – driven by markets for wood or land to grow cattle feed, palm oil and other crops. And it's not just animals and plants that feel the effect of environmental destruction: when the environment suffers, people also suffer, and usually that means the poor. There are countless manifestations of this fact, from the **murder and persecution** of indigenous people that goes hand in hand with deforestation, to the cancer and blindness that result when industrial effluent from chemical works or factories is pumped untreated into rivers used for water supplies, such as has happened around Bangladeshi leather tanneries (see p.197).

Besides killing and incapacitating many people, these kinds of problems have forced millions of people from their homes. Though **environmental refugees** are not specifically recognized by the Geneva Convention, there may now be more of them than political refugees: 25 million compared with 22 million, according to recent analysis by the author and environmental ecologist Norman Myers. And this figure is set to rocket as climate change kicks in.

Not everyone's convinced that buying and consuming less is the way to solve all this. People's immediate, man-made environmental problems only tend to start improving, globalization proponents point out, when they reach a certain level of material wealth (two academics from Princeton University put the threshold at an annual average income of $5000). Granted, such people admit, even the richer countries in the world have their environmental problems – in the UK, for instance, tens of thousands of inner-city residents die each year from the effects of **car fumes** (see p.316). But our air and water quality are generally getting better rather that worse, whereas the opposite is true in much of the developing world. The only way people there are likely to become rich enough to be able to pay heed to environmental issues, we're told, is through more trade – which necessarily involves people buying and consuming more.

But, even if it's true, there's at least one serious problem with this line of reasoning. Rich countries may have fewer local environmental problems, but they are incomparably worse when it comes to what is increasingly accepted as the most pressing of the world's environmental concerns – global warming.

WE'S BUYING, THE CLIMATE'S FRYING

Despite the occasional sceptical voice from within the scientific community (and, unsurprisingly, many from companies and industry bodies) there is now a very solid scientific consensus that by releasing CO_2, methane and certain other "greenhouse" gasses into the atmosphere – for example through burning oil or gas – humans are measurably warming up the planet. It's true, of course, that the world's climate has always been in a natural state of flux: the seas were once gas, ice ages have come and gone, and in around a billion years the sun is due to grow to 250 times its current size, boil the oceans into space and cause "iron rain, silicon snow and the emergence of a giant icecap made of argon", according to the *New Scientist*. But none of

Started in 1993 by members of Adbusters (see p.63), Buy Nothing Day embodies the "buy-less" approach to ethical consumerism – and it has become a global event. The challenge is to go 24 hours without buying anything. It's a commitment to consuming less, recycling more and challenging corporations to clean up and be fair. "Culture jammers" take the opportunity to stage pranks and protests in shopping malls, make a consumer monster (see www.consumermonster.com), start a Saturday job timed specifically to get fired from it (for refusing to sell anything on Buy Nothing Day, of course) and generally raise awareness of one's ecological footprint.

that changes the fact that we're currently having a serious effect on the fragile ecological balances upon which we all depend, and that our energy-guzzling consumer lifestyles play a significant part in that.

It's difficult to overestimate the potential outcomes. A recent report from World Health Organization scientists suggested that more than 160,000 people *already* die each year from climate change's effects, and that figure could double by 2020. Some of the victims are elderly people killed by heat waves in Europe – the people we hear about on the news – but the majority are children and adults in the developing world. The risks to their health are posed by the higher rates of malnutrition, diarrhoea and malaria that are caused both by higher temperatures and "**natural disasters**" such as hurricanes, droughts and floods. It's hard to believe that we now create natural disasters, but that's what the evidence suggests. Figures from insurance giant Munich Re, for example, suggest that, globally, the cost of natural disasters is doubling every ten years.

The effect on biodiversity could be even worse. A study published in science journal *Nature* in January 2004 concluded that, if "mid-range" predictions for climate change are correct, 15–37% of the world's plant and animal species will be "committed to extinction" by 2050.

In the longer term, according to current UN models, vast areas could disappear under **rising seas** caused by melting ice caps and expanding desert. Low-lying areas in rich countries will probably get flood barriers to protect them, but it's unclear who will fund such projects in **Bangladesh**, where 20 million people may be displaced, or how we'll protect islands such as those of Tuvalu, which will in all likelihood be completely submerged under water within a few decades (perhaps the first case of states disappearing physically rather than politically).

Of course, a different climate may also have some positive repercussions, but the costs are likely to be incomparably greater and will be felt the worst by the people least able to afford them. (Any Brits excited by the prospect of warmer summers should be aware that climate change could divert the gulf stream this century, leaving Britain as cold as equivalent latitudes in Russia or Canada).

Solutions great and small

The **solution** to human-induced climate change is, of course, not individual action but some sort of multilateral, international framework for reducing the world's total CO_2 emissions and sharing out "carbon credits" equitably between countries. **The Kyoto Protocol** – which aims to get the rich countries that produce most of the greenhouse gasses to reduce their emissions – is a step in the right direction, though certainly a long way from what's needed.

Unfortunately, the Kyoto Protocol looks relatively likely to fail, because the US government headed by George Bush has refused to sign up, despite the fact that his country produces a quarter of the world's CO_2. So one thing we can do as consumers is to avoid the companies that bankroll the Bush administration (see pp.80–81). And we can try and favour specialist "ethical" businesses, since the mainstream business community has done a great deal to get solutions to global warming *off* the agenda. In May 2001, for example, Thomas J Donohue, President and CEO of the Chamber of Commerce of the United States of America, which speaks on behalf

Paani Laupepa of the low-lying nation of Tuvalu looks out at the rising ocean that is expected to cover his country within decades. "The question is not if but when we'll be drowned."

of "three million businesses", wrote a letter to Bush claiming that "Global warming is an important issue that must be addressed – but the Kyoto Protocol is a flawed treaty that is not in the U.S. interest."

But even though the real solution has to be political, the fact remains that the things that we buy and consume as individuals – especially our household power and transport – contribute directly to global warming, including the deaths and disasters outlined by the World Health Organization and the UN's Intergovernmental Panel on Climate Change. Each of us in the UK produces 100–300 times more CO_2 than the average person in most poor countries. And yet it's the latter who are feeling the negative effects of climate change.

We can each limit the greenhouse gas emissions we're responsible for, not just by buying less, but also by favouring **green electricity** tariffs (see p.274), and **energy-efficient appliances** (see p.282) and **transport** (see p.324). And we can also try to favour progressive businesses who are making conscientious attempts to reduce their own greenhouse contributions – after all, most of us do more harm to the climate via the companies we support (including farms, since agriculture accounts for a fifth of the world's CO_2 emissions) than we do directly.

#5: BUY LOCAL
Thinking small

The idea of "buying local" whenever possible is often thought of as a core tenet of ethical shopping. Proponents of this strategy accept that trade is an essential and potentially beneficial part of life, but claim that it'll be more of a force for good if trading networks are local, creating **accountability** (people are less likely to rip off or exploit their neighbours) and **collaboration** (everyone sharing the goal of furthering the wellbeing of the community). On an international scale, they argue, vast distances and powerful financial interests come between the parties engaged in the "real" exchange – the producers and the consumers – and wealthy countries and companies have the political and economic clout to determine the terms of trade. Hence poor-country workers end up with little for their efforts except bad pay, appalling working conditions and exported natural resources.

Furthermore, localizers point out, global trade is inherently eco-unfriendly, both directly – as it relies on the burning of a vast quantity of **transport fuel**, contributing to climate change – and indirectly, since it separates consumers from the mess their goods are making, removing any pressure on them to act accordingly. The environmental impact is compounded by the fact that world trade is inherently tied up with a corporate-driven consumerism which encourages us all to buy and use as much as possible. And, as mentioned later on, there's the question of **food security**: our long-term ability to feed ourselves. As we become ever-more reliant on transporting food from abroad, the oil that facilitates that transport gets closer to being exhausted.

For all these reasons, the argument goes, as well as numerous others, the best way forward is a new era of "**localization**", which shoppers can help realize by favouring local goods and services wherever possible. Obviously, there will always be some national trade (it wouldn't make

> ❝ *Localisation ... has the potential to increase community cohesion, reduce poverty and inequality, improve livelihoods, social provision and environmental protection and provide the all important sense of security.* ❞
>
> Colin Hines, author of *Localization: A Global Manifesto*

> ❝ *The problem with localisation is that it would trap the poorest economies in their current subordinate relationship to the rest of the world, and would require a whole new coercive apparatus to impose it. It is a backward looking and reactionary reformism.* ❞
>
> Paul Hampton, Workers' Liberty

sense for every town to make its own buses, say) and some international trade (not every country has the minerals and metals necessary to make buses, nor the climate to grow coffee). But whenever home-produced is available – in agriculture, clothes production, or whatever – that's what ethical shoppers are to go for.

Overall, localization might mean that we'd end up **producing and consuming less**, the argument continues, but that's not a bad thing, since, as we've already seen, the world simply cannot sustain the West's ever-rising current consumption levels. Moreover, our food would be fresher; local engagement with politics and environmental problems would be stimulated; perhaps we'd even be happier. **Poor countries** would in theory also benefit: no longer reliant on cash-crop and manufacturing exports, they'd be able to grow their own food, protect their environments, shape their own development and benefit from processing and using their own natural resources.

One step forward or three steps back?

Most progressive writers and thinkers agree that a move towards localization for **fresh foods** would be a good idea on the environmental level. This may not *always* be the case – sometimes the efficiency of foreign growers may more than offset the environmental costs of transportation. But no one can deny that **air-freighting** out-of-season strawberries or mangetout from the southern hemisphere to a UK supermarket is a heavy and unnecessary burden on the environment; or that locally farmed vegetables are a better option, in terms of minimizing climate change, than those trucked from the other side of Europe. (For more on food transport, see p.100.)

But when it comes to the bigger aims – favouring locally produced dried foods, clothes, shoes and other goods with an aim to winding down global trade completely – the proponents of localization are increasingly standing on their own. For a start, these kinds of goods are usually shipped, not flown, so the environmental costs, though certainly not negligible, are as much as fifty times lower per kilogram than the aforementioned mangetout. But the point where most people part company with the local-izer is the claim that a reduction in international trade would be good for the developing world. Will it really help Bangladesh if we produce our clothes in Birmingham?

Clearly there are many problems with the current system of globaliza-tion, such as the gung-ho opening of financial and capital markets that the International Monetary Fund has forced on many poor countries as a condition of borrowing money. Or the patent laws which stop life-saving drugs getting to dying people in the poorest countries. But does that make global trade a bad thing? Not according to groups like Oxfam, which

> ❝ 30 years ago, South Korea was as poor as Ghana. Today, thanks to trade led growth, it is as rich as Portugal. ❞
>
> Mike Moore, ex-Director of the World Trade Organization

> ❝ Trade is the fuel for growth but not the engine ... we need development-led trade policies ❞.
>
> Michael Herrmann, UNCTAD specialist in least developed countries

have spent the last few years campaigning hard to get *more* access to world markets for producers in poor countries (for example by ending European farm subsidies).

And it's not just Oxfam. Numerous anti-poverty groups and left-wing political writers have expressed concern that, without trade, poor countries can only get hard cash via **aid** – which is not only insufficient, but puts recipient countries under the thumbs of the donors and is no kind of long-term solution anyway. Without hard cash, these critics of localization claim, poor countries won't be able to invest in home production and they'll end up being locked into their current position of exporting raw commodities, such as min-erals and cash crops, with all the lucrative processing and manufac-turing – the creation of the actual finished product – done elsewhere.

Certainly, increased international trade can cause problems in the developing world, the argument goes, from poor labour and environ-mental conditions to the eroding of local cultures and, in some cases, unemployment. And, certainly, trade in itself is no immediate answer to poverty: for example, a 2004 report by the United Nations Conference on Trade and Development (UNCTAD) pointed out that the world's least developed countries have opened their markets to external trade during the last few years but have gained very little – or even lost out. But, overall, there are more cases of countries becoming rich through embracing international trade – such as the "Tiger" economies of East Asia – than there are of those which have avoided it.

On a broader – and more controversial level – there's also the argument that global trade, for all its many current problems, is catalyzing the kind of multilateral, rules-based system of **international integration** that will be essential if the world is ever to combat global-scale issues such as climate change effectively. The **World Trade Organization** (WTO), via which international trade rules are negotiated and disputes are settled, has rightfully been attacked for – among other things – its lack of transparency and accountability. Most deals are brokered behind closed doors, where the coercion of poor countries by rich countries seems almost inevitable; and the judges in the dispute procedures and accountable to no one.

But, for all its numerous problems, the WTO is a forum in which poor countries *can* combine forces and demand a better deal, as happened at the 2003 meeting in Cancun, which saw the emergence of the "G21" group of developing countries. In 2004, the practices of both the EU (for its sugar export subsidies) and the US (for its cotton subsidies) were even declared illegal at the WTO after objections by Brazil. These kinds of developments would have been unimaginable before the existence of the rules-based system brought about by world trade.

So, once again, a simple approach – buying local – turns out to be less straightforward than people sometimes suggest. Whether favouring local goods is "more ethical" depends on the individual product and transport method as well as your individual views on the impact of world trade on everything from poverty to **labour rights** (see p.51) and **oppressive governments** (see p.72).

03

SHOULD WE BUY FROM ...

SWEATSHOPS ETC
Made in the third world: exploitation or opportunity?

One of the most debated issues in ethical shopping is whether, with the current world order being what it is, buying goods produced in poor countries is good or bad for the people in those countries – not to mention for workers at home. Though it's rarely posed in such stark terms, this is the question that consumers end up asking themselves after hearing reports of **sweatshop labour** in Far Eastern garment factories or the **appropriation of water and land** for the growing of cash crops in Africa. In the case of some specific countries, there's also the further question of whether we're supporting an oppressive regime (a related but separate issue, discussed on p.72) but for the rest it's mainly a matter of whether buying goods produced in poor countries amounts to the exploitation of poverty, or the provision of an opportunity out of poverty.

In fact, most of what we consume in the UK is still produced at home, and most of the rest comes from the EU. But as globalization rolls onwards, a growing chunk of our goods come from the developing world, where **wages** are low and **labour and environmental regulations** tend to be slack, or at least not properly enforced. Sweatshop-produced trainers, toys and footballs have garnered most of the media attention in the area of worker exploitation and child labour, but really this issue covers everything from cut flowers to car parts, bananas to silk, tobacco to electronic equipment. A report by the New York-based National Labor Committee, for example, found serious abuses in Chinese export factories manufacturing products ranging from bicycles (15-hour shifts, 7 days a week with no overtime pay) to handbags (guards beating the workers for being late).

The question of whether or not sourcing goods from cheap factories and farms in the third world is ethical could (and does) fill many books on subjects ranging from economics to cultural imperialism. The following few pages can only serve to briefly outline the debate.

The problems

Few people would deny that labour conditions in poor countries are generally very low when judged by Western standards. Some of these issues are widely discussed, such as the hours worked and wages received in sweatshop-style export factories and farms in Asia, Latin America and Africa. Countless reports – not just investigative exposés, but studies from the Western companies using third-world suppliers – have shown that manufacturers in Asia and Latin America often demand truly incredible working weeks of 120 hours or more. In many cases, up to half of the hours worked count as unpaid overtime, and for each "official" hour worked, the pay can be as little as 10p – hence the shocking **wage inequality** reflected in much-quoted statistics such as the supposed fact that it would take a Bangladeshi garment worker sewing Disney clothes more than 200 years to earn what the company's CEO get each hour. According to sweatshop campaigners, common phenomena include workers suffering injuries due to tiredness and even pregnant women miscarrying due to overwork.

To compound the problem, workers are commonly not paid on time, or have **wages deducted** for making mistakes or for being a few minutes late; 2003 figures from the Department of Labor and Employment in the Philippines, for instance, showed that nearly half the companies inspected that year had failed to pay workers properly – and those are just the official figures. And, importantly, in this era of "flexible" labour, **job security** is an increasingly rare phenomenon: millions of workers have no contract, and even those who do have one can be dismissed for being ill, late or pregnant – or simply because a factory has become financially unsustainable after a big company has placed its orders elsewhere. This may be against the law, or against a company's policy, but this doesn't seem to stop it happening.

Less discussed, but just as important, is **health and safety**. A staggering number of workers – more than two million – die every year due to work-related accidents or illnesses, according to the UN's International Labour Organization (ILO). This is an international problem, but poor countries bear the brunt of it: the rate of fatal workplace accidents in developing countries in Asia, for example, is four times higher than in the industrialized world. The same can presumably be said for the hundreds of millions more affected annually by non-fatal health problems, such as the three million farmers around the world who (according to World Health Organizaiton estimates) suffer acute **agrochemical poisonings** each year.

Less dangerous but equally demeaning conditions include unsanitary toilets available only at certain times of day, round-the-clock surveillance, and crowded, dark dormitories. Sometimes humiliation tactics appear to be a deliberate policy: according to Oxfam

Community Aid Abroad, for example, Indonesian women working in some export factories don't take their entitlement of two unpaid days of menstrual leave per month, since to qualify they have to remove their underwear in front of (female) factory doctors to prove that they are indeed menstruating. Even more seriously, **verbal and physical abuse** is widely reported, ranging from minor offences to serious sexual assault.

Perhaps most significant of all, however, is the fact that collective bargaining for better terms and conditions through **unions** and other groups – something recognized by the ILO as a fundamental worker right – is often impossible. In some countries only a state-controlled union is allowed (such as the All-China Federation of Trade Unions, which is so much a tool of the state that it has reportedly turned down offers of increased wages from foreign companies, to help keep China cheap and business friendly). In others, free unions are legal but rarely tolerated in reality: organizers are usually simply fired, but in many cases they're harassed, beaten, jailed or even killed. According to the International Confederation of Free Trade Unions (ICFTU), 213 trade unionists were assassinated or "disappeared" worldwide in 2002 alone.

Buy "Western" instead?

Reports of these kinds of conditions have caused a minor uproar in the West since the mid-1990s, but the question remains as to how we should respond. For many people, who feel that benefiting materially from such harsh conditions is unacceptable, the obvious conclusion is that we should where possible support "decent" jobs by favouring goods produced in, say, Europe or America, and avoiding goods imported from countries where the poor are exploited and the environment polluted.

But the idea of helping third-world workers by simply shunning their products is obviously problematic since, for one thing, these jobs are clearly in big demand. True, even some of the more ethically aware Western brands have found themselves in court for using sweatshops that exploit **indentured labour** (whereby workers are conned into signing away a large proportion of their wages in return for securing the job, putting them in a vicious cycle of debt and making it impossible to leave). But this is the exception rather than the rule – the vast majority of workers are taking these jobs by choice.

And no wonder, globalization advocates argue, since jobs in the export sector are usually the best thing going. According to right-leaning think-tanks such as the Institute for International Economics, American and European firms in poor countries pay on average around twice what equivalent local firms offer. Of course, these wages still sound shockingly low to those in the West, but the alternative for a worker is either even worse pay from a domestic firm, or rural work. The latter, despite Western middle-class idealization of "simple" countryside living, usually involves grinding poverty and hard labour – hence the tens of millions of **subsistence farmers** voluntarily leaving home each year to head for the cities and factories. (Furthermore, converting third-world wages into Western currency can slightly exaggerate the inequality, because in countries where, say, 25p per hour is a standard wage, 25p tends to buy a lot more than it would do in the UK, a fact that backpackers on six-month trips around Asia are all-too aware of.) And it's not just wages that are better in export jobs, pro-globalizers claim. Other problems such as health and safety risks and child labour – widely associated in Western eyes with, say, Gap clothes factories – are actually most problematic in areas where Western companies aren't involved, such as artisan mining and small-scale farming (see overleaf for more on child labour).

The same people also argue that sweatshop-style jobs can be an important part of **economic development**, pointing out that in the 1960s the West's shoe sweatshops were in **Japan**, which is now a bigger economic power than the UK, and has strict labour and environmental legislation. In the 1970s and 1980s, they were in **Taiwan** and **South Korea**, which have since become specialists in microelectronics and are among the richest countries in Asia. By the same token, what we now call sweatshop conditions were standard in

CHILD LABOUR

With more than 350 million children aged 5–17 classed as "economically active" by the International Labour Organization, children account for a substantial proportion of the global workforce. Around half of this total is considered to be acceptable: 15- and 16-year-olds working full time in safe conditions, or younger children doing a few hours after school. But much of the rest, in the ILO's words, "is not jobs for kids ... it is adults exploiting the young, naive, innocent, weak, vulnerable and insecure for personal profit".

While the issue is widely associated in the West with stitching footballs and sports shoes, in reality the problem is much more diverse, the most widely affected industries including **silk**, **carpet weaving**, **brassware** and **glassware**, **precious stone cutting**, **mining**, **leather tanneries** and **farming**. A frightening 170 million children are involved in work classified as hazardous, and of these more than a third – roughly an equivalent number to the entire population of the UK – are aged eleven and under. At the most shocking end of the spectrum, at least eight million children are stuck in what the ILO describes as the "unconditional worst forms of child labour": armed conflict, forced and bonded labour, prostitution, pornography and illegal activities.

While (nearly) everyone agrees that it's imperative to end all dangerous and degrading forms of child labour, there's no consensus on the best response to the hundreds of millions who are working in safe, or at least relatively safe, conditions. Studies by the ILO have shown that if all child workers were put through **education** instead of working, the result would be an enormous boost not only to the children's quality of life, but also to the economy of their countries. However, in most cases, no one is offering to pay for these children to be educated and, until someone does, a clampdown may simply exacerbate the problems, forcing it underground and further marginalizing and impoverishing the children involved. After all, child labour tends to be primarily a **symptom of poverty** (though interestingly it appears to be more common in households which own land), and banning it is unlikely to help reduce this poverty.

So where does all this leave the concerned shopper? One thing worth noting is that the vast majority – probably around 95% – of child labourers are not working in the formal economy creating goods for export to the West. They're working largely for a local or domestic market on **subsistence farms**, or producing silk, bricks, cigarettes or matches; a large number are also working in "domestic service". As such, some people say that the best way forward is to encourage more global trade – since child labour is a symptom of poverty, and world trade, they argue, is the best way to make countries richer. Others claim that it's none of our business – it's a cultural issue and we shouldn't meddle. This debate is bound to run and run.

But what about the 5% of children – still a number in the millions – who *are* producing goods for the West, making clothes, carpets, shoes and furniture, tanning leather and mining and polishing gems? Should we demand that all our goods are "child labour free"?

For **factory-produced goods**, at least, the obvious answer is yes. If global trade, as its advocates claim, is providing valuable and in-demand jobs in the poor world, then surely it would make sense for these jobs to go to poor adults rather than poor children (not least as the adults may then be able to afford to send their children to school). But in other areas, such as more **craft-based industries**, there's an argument to say that an unqualified demand for child-labour-free goods may add up to refusing to do business with the poorest people, hence worsening their position.

Partly, it all depends on who's in charge and what other opportunities – if any – will be offered to children who currently *are* working. A faceless directive from a corporate headquarters to stamp out all child labour – or to pull out from regions where child labour is widespread – may do more harm than good, with desperate children left with no option but to turn to dangerous work, crime or even prostitution. According to Oxfam, this is exactly what happened in Pakistan, where large numbers of child labourers were found to be making Western footballs a few years ago.

But local schemes set up specifically to deal with the problem – such as the RUGMARK label for South Asian rugs (see p.306) – have shown that with appropriate monitoring and focus it's possible to reduce child labour constructively, using a labelling scheme both to inform Western consumers and fund education for ex-child labourers.

A billboard promotes a private "EPZ" in Ho Chi Minh City, Vietnam. These special no- or low-tax areas are designed to attract foreign business, and they're associated with the worst type of sweatshop abuse.

Europe and the US a century ago. Industrialization may not be very pretty in its early stages, but every country wealthy today, we're told, has been through this process – and only once people become wealthier will they be able to demand better environmental and labour conditions.

Things aren't quite this simple, of course. For a start, it would be naive to think that everyone is happy as Larry to work under such harsh conditions. **Strikes** are not uncommon in export factories (at least in areas where unions aren't suppressed) and there is no shortage of outspoken workers complaining about the labour abuses. Similarly, despite the fact that some multinationals might pay *relatively* high wages, many have successfully lobbied governments for exemption from having to match the minimum wage. They also frequently choose to use factories based in the notorious **export processing zones,** or **EPZs,** where labour law is even slacker than elsewhere.

In the words of the ICFTU, EPZs "have become a symbol of crude free market globalisation, where workers are made to take amphetamines to get them to work harder and faster, where violence and abuse are a daily reality for thousands upon thousands of workers, and where attempts to form unions and bargain collectively for a fair deal are often met with reprisals, sackings and even death threats".

> ❝ *Globalisation has the potential to bring prosperity to people across the world, but today crude free market globalisation is pushing standards down and leading to massive exploitation.* ❞
>
> Guy Ryder, General Secretary, International Confederation of Free Trade Unions

Furthermore, while Taiwan and South Korea may have got richer through sweatshop-style manufacturing, they did so at a time when there was less global trade, and hence much less **competition between poor nations.** Today, poor countries struggling to make money through sweatshops have to deal with the fact that other poor countries can try and undercut them on price (and labour conditions), hence slowing development down. Today, it's a "race to the bottom", campaigners claim, with real-terms minimum wages in some areas of China (the leader of the "race") having fallen in the last ten years. According to many campaigners, even where higher wages are *officially* paid, they are sometimes simply balanced out by forced unpaid overtime (more on this in the next chapter).

Also, you cannot isolate this discussion from a whole range of bigger issues. The poverty of many poor countries is inextricably linked to a whole host of factors: the unsustainable **debt** foisted on them decades ago by the West; colonial and post-colonial **wars;** the rich world's **farm subsidies** that erode poor-country agricultural societies; currency instability helped along by Western banks and speculators and the International Monetary Fund's strong-arm opening of poor-world financial markets. And so on.

So when ex-farmers "voluntarily" take 14-hours-per-day shifts producing lampshades for Britain, or green beans for the US, they may be doing it "out of choice", but that choice may have been shaped by an unjust global order which has made their previous life impossible. And even if export factories and farms are comparatively high for those people who choose to work in them, they may bring nothing but misery to others, such as villagers who find their water is being drained by a nearby plantation, or their air and rivers being polluted by factory effluent (poor-world environmental regulation and enforcement is incomparably less strict than that in the West).

Still, even with all these evident problems in mind, the case for trying to help third-world workers by simply avoiding third-world goods is clearly problematic – as we've already seen (see p.48).

Demanding better standards

If shunning third-world goods is unconstructive, how about using our power as consumers to demand that companies improve conditions throughout their supply chains? Certainly this seems like a more sensible strategy, though – as ever – not everyone is convinced it's a good idea. Free-marketeers claim that, while it's laudable to desire better standards and wages for third-world workers, their "cheapness" is exactly what allows them to undercut the West and create jobs and wealth – it's their **comparative advantage**, to use the economics jargon. If Western consumers demand better labour and environmental standards, they risk limiting this advantage, thereby reducing the incentive for companies to invest in, and provide jobs in, developing countries. Hence the fact that, in international trade negotiations with the West, governments of poor countries have often objected to the idea of making trade deals conditional on the enforcement of better labour or welfare conditions – they claim the main beneficiaries of this would be workers in Europe or the US, as it would increase the cost of doing business in poor countries.

However, the argument that consumer pressure for better standards is likely to harm third-world workers isn't very convincing. For one thing, to those who believe in the free market, it ought to be clear that the improvements that could be made – such as clamping down on abusive managers and ending humiliating restrictions on when workers can visit the toilet, two problems that have been reported everywhere from Mexico to China – don't cost much economically. Indeed, they may end up saving money, since, as numerous recent studies have shown, workers treated with respect are more productive than those who aren't (no surprise there).

Another thing that costs very little – at least, if the companies have got nothing to hide – is **transparency**. Hardly any big companies that make use of cheap developing-world manufacturing reveal exactly where their products are made, which means that it's difficult for anyone other than investigative journalists to get an independent view of conditions. As Labour Behind the Label told Rough Guides, "no company produces a complete map of its supply chain". Usually, the excuse is not wanting to give away valuable business secrets to their competitors – it would be "a little like giving your playbook to the opposing team before a game", according to the Nike website. But it's hard to believe that big businesses operating in the same countries, and sometimes the same factories, cannot find out relatively easily where their competitors' goods are produced.

Even those improvements which will cost money, such as better **health and safety**, and ensuring that **wages** are high enough to provide a decent standard of living, are likely to be small costs in comparison with the money saved by sourcing from poor countries in the first place. Indeed, labour costs are as much as fifty times lower in poor countries than rich countries so, even when you factor in transport and import costs, it's likely that there is plenty of room for improvement before it becomes economically unviable for companies to source from the developing world – as many fair-trade suppliers are already showing.

BIG BRANDS, BIG BUSINESS
No logo, pro logo and CSR

In general, the bigger, more visible and more strongly "brand-name" a company is, the more it's disliked by those who describe themselves as ethical shoppers or consumer activists. This is due to widespread distrust both of transnational companies themselves and the logos, advertising and chain-store outlets associated with them.

> **❝** Quite simply, every company with a powerful brand is attempting to develop a relationship with consumers that resonates so completely with their sense of self that they will aspire, or at least consent, to be serfs under these feudal brandlords. **❞**
>
> Naomi Klein, *No Logo*

Anti-corporate, anti-advertising sentiment is nothing new, of course, but it's been running at an all-time high since the 1990s, and especially since the publication of **Naomi Klein**'s bestseller – *No Logo* – which catapulted modern branding strategies and global supply chains firmly into the public consciousness. Klein made the case that big companies are getting bigger, and that their focus is shifting away from real-world activities such as employing staff and manufacturing products (which they increasingly "outsource" to exploitative contractors in the developing world) and towards the insidious process of branding: using logos and advertising to make people think that their produce "means" something. This has inherent problems, she argued, but it's especially ugly when you consider that the companies constantly appropriate people's icons and aspirations for their advertising and logos, which they force ever further into our public spaces – from concert halls to classrooms.

Though Klein has never really been an advocate of ethical shopping (she tends to be far more concerned with political issues such as the deals brokered at the World Trade Organization and the International Monetary Fund), her arguments have undoubtedly entered the ethical consumerism debate. The heavily branded companies she criticized – such as Starbucks, McDonald's, Nike and Gap – may not ever have been popular among ethically minded shoppers, but since *No Logo* they're at the top of most people's list of companies to avoid.

All this raises an important, though rarely asked, question: are the big brands – indeed, big companies in general – less or more ethical than the rest? How do they compare with manufacturers of **non-name-brand** goods, or less high-profile retailers?

Branding as accountability?

Klein's critics, as exemplified by the "Pro Logo" writers at *The Economist*, say that she has it all wrong. In practice, they claim, the more heavily branded a company is, the more visible it is, and the more accountable to consumers it becomes. One foot wrong from a famous global brand and consumers can take revenge within hours. "Even mighty Coca-Cola has been humbled", they point out: "Told of a contamination incident in Belgium, its then-boss, Doug Ivester, is said to have dismissed it with the comment: 'Where the fuck is Belgium?' A few months later, after a mishandled public-relations exercise that cost Coke sales across Europe, he was fired."

No group better sums up the anti-brand ethos than Adbusters, a self-proclaimed "global network of artists, activists, writers, pranksters, students, educators and entrepreneurs who want to advance the new social activist movement of the information age". It's best known for the striking, witty series of spoof ads it designs, which often adorn the cover of *Adbusters* magazine, its print outlet for ecological, anti-corporate and anti-brand comment. But it also runs PowerShift, an "advocacy advertising agency", which helps like-minded organizations to promote their cause visually. At the time of writing, US commercial television networks were refusing to sell Adbusters airtime for its 15-second public-health broadcast about the fat content of Big Macs.

Indeed, *The Economist* writers continue, branding is "an effective weapon for holding even the largest global corporations to account". And this accountability extends to ethical matters, so that when Klein and others attack heavily branded companies for, say, exploiting sweatshops, these companies fear a consumer boycott and are forced to clean up their act. Nike has been forced to "revamp its whole supply chain" due to just such a fear, they point out – but only because its branding (the ubiquitous name and swoosh logo) makes it such an easy target. Had it produced unbranded, no-name prod-

CSR: ETHICAL BIG BUSINESS?

One of the defining business buzzwords of the last decade has been **CSR**, or **corporate social responsibility**. There's no single definition of what this means, but it usually involves a company "aligning its business operations with social values" by drawing up codes of conduct and "reporting", which refers to companies publishing public, self-penned documents assessing their social and environmental "performance".

This issue splits those in the ethical shopping movement down the middle. While most people agree that a company prepared to acknowledge ethical issues is better than one which is not, some see CSR as primarily "greenwash": a cheap smokescreen to satisfy ethically minded consumers, get rid of annoying protesters, and to persuade governments that there's no need for the thing that big companies really fear: laws and regulations that *force* them to behave well all the time.

It's certainly true that CSR contains a fundamental limitation, at least in the case of companies owned by shareholders – it can only include things that are likely to increase profits. Doing anything else would violate the basic obligations of company directors to their shareholders: to maximize returns. So while a company's CSR report may talk about wanting to be a "good corporate citizen", this can only go so far. If it can be shown, for example, that improving conditions for workers will raise productivity, avoid the cost of strikes or high staff turnover, or reduce the chance of a consumer boycott, then changes will probably be made – and the company will make a proud public statement about its solid commitment to its workforce. But if it looks set to harm profits, then things will stay as they are.

And can CSR claims be believed anyway? According to many anti-

ucts, it wouldn't have been so vulnerable to consumer pressure. In fact, it probably would never have had investigative writers visiting its factories in the first place.

Commentators who take this line admit that there are clearly jarring contradictions between, say, the inclusive, one-world imagery cynically used in a big sportswear company's marketing campaigns and the reality of its factories. But surely, they argue, the important issue is simply how good or bad the working conditions are, not whether they're at odds with a few Western adverts, which everyone

poverty NGOs, the answer is often no. "Corporate practices do not match ethical policies", wrote Oxfam recently about the sportswear industry.

At almost the same time, Christian Aid examined the ethical claims of some high-profile companies such as British American Tobacco (on worker health and safety in their developing-world plantation), Coca-Cola (on their promises not to harm local communities by extracting too much groundwater) and Shell (on its social impact on communities in Nigeria and elsewhere). They concluded that in each case the claims were not reflected on the ground and that in general CSR was proving "a completely inadequate response to the sometimes devastating impact that multinational companies can have in an ever-more globalised world – and that it is actually used to mask that impact".

To try and prove that their codes of conduct are enforced, many of the more progressive companies employ **independent monitors** – professional auditers examining labour rights in Chinese supplier factories, for example. But even "independent" auditors can be contentious: while some companies employ expert, non-profit monitors such as Verité (www.verite.org) in interviewing staff about violations, others employ companies that may sometimes have a financial interest in not uncovering all the problems (exactly the kind of conflict of interest that lay behind the Enron scandal).

CSR's defenders claim that all this criticism and scepticism is unhelpful. They claim that this ethical approach to running a big business has already yielded some very positive results, and that it is sowing the seeds of wider change in a much more effective way than enforceable regulation could ever achieve.

knows are a load of marketing claptrap anyway.

Few people would disagree with that last point. But are big, visible brands and retailers *really* more conscientious and good for the world than the non-name-brand equivalents? Well, it's undoubtedly true that as a group – and especially those with high-profile brands that have been targeted by activists – big companies have issued more ethical statements and introduced more **codes of conduct** than less visible companies. Indeed, the field of CSR, or **corporate social responsibility** (see pp.64–65), is now thriving – the UK has a Minister for Corporate Social Responsibility, and is soon to open a CSR Academy. And it's mainly the big companies that are driving all this.

Take food retail. Nearly all the major supermarkets are signed up to the Ethical Trading Initiative (see pp.68–69), which aims to ensure good labour practice in their developing-world suppliers. You won't find your local corner shop or florist on the list. Or take the clothes

A protester outside the US supreme court takes a stand against what many see as our "brand new world", on the day of Nike vs Kasky (see box on p.207). But how do the corporate giants compare to smaller, non-name companies?

sector. Many involved in the social and environmental auditing of developing-world factories treat it as a given that conditions are worse in the small-business-dominated, non-name-brand garment sectors, where margins are tighter, consumer pressure non-existent and campaigners nowhere to be seen. One person who works for an auditing body told Rough Guides, "it's common knowledge … that non-name brands tend to be bottom feeders".

Even the most despised big firms may be better in many ways that their small-scale rivals. McDonald's uses free-range eggs, shuns milk from cows that have been injected from the controversial protein known as "bovine growth hormone", and doesn't use eco-unfriendly polystyrene in its packaging. Can your local burger joint say the same? And can your local café claim to have as good a coffee sourcing policy as that of Starbucks (see p.161).

Of course, the argument continues, the big companies are a very long way from perfect. As already discussed, many of them refuse to publish their list of developing-world suppliers. And, inevitably, some of their ethical policies are overblown PR efforts – in a recent case, Nike settled out of court after exaggerating its ethical standards (see box on p.207). Still, surely their efforts are better than nothing? Surely a code of conduct and a team of factory auditors is better than the code-free, no-promises approach of the faceless companies that supply bargain stores and street markets?

As one economist from the Bank of England put it, while we might push for global *regulation*, in the meantime we can at least have global *reputation*. And without reverting to small-scale localization (see p.46), in which you might know the individuals who grew your food and sewed your T-shirt, that reputation is most precious to the bigger, more visible brands and retailers.

One hand gives, the other takes away...

The obvious conclusion to the above case is, sure, avoid big brands and shops if you think that advertising is inherently distasteful, that global logos and high-street chains are destroying cultural diversity

THE ETHICAL TRADING INITIATIVE

While some people use the term "ethical trade" to mean the same thing as fair-trade, others use it to refer specifically to something quite different: the **ETI**, or **Ethical Trading Initiative**. Set up in 1998, this is one of the more widely respected corporate social responsibility initiatives, a project that brings NGOs and trade unions together with companies, in order to help the latter develop and implement credible codes of conduct relating to **labour and human rights practices** in their supply chains. The ETI membership includes many household-name companies, all of which have committed to implementing a "base code", which covers nine areas and specifies that:

▷ Employment is freely chosen

▷ Freedom of association and the right to collective bargaining are respected

▷ Working conditions are safe and hygienic

▷ Child labour shall not be used

▷ Living wages are paid

▷ Working hours are not excessive

▷ No discrimination is practised

▷ Regular employment is provided

▷ No harsh or inhumane treatment is allowed

Significant is the reference to a **living wage**, which ETI defines as one which "should always be enough to meet basic needs and to provide some discretionary income". This is a commitment that is missing from most corporate codes of conduct, and its presence here is one reason why many labour and anti-poverty groups describe the ETI rules as

and homogenizing public space, and that big firms are draining money from local economies. But don't try and fool yourself that the no-name alternative is any better in terms of workers' rights or environmental awareness – in all probability it's considerably worse.

It's a fair point. As ever, though, it's not quite so simple. For one thing, it's not necessarily true that the big, visible companies are the most ethically enlightened. The world's biggest chain retailer – **Wal-Mart** (which owns Asda) – is often given as an example of exactly

constituting "a model code". However, that's not to say that the same groups hold up the companies which belong to the ETI as examples of model "ethical traders". Indeed, the list includes many names that have long been the bane of anti-sweatshop campaigners and trade unions – such as Asda, owned by union-bashing Wal-Mart.

And though the ETI rules specify that the implementation of the code should be independently monitored, some commentators have questioned how consistently and effectively this happens.

ETI MEMBERS

ETI members include a number of major companies as well as international trade unions and a plethora of charities and NGOs (including the Fairtrade Foundation as well as Oxfam and Save The Children). Following are some of the better known corporate members. For a full list, and for more information about every aspect of the ETI, see: www.ethicaltrade.org

▷ ASDA	▷ Gap	▷ Sainsbury's
▷ The Body Shop	▷ Levi Strauss & Co	▷ Somerfield
▷ Boots	▷ Marks & Spencer	▷ The Tea Sourcing
▷ Chiquita	▷ Monsoon	Partnership (includes
▷ The Co-operative	▷ Mothercare	Taylors, Tetley,
Group (CWS)	▷ New Look	Twinings and others)
▷ Debenhams	▷ Next	▷ Tesco
▷ Fyffes	▷ Safeway	▷ WH Smith

how ethical businesses *shouldn't* behave. True, it now has a code of conduct, but at the time or writing it is "silent on trade union rights", according to Oxfam. The right to organize is a fundamental ILO right, but one which Wal-Mart famously doesn't recognize (see pp. 179–180).

However, even if you're prepared to accept, for the sake of argument, that big, visible companies *are* more likely to be ethically accountable than their smaller, no-name rivals, there remains a case for saying that – very often – their whole way of doing business may still be contributing to lower labour and environmental standards. This view has been put forward by numerous pressure groups such as Oxfam, and holds that, once a brand or retailer has grown big enough, it can exert extraordinary leverage over its suppliers, forcing them to produce faster, more cheaply and more "flexibly" (being able to turn around big orders very quickly, for example).

Once that leverage is available, critics of corporations maintain, a company will invariably exercise it, no matter how many factory auditors it employs or CSR reports it publishes. This allows the brands and shops to pass savings on to consumers and shareholders. But the cost is shouldered by the suppliers, who – in order to meet their ambitious production targets, and stay on good terms with the big buyers – have to cut corners. The result, for workers, is very often more overtime, less job security, frozen wages, less spending on health and safety in the workplace, and poor environmental standards.

While decent codes of conduct are to be welcomed, says Oxfam, they may be ignored on the ground, because the big brands' "supply-chain purchasing practices are undermining the very labour standards that they claim to support". A 2003 World Bank document seemed to agree, pointing to a frequent and unresolved "tension among price, quality and delivery time on the one hand, and CSR requirements on the other".

On a different level, there's also a fundamental limitation with thinking of corporate size and visibility as a form of accountability: most branded products are made from virtually **untraceable commodity** supply chains over which brands have no ethical control.

So, for instance, even if a big clothes company is relatively "ethical" in its factories, its codes are unlikely to cover the farmers growing the cotton they use. Likewise, even the most ethically enlightened electronics brand can't claim to know the provenance of the bauxite or coltan used in its new laptop series. This might all seem a touch pedantic, were it not for the fact that extraction of coltan – a black, tar-like mineral used in mobile phone and computer circuit boards – has for years been funding murderous civil war in central Africa. Besides, minerals mining is overall one of the most dangerous, exploitative and ecologically damaging of all industries (faceless mining conglomerates don't feature much in the mainstream press, but they do crop up in reports on human rights and the environment).

According to many campaigners, what these "invisible" commodity sectors need is a clear and strict **international legal framework** to enforce decent standards and hold companies that behave badly to account. But big business is not often in favour of this. Indeed, the same high-street brands who claim to be ethical trailblazers are often major players in the corporate lobby groups which spend millions lobbying *against* any across-the-board enforceable regulations. The UN's proposed **Human Rights Norms For Business** are a good recent example: they have met fierce resistance from big business-dominated trade groups such as the International Chamber of Commerce. Furthermore, as discussed below, in many cases big business bolsters its lobbying case by giving money to politicians. Even where they are making positive developments in their own supply chains, then, companies may be having a negative effect elsewhere.

So, once again, there are no simple answers for ethically minded shoppers. Big brands and retailers do generally have more developed ethical policies than those producing no-name goods, but their codes only go so far, and arguably their aggressive buying practices, lobbying and political donations (not to mention their invasive advertising, fat-cat pay and other corporate trappings) offset the good they do with their moral efforts. Thankfully, however, in a growing number of cases, we can get the best of both worlds by favouring ethical specialists and formal certification schemes such as, for food, Fairtrade or, for wooden products, the Forest Stewardship Council (see p.296). The rest of this book lists many such firms and schemes.

OPPRESSIVE REGIMES
To trade or not to trade?

As mentioned in chapter two, some of the first well-known boycotts of companies were primarily a means of boycotting a government – that of South Africa – in protest at the apartheid regime. People still debate the degree to which Western consumers contributed towards apartheid's eventual fall (they were just one of many political and economic pressures applied), but most agree that they did help. That success triggered a new approach to ethical shopping: avoiding products – and services, in the case of holidays – from countries with oppressive governments.

The logic is straightforward. A government always benefits from its country's exports – via corporation tax, export tariffs and the like. So when we buy goods imported from a country where the regime in power is oppressing its own people, we may be adding to the government's coffers and tightening its grip on power. Likewise if we give our custom to any multinational company that does business in the country in question.

If, on the other hand, we avoid all goods from oppressed countries (and the big businesses operating in them), us shoppers can help to isolate the governments economically, cutting off their much-needed cash supplies, weakening their grip on power and giving their people a better chance to rid themselves of their tyrants. Even Western governments seem to acknowledge the potential power of such a tactic. The US Department of Commerce Bureau of Industry and Security operates the Office of Antiboycott Compliance, which aims to "encourage, and in specified cases, require US firms to refuse to participate in foreign boycotts that the United States does not sanction".

But boycotting countries is always going to be a thorny issue. For one thing, it's difficult to know which countries to avoid. There is, after all, no single and uncontroversial measure of the "oppressiveness" of a country. And where should we draw the line? If we're going to boycott "oppressive regimes", then shouldn't we really also be boy-cotting the Western countries that fund, or otherwise support, such regimes? This would certainly seem the logical conclusion, but if we're taking foreign policy into account (not to mention crimes against the global environment), then not many countries would be left on the thumbs-up list. What about the UK, for instance? Considering that the current government has, among other things, fought a war of questionable legality in Iraq and maintained a special relationship with a US administration hell-bent on derailing the international response to climate change, should ethically minded Brits boycott goods from their own country?

Unintended consequences

Besides these conundrums about moral consistency, there's also the risk that boycotting oppressive regimes may actually be counter-productive. While hitting a government where it hurts is fine in prin-ciple, inevitably it also means harming the population – at least in the short term. Indeed, oppressed countries are usually also poor, and have a terribly unequal distribution of wealth, so if Western con-sumers refuse to buy goods from such countries, it may well hit fac-tory and agricultural workers much harder than the government itself. If so, the effect could be a double whammy: the poor will go hungry and also find themselves *even more* reliant on the regime in question than before, leaving them less able to do anything about it.

No single boycott of a country has ever been big enough (and inde-pendent of other international pressures) for us to know whether this argument stands up. But we can perhaps get a sense of the effects of a boycott on a country's people by looking at what happens when *states* impose trade sanctions on each other. Take Iraq, which was subject to around a decade of international sanctions (imposed by the UN but driven by the US and UK) to "contain" the military capa-bilities of dictator Saddam Hussein. This case was unusual in that it involved an "Oil for Food" programme (through which Iraqi oil could be exchanged for humanitarian goods), in theory ensuring that

OPPRESSIVE REGIMES LISTS

There is no definitive list of oppressive regimes, but there is a huge amount of research available as to how the various countries of the world compare on **human rights** issues, political openness and other such criteria. Much of this research is carried out by non-governmental organizations such as Amnesty International, Human Rights Watch and Freedom House. Governments also sometimes release surveys of this kind of information.

A number of organizations concerned with ethical consumerism use all this data to maintain their own lists of oppressive regimes, which shoppers and investors can choose to take into account if they so desire. Following are two examples of lists from respected groups: the Ethical Investment Research Service (see p.246) and ECRA – the research body behind *Ethical Consumer* magazine (see p.362).

Such lists are always **controversial** – not just inherently, but because, in practice, they're very prone to going out of date, since they're time-consuming to compile and rely on third-party on-the-ground research. The following may have been updated by the time you read this.

ETHICAL INVESTMENT RESEARCH SERVICE OPPRESSIVE REGIMES LIST

CATEGORY A (THE WORST OFFENDERS)

▷ Afghanistan	▷ Colombia	▷ Kenya	▷ Sudan
▷ Algeria	▷ Democratic	▷ Libya	▷ Syria
▷ Angola	Republic of	▷ North Korea	▷ Tunisia
▷ Bahrain	Congo	▷ Oman	▷ United Arab
▷ Brunei	▷ Egypt	▷ Pakistan	Emirates
▷ Burma	▷ Iran	▷ Rwanda	▷ Vietnam
▷ Cameroon	▷ Iraq	▷ Saudi Arabia	▷ Yemen
▷ China	▷ Kazakhstan	▷ Somalia	▷ Zimbabwe

CATEGORY B

▷ Burundi	▷ Cuba	▷ Eritrea	▷ Haiti
▷ Cambodia	▷ Equatorial	▷ Ethiopia	▷ India
▷ Chad	Guinea	▷ Guinea-Bissau	▷ Indonesia

▷ Israel	▷ Nigeria	▷ Serbia &	▷ Turkey
▷ Lesotho	▷ People's	Montenegro	▷ Uganda
▷ Liberia	Republic of	▷ Sierra Leone	▷ Uzbekistan
▷ Mexico	Congo	▷ Sri Lanka	▷ Venezuela
▷ Morocco	▷ Peru	▷ Tanzania	
▷ Nepal	▷ Senegal	▷ Togo	

ECRA OPPRESSIVE REGIMES CATEGORY

ECRA make no distinction between the bad and the *really* bad. For the most up-to-date version see:
www.ethicalconsumer.org/magazine/buyers/categories.htm

▷ Afghanistan	▷ Egypt	▷ Kuwait	▷ Senegal
▷ Algeria	▷ Equatorial	▷ Laos	▷ Somalia
▷ Belarus	Guinea	▷ Lebanon	▷ Sudan
▷ Brazil	▷ Eritrea	▷ Liberia	▷ Swaziland
▷ Burma	▷ Ethiopia	▷ Libya	▷ Tanzania
▷ Burundi	▷ Fiji	▷ Malaysia	▷ Thailand
▷ Central African	▷ Guatemala	▷ Mexico	▷ Togo
Republic	▷ Indonesia	▷ Nigeria	▷ Tunisia
▷ Chad	▷ Iran	▷ Pakistan	▷ Turkey
▷ China	▷ Iraq	▷ Qatar	▷ United Arab
▷ Côte d'Ivoire	▷ Israel	▷ Russian	Emirates
▷ Democratic	▷ Jordan	Federation	▷ Uzbekistan
Republic of	▷ Kazakhstan	▷ Rwanda	▷ Vietnam
Congo	▷ Kenya	▷ Saudi Arabia	▷ Zimbabwe

If you'd rather go straight to the source and get information about specific countries, try:

Amnesty International Library www.amnesty.org/library
Human Rights Watch www.hrw.org
Freedom House www.freedomhouse.org

Or read the out-of-date but very informative *Observer Human Rights Index 1999*, available online at www.guardian.co.uk

the poor of the country didn't feel the brunt of the sanctions. And yet by all accounts the results were still a human catastrophe. Denis Halliday, former UN humanitarian co-ordinator in Iraq, described the sanctions as "genocidal", pointing to "the death of some 5–6,000 children a month" through malnutrition, disease resulting from damaged water infrastructure, and so on. It seems that the sanctions were bad for nearly the whole population, except perhaps Hussein, whose government seemed only to tighten its grip.

True, this is an extreme case. And it's worth remembering that a similar argument was initially used by Margaret Thatcher and Ronald Reagan to try to discourage people boycotting South Africa. But it demonstrates that the effects of economic isolation are not necessarily positive. A very different but equally useful example is Cuba, which since October 1960 has faced a trade embargo from the US. Critics of the embargo regularly and rightly point to the fact that the negative effects are felt not by the government but by the Cuban people. (Curiously, many of these critics also rail against the increase in world trade brought about by globalization.)

Trade as Trojan horse?

A more controversial argument against consumers shunning oppressive regimes and the companies doing business in them is the claim that even if international trade may help a bad government in the short term, it may ultimately be the best way to "open up" a repressed country – especially when big foreign businesses are involved. After all, global trade encourages communication, transparency, clear property laws and other factors which those on the right tend to see as likely to bring about democracy and respect for human rights.

On one level, such an argument is patently absurd; there have been countless examples of oppressive and corrupt governments feeding off international trade while their people get nothing except pollution, further oppression and increasing inequality. Just think of **Nigeria**, where infamous dictator General Abacha personally creamed off a staggering amount of public money (an estimated $4

Activists of the Tibetan Youth Congress shout anti-China slogans during a rally in New Delhi on December 8, 2002. Campaigners such as these call on Western consumers to avoid Chinese goods until China stops human rights abuses among its own people and the people of Tibet

billion) in the 1990s, almost all of it from oil sales to the West.

And yet, despite a few notable exceptions, measures of economic "openness" – such as the Index of Economic Freedom compiled by the right-wing combo of The Heritage Foundation think-tank and *The Wall Street Journal* – *do* tend to equate roughly with measures of political freedom. And foreign trade often encourages this kind of economic openness.

This is a wide and heated debate. Take **China**, for example, which is swiftly becoming the "factory of the world", and which features high up on every list of oppressive states thanks to its appalling record on torture, deaths in custody, prisoners of conscience, unfair trials, detention without charge or trial, and executions, among other things. Some human rights campaigners claim that increased foreign trade is gradually helping to make China's government more open,

OPPRESSIVE REGIMES

> *The rise of democracy in South Korea and Taiwan attests to the power of the market in generating political liberalization. Both countries have moved from closed, authoritarian regimes to open-market democracies without bloody revolutions and without the threat of economic sanctions ... will China follow?*

James A Dorn, *The Cato Journal*

> *We have reached the point where the most ardent defenders of Chinese communism are US capitalists.*

Trade unionist Mark Anderson in 1996, on the US's decision not to make China's "most favoured nation" trade status conditional on human rights improvements

less oppressive and more vulnerable to pressure from the rest of the world (for example through the World Trade Organization, which China recently joined). But the regime's human rights standards are still extremely bad, and many critics, not least those in the Free Tibet movement, are calling for the international community – consumers included – to use a trade boycott as a way of putting pressure on the Chinese government to make much more radical improvements.

So what can you do?

There's no golden rule that says whether trade will be a blessing or a curse for the people living under an oppressive government. It depends on the specific regime, and the specific circumstances, such as the products being exported (natural resources, for example, seem to spell much more trouble than manufacturing). And it depends on the speed with which an economy opens up to international trade: a recent study by Israeli academics suggested that the faster the transition, the greater the amount of corruption it creates.

If a boycott is called for from within the country itself, by opposition groups which represent the majority of the population, then there can be little question that it's the right thing to do. This was the case in South Africa, and at the time of writing is the case with **Burma** (Myanmar).

There, pro-democracy leaders won free elections by a landslide nearly 15 years ago but have been prevented from taking office by a brutal military regime. They are calling on the world's companies, shoppers and travellers to boycott the country (see p.339).

But in most other cases the picture is less clear, and citizens of the countries in question are sometimes shocked and offended to find their homeland – including all the companies their friends and families work for – on an international boycott list. Ask people from Venezuela, China and elsewhere whether they support Western consumers boycotting all big companies that operate in their country, and you're unlikely to get a very positive response.

So, once again it's a matter of making your own decisions, and once again it's true that making your views known politically is arguably far more important that simply buying or not buying. If you do decide that shunning certain countries is the way to go, the box on pp.74–75 shows the governments that certain organizations define as being oppressive; pp.32–33 list a few current high-profile country boycotts.

POLITICAL DONORS
Voting with your wallet – literally

Though we might get upset about what certain politicians get up to, most of us continue to fund those same politicians via the companies we support (as well as the unions we're members of, but that's outside the scope of this book). This issue affects many countries, including the UK, but it's perhaps most pressing in the US, where campaign contributions are huge and where the politicians influenced by these donations have more influence on the world than anyone else. So, for example, we might lament George Bush's stance on climate change and the International Criminal Court, to pick just two of many possible objections, but we continue to buy from the huge list of companies which support him and his party (see box overleaf).

Financial contributors don't determine the outcome of every decision made in Washington, of course, and a causal link between contributions and policy decisions is extremely difficult to prove. However, as with advertising, we can be sure that companies only spend money on political donations when they expect something in return. And research by organizations like the US's Center for Responsive Politics certainly suggests that there is a very real link

WHO ELECTED GEORGE W BUSH? YOU DID!

Maintained by *Ethical Consumer* magazine and drawing on research from OpenSecrets.org, the Boycott Bush website encourages consumers to shun companies who have donated the most to George W Bush's election campaigns. The project was launched on Bush's rejection of the Kyoto treaty, but also objects to his "illegal invasion of Iraq and other regressive steps such as opposing weapons proliferation treaties". Following is their list of major UK brands owned by the top-25 Bush donors at the time of writing.

▷ **Computers, internet and media** AOL, CompuServe, Netscape Navigator, Microsoft, Walt Disney

▷ **Couriers:** UPS, FedEx

▷ **Electrical goods** Hotpoint, GE-branded consumer electrical goods

▷ **Food and drink** Carte Noire, Kenco, Maxwell House, Ribena, Horlicks bedtime drinks, Lucozade energy drinks, Budweiser, Michelob and Bud Ice beers, Dairylea, Philadelphia, Dime bar, Marabou, Milka, Suchard, Terry's, Toblerone, Bird's custard, Kraft foods, Doritos, Walkers crisps, Pepsi, Quaker breakfast cereals, Sugar Puffs, Granose, Protoveg and Realeat meat substitutes, So Good soya yoghurt (not So Good soya drink)

▷ **Medicine and personal hygiene** Anadin painkillers, Benadryl, Sudafed decongestant, Calpol, Diflucan antifungal, Feldene P gel, Listerine mouthwash, Rappell, TCP throat pastilles, Euthymol toothpaste, Aussie shampoo, Aquafresh and Macleans toothpaste, Beechams cold remedies, Contac cold and 'flu remedies, Eumovate eczema treatments, Oxy acne treatment, Panadol paracetamol, Lactacyd Femina feminine cleansers, NiQuitin nicotine patches, Solpadeine painkillers, Zovirax coldsore

between contributions and voting patterns. Anyhow, altruism doesn't seem like a very likely motive, and nor does ideology, considering that many companies – such as Microsoft and AOL – are associated with donating heavily to all parties with any chance of getting elected.

Some people claim that political donations from companies are not a bad thing – the necessary counterbalance to equivalent donations from trade unions. But even if you agree with that, it doesn't

treatment, Coppertone sun lotion, Amway toiletries and cleaning products, Nutrilite vitamins and food supplements, Artistry skin care and colour cosmetics, eSpring system, Magna Bloc therapeutic magnets, SA8 laundry detergent

▷ **Store cards owned by GE Capital Bank** includes those offered by Monsoon, Kwik-Fit, Laura Ashley, New Look, Debenhams and House of Fraser

▷ **Supermarkets** ASDA

▷ **Tobacco** Marlboro, Parliament

▷ **Travel and transport** BP, Esso and Mobil-branded lubricants, Texaco petrol, Ford, Land Rover, Range Rover, Mazda, Volvo, Jaguar, American Airlines flights

Note that, technically speaking, it's not necessarily the companies that make the donations: due to US political contribution laws, it's very often organizations "affiliated" with the company, or their employees. But the effect is the same. Also note that some of the businesses listed above (such as AOL) have given more money to the Democrats than the Republicans – not that trying to buy influence with all the candidates is much better. Finally, be aware that this list looks at the period 2000–04. At least one company listed – BP – has promised to stop all political donations.

For the most up-to-date list, methodology and background on the campaign, go straight to the sources:

Boycott Bush www.boycottbush.net
Open Secrets www.opensecrets.com

change the fact that as consumers we have a choice: we can either buy goods from companies giving money to politicians we dislike, or we can shop elsewhere. The only problem is that it can be hard to pin down exactly who's giving what to who, not least because the political funding may not come from the company itself, but from individual directors or (in the US) from **PACs** – Political Action Committees. Luckily, however, there are a number of websites that will help you navigate the murky world of political giving:

Center for Responsive Politics (US donations) www.opensecrets.org
CleanPolitix (UK donations) www.cleanpolitix.com
PoliticalMoneyLine (US donations) www.tray.com

Beyond donations: lobby groups and think-tanks

Even when companies aren't donating directly to politicians, they may be having an even greater – and even less transparent – impact on government policy and media content through their contributions to corporate lobby groups and think-tanks. We've already seen how even the most mainstream business groups – such as the US Chamber of Commerce – have taken a firm stance against the Kyoto Treaty and the UN's Human Rights Norms for Businesses. A number of similar examples crop up elsewhere in this book.

However, more sinister than these giant groups are the small but highly influential think-tanks – many of them funded largely or entirely by corporations – which exist solely to push for big-business-friendly agendas on everything from animal testing to nuclear power. It's beyond the scope of this book to look into this area – not least because accurate information about which companies are giving to which think-tanks is very difficult to come by. But if you fancy exploring the issue, check out Disinfopedia. You'll never look at big companies (or right-wing politicians) in the same way again.

Disinfopedia www.disinfopedia.org

PART II

PRODUCTS & COMPANIES

FOOD & DRINK
CLOTHES, COSMETICS & JEWELLERY
FINANCE
HOUSEHOLD
TRAVEL & TRANSPORT
GENERAL FAIR-TRADE SHOPS

04

FOOD & DRINK

No consumer area is so politically charged as food, which is at the centre of debates ranging from farmer exploitation, animal welfare and unfair international trade rules, to public health, biotechnology and environmental degradation. Some of these issues are discussed in general terms in the first section of this book, but this chapter looks in more depth at the wider implications of the food and drink we buy. It covers some general topics – intensive farming, organics, food miles, GM (genetic modification), and the environmental burden of meat production – before focusing on specific foods and drinks (from p.126) and the pros and cons of different places to shop (see p.175).

"CHEAP" FOOD VS ORGANICS
Is organic food and drink more ethical?

Agriculture has undergone a remarkable transition in the last sixty years. In the aftermath of World War II, the UK's drive to produce as much as possible as quickly as possible saw massive **state subsidies** awarded to the biggest, most industrialized farms. Small producers that relied heavily on manpower and produced a range of crops and animal products were gradually eclipsed by larger businesses that focused on just one or two crops or meats and relied primarily on technology, economies of scale and large quantities of **agrochemicals** (such as fertilizers and pesticides).

One impact of this process of industrialization has been a massive decrease in the number of farm workers. Indeed, there are now nearly half a million **fewer agricultural jobs** in the UK than there were a few decades ago – and although the amount of food we import has played a part in this, the main factor has been the increased "efficiency" allowed by technology and chemicals. Depending on who you ask, this reduction of the farm workforce is either a disaster (as family traditions have been destroyed and thousands of workers have lost their jobs) or a good thing (since fewer people are subjected to back-breaking work in rainy fields).

Another impact of subsidized industrial agriculture has been **a fall in the price of the food in our shops**. The average UK household is now estimated to spend less than one-tenth of its total budget on food. This compares with around one-third just fifty years ago, and that's despite the fact that we're eating posher, more "exotic" ingredients than ever before. Of course, much of this drop in how much of our money we spend on food is down to increasing wages and the fact that prices are kept artificially low by our tax-funded subsidies. But even taking these factors into account, food has become significantly less expensive as farming has got more industrial.

Most people would agree that cheaper food is a good thing (despite

BODY AND SOIL

Soil may not seem like the most interesting thing in the world, but earth is pretty amazing stuff, and it's at the centre of debates about organic and industrial farming. Despite its dull appearance, soil is absolutely packed **full of life**. The UN's Global Biodiversity Assessment suggested that a single gram of soil "could contain 10,000 million individual cells comprising 4,000–5,000 bacterial types, of which less than 10% have been isolated and are known to science", and that's before you consider snails, earthworms, termites, mites and other invertebrates. But soil not only *contains* life, of course, it also gives it: without fertile earth, there'd be no plants, no animals and no humans.

The world is covered by an extremely thin and delicate skin of this fertile dirt, just a few feet deep. And yet humans have been rather cavalier in their treatment of it: battering it with intensive, chemical-heavy agriculture, urbanization and deforestation. According to a report by the UK's Royal Commission on Environmental Pollution, around 10% of the world's total soil has been lost through human-induced causes. Even more amazingly, in just the last 40 years, nearly a third of the world's arable crop land has been abandoned due to soil erosion. Considering that it takes around 500 years to form just a few centimetres of soil in agricultural conditions, we're clearly losing our life-giving earth far quicker that it can be replaced, in the process endangering the future world's ability to feed itself.

It was precisely these worries that led to the establishment of the organic movement; hence the fact that its longest-standing organization is known as the Soil Association.

Source: All figures quoted in Biodiversity for Food and Agriculture, *a report by the Sustainable Development Department of the United Nations Food & Agriculture Organization*

the worsening problem of obesity in the UK). However, according to a growing number of commentators, we're not getting something for nothing. The hidden costs of industrial farming – to **human health**, the **environment** and long-term **food security** – are big and getting bigger.

In the words of the staff writers at *Nature* (a peer-reviewed science journal, not a bastion of eco-warriors), "Mainstream agronomists now acknowledge … that intensive farming reduces biodiversity, encourages irreversible soil erosion and generates run-off that is awash with harmful chemicals – including nitrates from fertilizers that can devastate aquatic ecosystems." In other words, soil and food experts are worried that intensive agriculture is wasting irreplacable soil, reducing the number of animals, birds, insects and plants in farming areas, and killing fish and plants in nearby streams and rivers. And that's before you consider the impact on **animal welfare**, and the massive wastefulness that accompanies intensive animal farming (more on this later).

Some saw these problems coming right from the beginning. As agricultural industrialization took off, a small bunch of philosophically minded farmers, worried primarily about the potentially damaging effect on soil, planted the seeds of the **organic movement**, which, after decades on the fringe, has seen an amazing boom recently, with annual sales in excess of £1 billion and rising every year.

ORGANIC QUESTIONS AND ANSWERS

What *is* organic food?

Since the EC passed legislation on it in 1993, the term "organic" has been governed by strict legal **definitions and regulations** across the European Union. Any product labelled as organic – wherever it was produced – must have been grown or raised according to a set of minimum EU standards, and possibly even extra standards imposed by the individual country and certification body (see box overleaf).

As most people are aware, at the core of the organic movement is a policy that shuns synthetic **fertilizers, pesticides, herbicides, fungicides** and other man-made "inputs". Instead of these, organic farmers rely on a mixture of special growing techniques and "natural" alternatives. In place of chemical fertilizers, for example, soil fertility is maintained by using **animal manure** and through **crop rotation**.

Crop rotation is a farming technique in which the same field is used for growing different crops in successive months or years, to "fix" nitrogen (using plants that can take nitrogen from the air and put it into the soil) and ensure that the nutrients some crops take from the earth are put back by others. It can also reduce the need for pesticides and herbicides, though other techniques are usually also necessary. These range from manual weeding to the introduction of predatory insects to a crop (to eat the pests) or the use of "natural" pesticides such as the *Bt*, derived from type of beetle.

Organic rules also ban artificial **sweeteners, colourings, preservatives** and **flavour enhancers** as well as hydrogenated fats and genetically modified ingredients. But this doesn't tell us the whole story. The organic "idea" is more a whole agricultural philosophy, taking in **animal welfare** and **social justice** as well as environmental and health concerns (see box).

In the case of prepared foods, to bear an organic label they must contain at least **95% organic ingredients**; the rest, where applicable, may be non-organic, but only from a list of approved ingredients.

Who enforces the rules?

Anyone who produces, imports, packages or processes organic food has to register with an official **certification body**, which will inspect them at least once a year. In the UK, there are currently ten certification bodies, all of which impose minimum standards defined by the UK government,

THE ORGANIC CHARTER

Though the exact details of organic rules vary around the world, the general principles and aims – as set out by the **International Federation of Organic Agricultural Movements** (www.ifoam.org) – are pretty well consistent. They fall into three main categories:

▷ **Environmental sustainability** Organic farming aims to limit or reverse the environmental damage caused by agriculture. Besides eliminating synthetic agrochemicals, this involves minimizing water waste and pollution; using reusable and recycled substances wherever possible; taking care of the soil; and encouraging biodiversity. Wherever possible, closed-system, self-sufficient farming is favoured, so manure from cows, for example, will be used as fertilizer for crops grown on the same farm. This limits pollution both directly and by reducing the need for polluting and energy-guzzling transport.

▷ **Humane treatment of animals** Good animal welfare guidelines are part of the minimum organic standards. Indeed, UK organic rules are actually stricter than those of the RSPCA's Freedom Food scheme (see p.124). All animals must have ample space and good conditions, and cruel practices – such as farrowing crates for pigs (see p.127), dairy calves being taken from their mothers on the day they're born and egg-laying chickens being kept in unnaturally large flocks – are banned. Routine use of antibiotics and other drugs is ruled out, making it harder to push animals beyond their "natural" limits of productivity. And feed, which itself must be mostly organic, must also be free from other farm animals (no feeding chicken to cows, say) and GM crops.

▷ **Socially just farming systems** Though less widely publicized, social considerations are taken seriously by the organic movement – at least on the theoretical level. The IFOAM guiding principles, for example, state that "social justice and social rights are an integral part of organic agriculture and processing" and list a set of standards ruling that organic producers and operators must have a policy on social justice, respect basic human rights and not use force or non-voluntary labour. Employees and contractors must "have the freedom to associate, the right to organize and the right to bargain collectively" and be provided with "equal opportunity and treatment". And any children employed by organic operators "shall be provided with educational opportunities".

and some of which add extra rules of their own. The best known of the ten, the **Soil Association**, is often described as having the most comprehensive rules.

Every organic product sold specifies the certifying body. Even if you don't see the name and logo, you'll see a code written in the form "Organic Certification UK3". For a list of the bodies and their numbers, see www.defra.gov.uk/farm/organic

Is organic food definitely better for the environment?

There's no single, definitive answer to this question, because environmental impact can be measured in so many different ways, and because the research into it is a long way from comprehensive. However, according to most non-partisan commentators – including a recent summary of the scientific evidence in *Nature* – organic farms are certainly more environmentally friendly in some ways.

Compared with conventional farms, for example, they tend to **encourage greater biodiversity**, such as insects, birds and other wildlife (because of the absence of pesticides and the fertility of the soil). They also tend to **use less energy** and create less global-warming CO_2 per kilo of produce (in part because man-made fertilizers are so energy-intensive to produce) and they **generate less waste** (such as fertilizer packaging). In some areas, such as phosphorous run-off into streams and the all-important question of retaining soil quality, a lack of many long-term comparative studies make the benefits difficult to prove beyond doubt, but, according to *Nature*, "many studies" suggest that organic production lives up to its promises.

The United Nations Food and Agriculture Organization (FAO) seems even more convinced, claiming in 2003 that "If organic agriculture is given the consideration it merits, it has the potential to transform agriculture as the main tool for nature conservation. Reconciling biodiversity conservation and food production depends upon a societal commitment to supporting organic agriculture." They also noted that organic farming "encourages both spatial and temporal biodiversity … conserves soil and water resources and builds soil organic matter and biological processes".

That's not to say that organic is *necessarily* the most eco-friendly farming system in the world – for now or for the future. A growing number of scientists advocate a middle ground that builds on organic concepts but doesn't rule out all synthetic inputs or GM processes – some of which, they claim, are less harmful (both to the environment and health) than the "natural" alternatives. Still, this middle ground isn't something that's being adopted and it's not something that we're offered in the shops: for now, the choice is basically between the produce of "conventional" or organic farms, and the latter are indeed better environmentally.

Still, even if organic *farms* are a good thing for the environment, that doesn't necessarily mean the same can be said of organic *food*. At least, not according to two arguments often made by critics of the organic movement. The first is that a huge amount of organic produce is **flown or shipped** into the UK from the other side of the world. This contributes unnecessarily to climate change, via the CO_2 emissions of the planes and boats that transport them. It's a fair point – Europe and North America account for practically all organic food sales, yet around half of total organic food production takes place in Asia, Australia and Latin America. But it's also perhaps irrelevant: a criticism of food imports as a whole, not organic farming. If we grew more organic food at home, there's be less need to import it.

The second argument is that organic farms tend to produce **less food per acre** than their more industrial counterparts. Therefore, if everyone went organic we'd either not have enough food, or we'd have to reclaim more land to use for farming by cutting down vast areas of forest, which of course would have terrible environmental consequences...

So organic farming couldn't feed the world?

No one knows exactly how much food an exclusively organic world could grow, but by most estimates it would be substantially less than the amount currently produced. Even such keen organic exponents as

Lord Melchett (former director of Greenpeace UK and himself an organic farmer) admit that it's an unknown quantity.

However, any question of feeding the world has to ask the question of how much food the human population actually needs. After all, much of what we currently produce ends up squandered in the rearing of **cheap meat**. Indeed, as discussed later in this chapter, the world's rainforests *are* already being chopped down to make way for more farmland. But this isn't to grow organic carrots; the crop of choice is intensively farmed soya (much of it GM), the vast majority of which is used in the inefficient and environmentally burdensome process of feeding up cattle.

On these grounds, some in the organic movement claim that if we gave up our desire for cheap, intensively farmed meat (which we would *have* to, since huge monocrop soya farms aren't exactly suited to good old crop rotation), an exclusively organic world could easily feed itself.

Others aren't convinced we'd even need to change our diet very much. Several food economists have pointed out that many small farmers in poor countries have massively *increased* their yields by adopting organic practices. As Nadia Scialabba wrote in a report for the FAO, "In developing countries … properly managed organic agriculture systems can increase agricultural productivity and restore the natural resource base."

Furthermore, it's clear that solving world hunger is as much a matter of **increasing political will** and **reducing waste** as of producing more. Even according to the cautious figures of the US Department of Agriculture (www.usda.gov), one-fifth of America's food ends up in the bin – enough to feed the people who starve each year twice over.

Still, even if a completely organic world could feed itself now, it may struggle in the future. After all, the global population is predicted to rise to at least ten billion by 2050, according to the UN. The main sticking point is the fact that organic rules currently ban the use of man-made fertilizers, which have been central to boosting world food productivity in the last few decades, and which – though they can cause serious environmental problems when applied irrespon-sibly – are not necessarily all that bad when used carefully.

Hence it is sometimes said that green-minded consumers should certainly support organic farming, but that they should accept that, in the long run, the rules may need to be made slightly more "flex-ible", to allow, for example, a certain amount of carefully regulated synthetic fertilizer.

HOW CHEAP IS CHEAP FOOD?

Supporters of organic and other "alternative" agricultural systems claim that, while organic food is undeniably more expensive, this is partly because the price we pay for conventionally farmed goods at the supermarket check-out doesn't reflect their true cost. In the words of Jules Pretty, a professor at Essex University, food "only appears cheap in the shop because we are not encouraged to think of the hidden costs … we actually pay three times for our food – once at the till in the shop, a second time through taxes [for subsidies] … and a third time to clean up the environmental and health side effects".

Here are some of the "external" costs – beyond the barcode price on on the packet – that we, or others, pay for elsewhere.

▷ **The financial cost** The industrial agriculture machine needs financial oiling at many points. In the UK, this happens most demonstrably via billions of pounds' worth of direct subsidies, the majority of which go to the biggest, most intensive farms (though, to be fair, some also go to organic farms). However, the taxpayer also bails out industrial farming in less direct ways, such as cleaning up the massive environmental damage it causes. According to Jules Pretty's calculations, the *measurable* among these extra costs – such as dealing with the damage done to the environment and to human health – amount to around £2 billion a year (£35 per person) and that's without the massive giant costs of crises like BSE and foot and mouth. Sadly, consumers who buy organic, opting out of the industrial farming system, still have to pay for all these extras.

▷ **The human cost** People debate the health risks posed by agrochemical residues on and in our foods (see p.156). However, less widely discussed

Why is organic food so expensive?

There's no way of avoiding it: organic food is more expensive. And, largely because of the higher labour costs, it looks likely that this will never change. However, it's pretty clear that the "real" difference in price isn't quite as great as it currently appears, for two main reasons. First, conventional non-organic farming comes with a number of "external" costs that our taxes pay for, from subsidies given to farmers

is the more measurable impact on farm and plantation workers who apply the stuff. Figures from the World Health Organization (www.who.int) and the World Resources Institute (www.wri.org) suggest that there are between 3.5 and 5 million acute pesticide poisonings annually, tens of thousands of which result in death. And the impact is particularly bad in the developing world, from where a significant proportion of our produce now comes: according to one study published in the *World Health Statistic Quarterly*, 99% of pesticide fatalities occur in poor countries, despite the fact that they only account for a minority of the world's pesticide use. The drive to make food ever cheaper has also arguably exacerbated the problem of child labour. An estimated 70% of the world's child labourers work in agriculture, especially on plantations growing coffee, tea and sugar (as well as tobacco and cotton).

▷ **The cost to animal welfare** When it comes to animal products, intensive farming is generally very bad news for livestock. And though things are slowly improving – veal crates and the worst battery farm cages are on their way out, for example – the conditions that many farm animals are subjected to are still atrocious. As described later in this chapter, they are often treated as mere commodities, living their short existences in chronically over-crowded sheds, never seeing natural light until being packed into a truck on slaughter day.

To this list we could also add the potential cost to human health of routine antibiotic use for livestock (see p.122) and the environmental cost of intensive meat farms (see p.119).

to the clearing up of their environmental mess (see box on pp.94–95) – not that organic shoppers are excluded from paying these costs, of course. Second, organic foods are usually treated as "premium products" by supermarkets, which means they charge a larger mark-up on them.

Whether organic food is worth the money is for each shopper to decide. But bear in mind that you can always **be selective**. Just because you have no intention, or lack the cash, to turn yourself into a 100% organic-only zone, it needn't stop you from just buying, say, organic animal products – which score a hat-trick in terms of animal welfare, antibiotics and pollution issues (all of which are discussed later on in this chapter). Also, bear in mind that organic produce can very often be found at sub-supermarket prices via box-schemes, greengrocers and farmers' markets (see p.181).

Is it better for the farmers?

Organic farming can certainly offer some advantages to farm owners and workers. For example, it removes the considerable **health risks** associated with over-exposure to agrochemicals – a huge issue on developing-world plantations, especially (see pp.152–153). It also means that small farmers are less likely to find themselves getting caught up in a spiral of **debt** driven by the cost of chemical inputs. This is a common problem since, as soil quality goes down and chemical-resistant pests develop, farmers can find they need to spend more on inputs each year. As the UN has reported, "the conventional food production model ties farmers into conditions of dependence on large corporations to buy agricultural inputs (seeds, fertilizers, pesticides) and to sell their produce".

That said, it's certainly not the case that life is rosy for all farmers and workers growing organic produce. Though the organic codes on worker welfare are much better than nothing, the organic food we import from the third world still generally comes from farms where the employees see little reward for the fruits of their labour. And, in the UK, too, while some farmers have profited from converting to

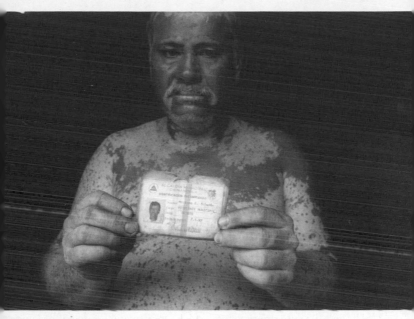

An ex-banana-plantation worker from the Chinandega (a farming area of Nicaragua) where widespread genetic illnesses, ranging from skin disorders to deformed babies, are blamed on decades of heavy pesticide use. Shocking pictures such as this aren't typical of non-organic farming, of course, and many of the worst agro-chemicals are no longer in use. However, around 20,000 farmers are still killed each year – and literally millions poisoned – by the ingestion of pesticides.

organic, many others have struggled to make a decent income from their produce. Some blame the supermarkets for taking too big a slice of the organic pie, others the subsidies and other external costs already described that allow conventional farming to appear cheaper than it really is.

Whatever the truth, there's a ever-increasing amount of organic **Fairtrade** products available – and these certainly offer farmers a better deal. And the Soil Association has recently launched it's own Ethical Trade label (see p.157).

Is organic food healthier?

Organic foods are widely marketed as safer and healthier, but the benefits are not universally accepted. The claims fall into two separate categories, the first of which relates to the potentially harmful effects of **pesticide residues** in our food. Unsurprisingly, organic foods carry incomparably fewer of these residues, and no one denies that this is a good thing. However, toxicologists aren't universally convinced that the levels of pesticide residues in conventional food – even those that exceed the official safety limits – are a serious cause for concern (for more on this topic, see p.156).

The second issue is whether organic foods are more **nutritious**. There have been studies showing organic food to be higher in levels of vitamin C, essential minerals, cancer-preventing phytonutrients and other beneficial things. But the differences tend to be slight, and there's a possibility that organic food may bring risks, too, such as – according to at least one study – a higher proportion of certain bugs in chicken meat.

Where to buy organic food and drink

Though the supermarkets now stock a pretty wide range of organic foods, there remains a strained relationship between organic farmers and the retail giants where most of their produce is sold. One point of contention is the issue of profit margins: like all farmers, organic producers feel that supermarkets' near-monopoly powers give them the ability to demand unreasonably low prices while making massive profits.

But beyond this, supermarkets also have various habits that many feel are the very antithesis of the organic philosophy: flying in produce from abroad, even when UK stock is available; packing fruit and veg in completely unnecessary plastic packaging; and contributing to the corporatization of the organic movement itself by favouring large organic suppliers rather than independent local farms.

For these reasons – and various others (see p.175) – you might prefer to buy your organic food via local box schemes, farmers markets and farm shops. To find them, turn to Where To Shop (see p.175). Or, for organic views and news, see:

Plan Organic www.planorganic.com
Links Organic www.linksorganic.com
About Organics www.aboutorganics.co.uk
DEFRA www.defra.gov.uk/farm/organic

NOT QUITE ORGANIC

Set up in 1991, **LEAF** (Linking Environment and Farming) is a UK farm certification scheme that aims to encourage an integrated and environmentally responsible approach to agriculture.

The rules are less strict than those of organics, but this, in theory at least, means that the scheme can appeal to the majority of growers who, for financial or other reasons, haven't decided to go properly organic. So pesticides are allowed, for example, but must be used responsibly. Though it's been around for more than a decade, the leaf "marque", as they call it, is one label that you're still unlikely to come across in most food outlets.

Waitrose is currently the only major retailer involved.

The **Wholesome Food Association** (WFA), meanwhile, has similar rules to organic certifications – including no synthetic inputs – but the system is based on trust rather that inspections and paperwork. The idea is that farmers interested in ecologically sound production and local sales can participate without the cost of official organic certification.

For more information see:

LEAF www.leafmarque.com
WFA www.wholesomefood.org

LOCAL FOOD VS IMPORTS
Meals and miles

Europe has been importing food and drink from far and wide for millennia – tea from China, spices from India, coffee from Ethiopia. But the globalization of modern food markets is on a completely different scale. These days we fly in fruit from the global South when it's **out of season** in the North, and we ship in goods that we could grow in the UK, but which can be **sourced more cheaply** from elsewhere.

Though only a small proportion of the food produced in the world is traded internationally – probably around 90% is consumed in the country where its grown – the distance travelled by the food we put on our plates in the UK is thought to have roughly doubled in the last two decades. Today, the contents of an average shopping basket of goods – including organic foods – can be the result of tens of thousands of miles journeying, by road, sea and increasingly air (see box overleaf).

For **food grown in the UK**, too, the distance from "farm to fork" is bigger than ever, not least because supermarket systems rely on everything being delivered to the shop via massive distribution centres. Since these are few and far between (Sainsbury's only has a dozen or so, for example), long truck journeys are inevitable. One much-cited study traced vegetables on sale in a supermarket in Evesham: they were grown just up the road, but had arrived via a huge round trip taking in Hereford, Dyfed and Manchester. Some defenders of the supermarket-style system – such as Tony Blair's "rural tsar", Lord Haskins – claim that this may actually be better than millions of half-full smaller vans making shorter journeys. But it's a contentious argument.

The most obvious problem with extra "food miles" is their **environmental impact**, especially in terms of global warming. Goods transport is one of the fastest-growing sources of greenhouse gases, and – in the case of air freight – there is no mechanism by which the importers and exporters pay for the environmental damage caused. Petrol used to transport food in vans or lorries at least has a tax payable on it, but aviation fuel – used, for example, to fly in out-of-season strawberries from South Africa to the UK– isn't taxed at all (see p.332). Yet, ironically, if global warming really kicks in, one of its most disastrous symptoms may be an impact on agriculture, in turn perhaps necessitating even more food transport – potentially a very vicious cycle.

It may not always be the case that local food is more eco-friendly. As economist Philippe Legrain argues, "growing Kiwi fruit in heated greenhouses in England gobbles up more energy than transporting them from New Zealand". This may be true, as long as they are shipped rather than flown. But the point only relates to "exotic" produce that is hard to grow in the UK – not the majority of food imports.

Environmental damage isn't the only criticism that local-food advocates make of our increasingly long-distance dining. In the case of shipping live animals, longer-than-necessary distances raise the likelihood not only of animal welfare abuses but also of the **spreading of diseases** such as foot and mouth. And these can end up costing astronomical sums of money: the total bill for the UK's foot-and-mouth crisis of 2001–02, including lost tourism revenue, is estimated to be around £10 billion.

In the case of fruit and vegetables, there's also the possibility of food losing **nutrients** en route. Studies by the Austrian Consumers Association, for example, found that "fresh" out-of-season fruit and vegetables are often significantly lower in vitamins and higher in harmful nitrates than genuinely fresh ones (or, indeed, frozen ones, which are usually put in the freezer within hours of being picked).

Poor-country imports

While the impact on climate change of unnecessary food miles is quite clear-cut, the effects on workers and local environments are more complex. First of all, there's the question already raised in

LONG-DISTANCE DINING

In a study called *Eating Oil*, the campaign group Sustain measured the miles travelled by our foods and the energy that the transportation consumes. One of their case studies looked at a basket of imported foods you might pick up in any UK supermarket:

FROM ABROAD TO THE UK

▷ 5kg of **chicken** from Thailand
   10,691 miles by ship

▷ 1kg of **runner beans** from Zambia
   4912 miles by plane

▷ 2kg of **carrots** from Spain
   1000 miles by lorry

▷ 0.5kg of **mangetout** from Zimbabwe
   5130 miles by plane

▷ 5kg of **potatoes** from Italy
   1521 miles by lorry

FROM THE UK TO THE DISTRIBUTION CENTRE

▷ 1kg of **sprouts** produced in Britain
   125 miles by lorry

▷ All the imports to the distribution centre
   625 miles by lorry

FROM THE DISTRIBUTION CENTRE TO THE STORE

▷ British sprouts, plus all the imports (total weight 13.5kg)
   360 miles by lorry

Add it all up and, collectively, these goods would have travelled almost **25,000 miles**, using up 52 megajoules of energy in doing so – equivalent to boiling the kettle for around 700 cups of tea. By contrast, an equivalent basket of seasonal produce from a farmers' market went only

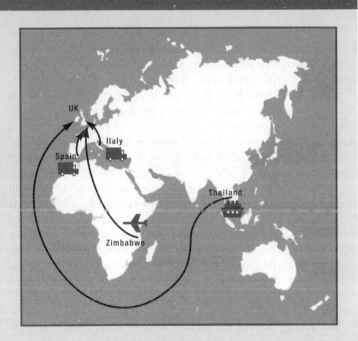

376 miles, using up just one megajoule (around 13 cups of tea).

Organic foods aren't likely to be any more local. The UK imports the overwhelming majority of its organic produce, partly because we don't produce enough, and partly because imports are cheaper. Sustain worked out that a basket of 26 imported organic products could have travelled nearly a quarter of a million kilometres, releasing as much CO_2 as "an average four bedroom household does through cooking meals over eight months".

For more information see:

Sustain www.sustainweb.org

chapter three (p.51): how much the people in the countries exporting food to us – whether it's beans from East Africa or chicken from East Asia – are benefiting or suffering as a result of this trade.

There's no doubt that many export farms are far from model workplaces – they are very often large, intensively run, monocrop operations which cause considerable environmental harm and which offer workers **wages and conditions** equivalent to manufacturing sweatshops. In many cases, the majority of the profits end up in the hands of a few rich owners, hence driving up **inequality**, and large plantations can put enormous pressure on already stretched sources of water and other resources. In some parts of Kenya, for example, cash-crop growing has been causally linked to the starvation of local people.

On the other hand, export farming can clearly provide **jobs and investment** in areas where they're badly needed. Hence it's not just big business and WTO advocates that are campaigning for increased international agricultural trade, but also many anti-poverty NGOs. In countries such as "Uganda and Vietnam, where smallholder production dominates, agricultural export growth in the 1990s contributed to rapid rural poverty reduction", wrote Oxfam senior policy advisor Kevin Watkins in a debate for *The Ecologist* magazine. He acknowledged that increased global food trade can cause environmental damage and, in some cases, raise inequality, and that these problems "have to be addressed". But he believes that "making common cause with protectionist lobbies and right-wing populists to exclude poor countries from rich country markets in the interests of 'self-reliance' is a prescription for mass poverty and inequality".

Then, of course, there's the impact of food imports on **UK farmers**, many of whom have been forced out of their jobs by foreign competition. Over 60% of apple orchards in the UK, for example, have stopped producing since 1970. Imports aren't the only driver behind this kind of trend (some would say bad financial planning by UK farmers is another significant factor), but they have certainly played an important role.

LET'S PLAY SWAP!

Regardless of what you think about the potential costs and benefits of our increasingly globalized food industry, the international trade in food is unquestionably sometimes more wasteful and environmentally damaging than it needs to be. For such is the weird and wonderful world of global commodity markets that countries often end up exchanging *exactly the same products.*

Local specialities changing hands, you might think. But no: even such "generic" products as milk are exchanged. In *Stopping the Great Food Swap – Relocalising Europe's Food Supply*, Green Party MEP Caroline Lucas documents this phenomenon, drawing on data from the UN's FAO Food Balance Sheets. Here are just a few of her examples:

▷ In 1998 the UK imported 60,000 tonnes of poultry meat from the Netherlands and exported more than 30,000 thousand tonnes to the same country.

▷ In the same year the UK exported 109,533 live pigs while importing 203,174.

▷ In 1997 we imported 126 million litres of liquid milk (powdered is another story) and exported 270 million litres.

To read the report online, visit:
www.carolinelucasmep.org.uk/publications/greatfoodswap.html

The implications of this are hotly debated. Farming groups tend to claim that, beside the pain felt by farmers forced from their land, we all lose through a disintegration of our national traditions and compromised long-term food security – since the price of imports depends on oil prices, an oil crisis could seriously jeopardize the availability of foods we depend on.

However, you can also look on the bright side: Britain currently has a historically low unemployment rate, and fewer people are in the kind of farm-labour jobs that most of us simply don't want to do. As for food security, it's probably fair to say that we could easily revive fallow UK farms, if oil prices or other factors necessitated it.

The ethical choice?

The environmental case for buying local food is very strong and – for anyone who prefers small independents over giant businesses – farmer's markets, farm shops and box schemes provide the ideal way to do this (see p.183). However, we shouldn't convince ourselves that avoiding the produce of poor countries is somehow doing them a favour. For all the inequalities of pay and the labour abuse that goes on in the international trade in food, unions in poor countries, as well as global anti-poverty groups working with them, are demanding more access to European markets.

The ideal solution would be to support global trade in food but demand that workers are treated well, resources are ethically managed, international trade rules are fair, and that the consumer (via regulation of producers) bears any environmental costs of the things they buy. This will only happen with political – rather than just consumer – pressure, but in the meantime we can at least buy Fairtrade imports wherever possible (see pp.154 and 158–167).

"Local" in supermarket-speak

If you do want to buy local food, be cautious of **supermarkets**, which often seem have their own peculiar definitions of the term. Friends of the Earth showed that most supermarkets use "local" to mean "produced in the UK" or produced as part of "a local traditional" – regardless of where that tradition is based. And, as already mentioned, even when food is genuinely produced locally, supermarket distribution systems can mean that the food has still spent a considerable amount of time travelling.

According to critics such as George Monbiot, the supermarkets are also guilty of causing **extra animal transport** to take place purely in the name of fooling their customers. "Scotch beef" and "Welsh lamb", Monbiot has written, "now come from animals pastured in

Scotland or Wales for just two weeks. They are trucked all over the United Kingdom so that the stores can change their designation and thus raise the price of their meat." This is not only profoundly wasteful and misleading, it's also cruel to animals and adds unnecessarily to the risk of spreading farm diseases.

To find more genuinely local food, see pp.181–188.

GM FOOD
To buy or to boycott?

Most people in the UK had never given much thought to genetically modified foods until 1999, when scientist **Árpád Pusztai** caused an outcry by claiming to show that young rats fed GM potatoes were showing signs of ill health. Pusztai's experiments are now widely accepted to have been "irrevocably flawed", as *New Scientist* put it, but the ensuing health scare about **frankenfoods** provided a springboard into the media and public consciousness for other related issues, such as GM food's ethical, environmental and economic implications.

By the time the government staged a **public debate** on the subject in 2003, the overwhelming majority of Britons were dead against biotechnology for food, and the big supermarkets had stopped selling most GM products.

Despite this, the first UK licence for the commercial cultivation of a GM crop was given out just a few months later. In the event, the licensee – Bayer CropScience – decided to abandon the UK as a potential market, which means that no GM crops are likely to be grown in Britain for some years to come. But modified ingredients and animal feed continue to be imported to, and sold in, the UK, and the arguments have broadened from questions over the safety and ethics of "tampering with nature" to claims that, by shunning GM crops, Western shoppers are inadvertently harming both the **environment** and people in the **third world**.

The following pages outline the cases for and against "biotech" food, before looking at how to avoid GM in the shops.

Health

There is nothing concrete to suggest that the current generation of GM food is more harmful or less healthy than any other foods, and the American population, as the biotech industry is always keen to remind us, has been eating it for years with no measurable side effects. However, critics such as **Michael Meacher** – the Environment

GM FOOD: WHAT, WHEN, WHERE?

Genetic modification is a kind of **biotechnology** in which the DNA of an organism, most commonly a crop, is altered. This can be done either by changing an existing part of the DNA or by adding a new gene from elsewhere – usually from a bacteria, a virus or another plant – allowing scientists to "cross" two organisms that couldn't cross in nature. GM has been a theoretical possibility ever since the discovery of DNA in 1953, but it was in the early 1980s that the techniques were actually developed, and in the 1990s that GM foods became a commercial reality.

Though the potential applications are very wide ranging, the only commercially available GM food crops at the time of writing are **soybean**, **maize**, **cotton** or **canola** (with wheat probably on the way soon). The majority of current modified plants are engineered to be **herbicide tolerant** – capable of dealing with special herbicides that would kill normal crops. The rest have been made **insect resistant**, with their cells modified to produce an insecticide known as Bt toxin. Some GM crops are both herbicide tolerant and insect resistant.

A public outcry has temporarily halted GM planting in Britain, but there's been no such hold up in much of the rest of the world. At the time of writing there are around six million farmers growing GM crops on roughly 75 million hectares (approximately twice the land space of the UK). **Monsanto** soya products account for the majority of these, with most of the planted area being in the US and Argentina, followed by Canada and China.

Minister sacked by Tony Blair after expressing scepticism about GM – claim that this isn't enough proof of their safety, pointing out that there have been no proper "human feeding trials", in the US or elsewhere, to rigorously screen the health of GM consumers.

Furthermore, not all scientists are convinced that the current laws, which require biotech firms to show that their crops are "substantially equivalent" to their non-GM counterparts, are enough to rule out potential increases in the levels of plant toxins or reductions in the levels of nutrients. And the tests that have been done have been largely carried out by the GM companies themselves, and have been, according to Meacher, "scientifically vacuous".

Overall, the scientific consensus seems to be that the risk of serious damage to human health is low. But if a danger were found at some point down the road – by which time the GM crop in question would probably have widely cross-pollinated with its conventional cousins – it could be almost impossible to solve.

Environmental impact

Environmental groups are leading the campaign against GM, but biotech advocates say they are shooting themselves in the foot, since GM technology could offer considerable environmental benefits. Their claims are numerous. Insect-resistant plants – with "natural" pest resistance built in – can mean **less pesticide** being pumped into fields, hence improving soil fertility and reducing both pollution and poisoning of farmers. Herbicide-resistant crops, meanwhile, allow for special "designer" weedkillers that are safe to use and quick to break down in the soil, and which make it easier for farmers to adopt **non-tillage** (plough-free) techniques, which reduce soil erosion and degradation.

GM could also make higher-yield crops possible or those able to grow in soil that's been left saline by irrigation (pumping water onto crops often results in salty groundwater rising up and damaging the soil). Both these technologies could help the world meet its ever-increasing demands for food without having to cut down forests to

Anti-GM food protesters ripping up biotech crops in Banbury, Oxfordshire

claim new farmland. And the applications aren't limited to food: biotechnology is already being used to research ecologically sound replacements for products such as bleach and formaldehyde.

The green movement is largely unconvinced by these claims. After all, in the case of herbicide-resistant crops, there's as much evidence to suggest they end up **increasing weedkiller use and harming wildlife** as there is to suggest the opposite. In parts of Argentina, for example, the development of weeds resistant to the "designer" herbicides has led to huge amounts of other herbicide being used, harming local peoples' health and crops. There's also the concern that different herbicide-resistant GM crops will cross-pollinate with each other, resulting in "**super-weeds**" resistant to multiple herbicides. Even the British government's **farm-scale evaluations** of three GM varieties suggested that two could be harmful to wildlife. And that was comparing them to their equivalents from conventional intensive farms;

a more meaningful study would compare GM crops to organically grown produce, environmentalists claim.

As for increasing the world's food supply, that's also a red herring, the greens argue. Most GM crops are simply supplying feed for the intensive livestock industry, the land for which is now one of the most important drivers of the disastrous clearance of Amazon rainforest (see p.117). Hence we should be looking to consume less meat and redistribute more, not simply increase production (more on this below).

There is one area where some GM critics concede that biotechnology may have proved environmentally beneficial. Pest-resistant crops – such as **cotton plants** engineered to produce Bt toxin, the pesticide based on a naturally occurring bacterium, and used by many organic farmers – are widely recognized to have helped reduce pesticide use in China and elsewhere.

But the question remains as to whether we should release any GM crops into the wild without absolute certainty that they won't cause environmental or health problems. After all, **contamination** (or "cross-pollination", depending on who you're talking to) is inevitable, as farmers in the US and Canada have already found. And even if this doesn't prove dangerous, it limits consumer choice and risks the livelihoods of **organic farmers**, since no GM-tainted crop can be sold as organic.

Some GM advocates, such as molecular biologist Conrad Lichtenstein, claim that organic farmers should simply embrace biotechnology: "GM technology … is by definition a very organic technology", he once wrote. "There is no contradiction between organic and GM." But organic farmers and consumers beg to differ.

Corporate control of the food chain

No part of the GM debate is as heated as the claims about the potential benefits for the world's poor. The biotech industry and the US government talk of **high-yield crops** able to resist harsh winters or droughts, which could reduce hunger and increase food security in regions struck by problematic climates and soils. And special nutritionally improved staples have already been designed to help farmers and their children get the vitamins and nutrients they are currently lacking.

True, these have so far failed to live up to their creators' promises. So-called **golden rice**, for example, aimed at combating the vitamin A deficiency which blinds and kills thousands of children in poor countries every week, needs to be consumed in vast quantities to have the desired effect. Still, it's "much better than nothing", GM scientist Michael Wilson told Rough Guides, and we should remember that this is only "first-generation" technology. At some stage, life-saving and environmentally beneficial GM crops are inevitably going to become reality and, by shunning biotechnology as shoppers, we risk being the "GM Jeremiahs" – in the words of the *Guardian* columnist Nick Cohen – who slow this essential process down.

It's a contentious case, made all the more contentious by the fact that many leaders of poor countries, as well as most anti-poverty groups, have spoken out against GM. In 1998, for example, a group of African delegates to the UN issued a joint statement saying that they "strongly object that the image of the poor and hungry from our countries is being used by giant multinational corporations to push a technology that is neither safe, environmentally friendly nor economically beneficial to us". ActionAid, meanwhile, considers GM crops to be currently "largely irrelevant for the poorest farming communities – only 1% of GM research is aimed at crops used by poor people – and they may pose a threat to their livelihoods". Indeed, as already mentioned, the vast majority of biotech crops are mainly serving to supply intensive meat farms, which, you might argue, are the single biggest threat to world food security (see p.116).

Even when pro-poor GM crops do evolve, some argue they are failing to deal with the underlying problems. In *So Shall We Reap*, for example, Colin Tudge writes that Vitamin A rice is the "heroic, Western high-tech solution to the disaster that Western commercial high-tech has itself created", pointing out that vitamin A deficiency doesn't exist "so long as people have horticulture", which has always been part of "traditional farming". The problem isn't low-tech rice, he claims, but a global agricultural ideology based on "obsessive monoculture" and global trade.

But the main concern of ActionAid is that "four multinationals dominate GM technology – giving them unprecedented control over their GM seeds and the chemicals that go with them". The companies in question are Monsanto, Syngenta, Bayer CropScience and Dupont, whose family trees can be traced at:

CorporateWatch
www.corporatewatch.org/genetics/familytree/familytree_click.htm

Like many other GM sceptics, ActionAid worry that near-monopolies on **seed distribution**, combined with a lack of education in some countries about the legal implications of using GM seeds (for example, the requirement to buy new seeds each year), allows the big companies effectively to force their products on farmers, who will then find themselves taking on avoidable debt.

Furthermore, the big companies are registering ever more **patents**, giving them the sole rights to perform certain types of genetic manipulation on certain plants. So even if public-sector organizations stumble across potentially positive GM crop developments, they are likely to find them all wrapped up in legal red tape.

The biotech companies tell us not to worry, and that they are out to create a better world. Yet they tend to behave in a way that suggests consumers would be right to be sceptical of such claims. For example, the firms spend millions on **political donations and lobbying**. According to the Center for Responsive Politics, by 2003 biotech firms have "close to $26 million in individual, PAC and soft money contributions since 1989". And, along with the Biotechnology Industry Organization (their main trade group), they "also spent nearly $143 million to lobby Congress, the White House and the Food and Drug Administration between 1998 and 2002". And that's only the start of it, according to campaigners. For full critical resumés of these companies, check out www.corporatewatch.org.uk.

In the short term at least, some farmers are clearly already bene-fiting from GM technologies – or thousands of them wouldn't be voluntarily choosing biotech crops in Argentina, China, India and elsewhere. And, in the longer term, it's quite possible that GM could be part of a solution for a better world. Certainly the UN Food and Agriculture Organization thinks so: "biotechnology is capable of benefiting small, resource-poor farmers" was one conclusion of their latest *State of Food and Agriculture* report.

But whether the world *needs* GM crops, whether they're part of the solution or the problem, and whether it's the industry or consumers who are holding up any potential positive benefits, is highly questionable. After all, if crops truly beneficial to the world's poor are proved to be effective and safe, and offered at reasonable prices and terms, it will surely take more than a few European fears about modified cornflakes to stop them being taken up around the world.

GM FOODS: WHAT'S IN THE SHOPS?

At the time of writing, no GM crops are commercially grown in the UK. And since Bayer CropScience decided to stop pursuing their goal of commercializing their **Chardon LL** modified maize (the only GM crop given government approval), it looks unlikely that there will be any British GM cultivation in the next few years. However, genetically modified crops are still imported from abroad, both as **ingredients** and as **animal feed**.

After a tightening of EU law in April 2004, all food derived from a GM organism must be **labelled** as such. And this includes all products that contain individual ingredients with a GM content of 0.9% or higher. So if a brand of biscuit, say, contained a small quantity of soya oil, which itself was 1.5% GM, a label would be required. If the soya oil, for "accidental or technically unavoidable" reasons, was 0.5% GM, no label would have to appear. In practice, though, this is all academic, since the major UK supermarkets, and many of the major food processors, have imposed their own stricter standards, and don't sell anything that would come close to requiring a label. The **Co-op**, for example, won't sell any foods containing ingredients consisting of more than 0.1% GM-derived produce.

The major exception to the EU's strict GM labelling rules relates to **animal products.** Despite the fact that most biotech crops are grown as animal feed, there's no requirement to label meat, fish, eggs or dairy products that came from farm animals fed GM crops. There's no evidence to suggest that GM DNA can be passed from animal feed into meat or milk, but anti-GM campaigners such as Greenpeace point out that this hole in the labelling laws makes it **impossible for consumers to boycott** biotech foods completely. That said, Marks & Spencer have stopped selling products from animals which have been fed GM crops, and it looks like others may follow their lead.

Similarly, no labels are required on food "produced with the aid of", but not actually containing, GM-derived substances. For example, the **chymosin enzyme** – "rennet" – used to separate the curds and whey in cheese production, is usually produced with modified yeast or bacteria (the main exception being traditional cheeses made with rennet from calves' stomachs). Finally, certain GM-derived foods produced before April 2004 may still be on sale and not labelled. But this only includes products – such as vegetable oil from GM rapeseed – that have been processed to the point of being chemically indistinguishable from the non-GM equivalents.

Similar rules apply in cafés and restaurants. Owners aren't obliged to specify GM ingredients on the menu but the staff must – in theory at least – be able to inform you, if asked, of any dishes that would require a label if sold in a shop.

Going GM-free

As explained above, most people in the UK aren't currently buying or consuming GM foods in any serious quantities. But if you'd rather be consuming none at all, including products from animals fed on GM crops, you may want to check-out Greenpeace's near-comprehensive online shopping guide, which gives thumbs up or down to hundreds of products, including supermarket own-brands:

Greenpeace GM Shopping Guide www.greenpeace.org.uk/Products/GM

Alternatively, buy organic, since the organic rules ban all use of GM technologies. Even this won't completely remove all traces of modification from your diet, since accidental contamination of organic food by GM crops has already been spotted. According to a study published by Mark Partridge and Denis J Murphy in the *British Food Journal*, out of 25 soya-bean "organic/health foods containing soya beans … ten tested positively for the presence of GM material"; eight of these were labelled organic. Still, it's about as close as you can get to sidestepping GM.

GM Links

To read more about the GM issues from various different perspectives, try the following websites:

Biotechnology Information Resource www.nal.usda.gov/bic
European Federation of Biotechnology www.efbpublic.org
Food Standards Agency www.foodstandards.gov.uk
Friends of the Earth www.foe.co.uk
Genewatch www.genewatch.org
Union of Concerned Scientists www.ucsusa.org

EATING ANIMALS
Waste, pollution and the ethics of meat

Beyond animal welfare concerns and the standard moral questions that surround killing animals for food, there are some serious **ecological problems** with our consumption of animal products – especially those which come from intensive farms.

FOOD & DRINK ▼

Many of the problems stem from the fact that most animal products are very **inefficient to produce**. Take beef, for instance. There's no single definitive figure, but producing a single kilo of intensively farmed beef typically takes around 10 kilos of grain for feed. Beef is among the worst culprits, but similar problems apply to most meats, farmed fish and, to a slightly lesser extent, dairy and eggs. Obviously all these foods have relatively high energy and protein levels, so a kilo of feed is not directly comparable to a kilo of meat. But even taking this into account, the simple fact remains: we get far less food out of most animals than we put in.

Animal produce *can* be made far more efficiently on **mixed, closed-system farms** of the type often favoured by organic growers. Chickens and some other animals can be fed on scraps that might otherwise go to waste. In some cases animals graze on land that would be no good for crops, with a diet largely consisting of grasses, perhaps supplemented with crop **by-products**. For these reasons, the most efficient food productions systems *do* actually include some animal products. But in reality, the majority of farmed animals consume feed that could be more effectively used elsewhere.

This is no minor issue. Global meat consumption has rocketed by around 500% since 1950 – the world today contains around **twice as many chickens as humans**, plus 1 billion pigs, roughly 1.3 billion cows and 1.8 billion sheep and goats – and there is no sign of this slowing down. According to agricultural commentator Colin Tudge, if the current growth rate of animal-product consumption continues, by 2050, livestock will consume as much food as the entire human population did in 1970.

This rising demand for animal feed has a number of implications, one of which is a growing demand for farmland to grow feed crops such as soya. This is already resulting in the clearing of **rainforests** in the Amazon and elsewhere, and looks set to become one of the worst threats to the world's biodiversity (not to mention the other environmental and human problems caused by deforestation).

A second implication, in the slightly longer term, is a threat to the

117

MAKING MEAT

The exact quantity of feed required to make each kilogram of meat or fish varies between breed and farming method – and there are also great differences between the figures favoured by campaigners, on the one hand, and the meat industry, on the other. The following "middle-of-the-road" estimates come from the non-partisan Council for Agricultural Science and Technology.

KILOS OF FEED REQUIRED TO PRODUCE 1 KILO OF FOOD

Farmed fish	1.5–2.0	
Poultry meat	2.1–3.0	
Pork	4.0–5.5	
Beef	10	

The amount of water required to produce certain meats is also often very high (though naturally the relevance of this varies from country to country). According to a study by D Pimentel, and published in *Bioscience*:

LITRES OF WATER REQUIRED TO PRODUCE 1 KILO OF FOOD

Potatoes	500	
Wheat	900	
Maize	1400	
Rice	1910	
Soya beans	2000	
Chicken	3500	
Beef	100,000	

food security of the world's poorest people. Unless rainforest clearance and/or a revolution in farm technology manages to keep up both with rising meat consumption and rising global population, we'll soon get to the point where there won't be enough crops to feed all the people and all the farm animals. At this point, demand will outstrip supply and the price of crops will rise. The price of meat will go up even more, of course (since meat farmers will have to pay more for feed). But such is global inequality that those who consume animal products will probably be able to absorb this rise in price far more easily than those in poor countries, who already struggle to buy enough basic crops to feed themselves and their families.

The environmental burden
Even if rainforests weren't at risk, the intensive production of animal products would create a range of serious environmental burdens. For one thing, the production of feed crops and the farming of animals uses up an astonishing amount of water. It can take 100,000 litres of water to make a single kilo of beef (see box). This isn't usually a big problem in the UK and many other rainy countries. But considering that fresh water stocks are already close to being exhausted in much of the developing world, it's a massive issue when the meat is produced there.

Secondly, the world's livestock produce more than 10 billion tonnes of mineral-rich effluent each year. While manure adds to soil fertility in closed-system, mixed farms, it can be a major polluter in intensive farms, finding its way into rivers and groundwater, and raising nitrogen and phosphorous levels higher than aquatic species can survive. Its ammonia content can also contribute to acid rain.

And then there's global warming. Astonishingly, farm animals are thought to account for around 10% of the world's greenhouse-gas emissions. Part of this contribution is due to the fact that meat production uses a lot of oil – to power farm machines, make fertilizer for feed crops, transport feed and animals, and so on. All told, meat requires around 10–30 times the total energy input per kilogram than

THE ETHICS OF VEGETARIANISM AND VEGANISM

Shopping for "ethical" meat is all well and good, but many would say the idea of being nice to an animal before unnecessarily electrocuting or slitting its throat is odd, to say the least. Most of us would be bothered by the idea of eating free-range cat and dog meat, after all, yet there's little difference between this and "ethically reared" meat from intelligent animals such as pigs. Why are we prepared to kill certain animals and not others? And is it really justifiable to kill any animals simply so we can have the pleasure of eating them?

This must be one of the longest-running of all ethical consumerism debates: exclusively non-animal diets have been relatively common in Asia since the development of ancient religions such as **Jainism**, and Europe first grappled with the concept just as long ago. **Pythagoras**, **Plato**, **Socrates** and **Ovid** all expressed doubts about meat. However, Western vegetarianism as we know it today didn't really take off until the beginning of the 19th century, when the tireless campaigning of the appropriately named **William Cowherd**, a reverend from Salford, started the ball rolling. The term itself was coined in 1847 by the UK's newly formed **Vegetarian Society**, which made a point of deriving it from *vegetus*, Latin for lively, rather than vegetable (though this seems a bit academic considering that both words come from the same Latin root). Numbers have grown ever since, and today surveys suggest that 4–6% of the UK population describe themselves as vegetarian, with many more consciously limiting their meat intake.

Besides individual views about killing animals unnecessarily, numerous more objective arguments can be made for vegetarianism. The two most convincing are the facts that most meat and farmed fish is **wasteful** to produce (as discussed above), and that **animal welfare** standards are usually very low (more on this below). Organic and other non-intensive meat and fish is available, of course, but it's more expensive, harder to find in restaurants and still ultimately more wasteful than non-animal foods.

Some other arguments, however, such as the idea that we're evolutionarily herbivore by design, are flawed. People disagree about the exact diets of our ancestors, but it's actually pretty clear that early humans, like the chimps they evolved from, ate at least some meat when it was available. As for claims of better **health**, vegetarians do tend to live longer and suffer fewer serious problems, but it's difficult to work out how much of this is due to a meat-free diet, and how much of it is down to other attributes that, according to the stats, happen to be common to most vegetarians, such as a wealthy class background and general health consciousness. Still, whatever the reasons, most vegetarian diets do tend to be very healthy.

But what about **eggs and dairy products**? Produced intensively, these too fall into the ecologically damaging category. The rearing of egg-laying chickens (p.130) and dairy cows (p.137) is associated with animal-welfare problems at least as great as those of the meat trade. Egg-laying chickens are killed after only weeks of life, ending up as meat in pet food, while dairy products rely on a constant stream of calves being born, most of which are slaughtered for meat (if they weren't, we'd end up with an ever-growing bovine population). So "lacto" vegetarians still kill animals, you might argue, and intensively farmed milk and eggs are not necessarily morally superior to, for example, organic, free-range chicken.

These contradictions lie behind the small but growing number of people going **vegan** – abstaining from all animal products, including dairy, eggs and even honey. Veganism grew out of the vegetarian movement in the first half of the twentieth century, and it generally sees itself as the logical conclusion of that movement, as is implied by the term "vegan": the beginning and the end of the word vegetarian. It is a much bigger commitment than vegetarianism, ruling out many foods and guaranteeing a considerable degree of inconvenience when eating out or travelling. But it's ultimately a more coherent ideology, at least from the animal-welfare and ecological perspectives.

Still, even veganism isn't enough for some, who ask why should we draw the line at plants? **Fruitarians** only eat foods – such as fruits, berries, olives, tomatoes – that can be eaten without deliberately harming any organism, and also save energy by eliminating the need for cooking, refrigeration or even washing up. This is one branch of ethical shopping that it's hard to see ever really taking off.

For more information, visit:

Vegetarian Society www.vegsoc.org
Vegan Society www.vegansociety.com
The Fruitarian Site www.fruitarian.com
Beyond Vegetarianism www.beyondveg.com

corn or soya. But it is also because cows and other livestock annually burp and fart out an astonishing 80 million tons of **methane**, which is a particularly problematic greenhouse gas.

THE ANTIBIOTICS ISSUE

Along with their diet, many animals in intensive farms – especially pigs and poultry, but also cattle and fish – routinely receive drugs. These are mostly **antibiotics**, both to stimulate growth and to prevent against the diseases that thrive in overcrowded conditions. Animal welfare campaigners object to this because growth promoters are thought to cause health problems and because they push animals beyond their natural limits. But equally troubling is the potential threat to human health via the growth of **antibiotic resistance**. As "super-bugs" in hospitals have shown, resistance to our most useful drugs is on the up. For instance, a significant proportion of cases of the biggest source of food poisoning in the UK, campylobacter, are now untreatable by antibiotics. Though not all scientists agree, many microbiologists think we're sitting on a time bomb.

Over-prescription in humans is certainly part of the problem – perhaps even the biggest part – but intensive farming is now widely accepted as a potential breeding ground for resistant bugs, which, once developed, may be passed on to humans via meat, milk or even possibly crops grown from animal fertilizer. With the chicken industry quietly having gone back on its much-publicized phasing out of antibiotic growth promoters (in 2003), it's good news that these products will be made illegal across the EU by 2006. But growth promoters only account for a small proportion of the hundreds of tonnes of veterinary antibiotics used each year, and there are no plans to phase out the rest, which are routinely administered on a prevention-is-easier-than-cure basis.

Drugging animals also raises the question of carcinogenic or otherwise harmful **drug residues** in our meat or milk. Strict regulations setting out periods of "withdrawal" for animals given drugs theoretically avoids this, but various studies have shown residues far in excess of the legal maximums, suggesting farmers don't always observe the rules.

If you want to avoid routinely administered antibiotics, buy organic or shop at Marks & Spencer, which claims to enforce a strict policy governing the use of antibiotics by their suppliers.

The solution?

Something is clearly going to have to be done about our excessive and rising consumption of intensively farmed animal products, and various groups claim they have the solution. **Vegetarians** (see p.120) advocate simply cutting out meat from our diet; **localizers** (see p.100) argue that we should move away from a global free market in food, encouraging countries to focus on self-sufficiency through ecologically friendly "mixed" farms; **GM exponents** (see p.107) look to biotechnology as a means of increasing crop productivity and therefore increasing supply to match demand; and some food economists have even suggested the implementation of a global "food-chain tax", to add to the cost of meat.

As for what individual ethical shoppers can do, the basic choice is simple enough: if you really want to reduce your environmental footprint – in terms of climate change, pollution, water use and deforestation – try to consume fewer animal products, especially those from intensive farms.

ANIMAL WELFARE LABELS
What do they mean?

Even if intensive meat production wasn't so problematic environmentally and economically, there are serious issues with the conditions that most animals are subjected to. Specific welfare concerns and the non-intensive alternatives are dealt with in the following sections on red meat (p.126), poultry and eggs (p.130), dairy (p.137) and fish (p.139). But first here's a quick look at two schemes that claim to guarantee better levels of welfare, one specifically – from the RSPCA – and one as part of a wider set of assurances from the National Farmers' Union (NFU). Ironically, neither are nearly as strict as the **Soil Association's organic standard** (see p.91), which remains the best guarantee of decent treatment of farm animals.

ANIMAL WELFARE LABELS

British Farm Standard

Launched just after the turn of the new millennium in response to massive public distrust of the agricultural sector, the **NFU's Little Red Tractor** scheme labels meats, dairy, veg and cereals that come from farms conforming to British Farm

**BRITISH
FARM STANDARD**

Standards, a set of "exacting" standards relating to the environment, food safety and animal welfare. In the latter area, the scheme sets out some very basic minimum standards – such as outdoor animals having access to shelter – but, according to campaign groups such as Compassion in World Farming, the rules still allow such **animal-unfriendly practices** as narrow farrowing pig crates, battery cages for laying hens, restrictive feeding practices, combinations of breeds and diets that can lead to animal health problems, debeaking of chickens, and tail docking and teeth clipping of pigs. Friends of the Earth have also complained that it doesn't rule out **GM** or cover the responsible use of **pesticides**. Find out more on both sides of the argument at:

NFU www.littleredtractor.org.uk
CIWF www.redtractortruth.com

RSPCA Freedom Food

Established in 1994, the Freedom Food scheme labels eggs, dairy, chicken, pork and some prepared foods. The idea is to label products from animals that – from farm through to abattoir – haven't been denied any of the basic "five freedoms": freedom from **fear and distress**,

freedom from **hunger and thirst**, freedom from **discomfort**, freedom from **pain, injury and disease**, freedom to express **normal behaviour**.

As interpreted by the scheme, these freedoms don't preclude many unpleasant practices – hens might still be debeaked and kept in high density sheds, for example – and this, combined with the fact that farmers pay to join, has led to criticism from some quarters. While Animal Liberation Australia's claims that the RSPCA is "in bed with egg industry … in the business of harming animals" are a little over the top, it's true that the scheme is laxer than you might imagine, considering who runs it. That said, the RSPCA clearly set the standards at a level which they thought would get the label into the mainstream, rather than limiting it to "premium" animal products. And the rules certainly imply a better than average level of welfare.

For more information, or a full list of products available at each supermarket, visit the RSPCA's website. Or for stricter animal welfare standards, go organic (see p.86).

RSPCA www.rspca.org.uk

LIKE A LAMB TO SLAUGHTER: ANIMAL TRANSPORT

Farm animals are often transported long distances by lorry within the UK, either on their way to slaughter – since most local abattoirs have been shut down since the 1970s – or to be fattened up elsewhere, sometimes just so supermarkets can add a misleading label about the animal's origins (see p.106). Whatever the reason, transport can cause enormous distress to the animals, which are packed into metal containers, often struggling for air and in some cases suffering injury or death on the way. Most UK supermarkets impose a **maximum journey time** for the animals used for their own-label meat, but with a couple of specific exceptions, they still allow around 8 hours for cows, pigs and sheep and 8–12 hours for poultry – far more than the EU vets and welfare experts suggest is acceptable.

Importing and exporting live animals is also big business, with millions of animals each year making huge journeys by road (England to Italy takes around 45 hours) or sea (Australia to the Middle East takes weeks). From the UK, exports are down since the foot-and-mouth crisis and since a 1997 law imposed a maximum 8-hour journey time for the worst vehicles. But Compassion in World Farming and other campaigners claim that unacceptable conditions are still endured by animals for prolonged periods.

RED MEAT
Pigs, cows & sheep

PORK PRODUCTS

Of the commonly available red meats, those from pigs pose the most pressing questions in terms of animal welfare. These are **highly intelligent** social animals – usually compared to dogs in the animal IQ stakes – often reared with no respect for their wellbeing. Pig farming techniques have become increasingly industrial over the past few decades. Farms are growing to epic sizes – in the US, there are now individual farms with more than a million swine – and the standard sow has been transformed into a meat-making machine. Relatively recently, female pigs would give birth to around five piglets a year, but 25 is not uncommon today. This is thanks to a mixture of **intensive breeding** programmes and the technique of removing piglets from their mothers very early, to maximize the number of possible pregnancies per year.

The UK is far better in terms of pig welfare than most of the EU, where many pigs still spend their whole lives in **sow stalls** – tiny barren cages, usually so small that the pig cannot even turn around – or chained to the floor using **tethers**. Routine "docking" of tail and clipping of teeth are also standard in much of Europe, to avoid the pigs biting each other – something they generally do only in cramped conditions with nothing to keep them entertained. Most of these techniques are due to be made illegal across the EU, but not until 2013.

In the UK, things have been improved by various bits of legislation – not least because of consumer pressure – but the situation is still far from rosy. Most pigs are kept in cramped, barren, dimly lit indoor conditions. According to Compassion in World Farming (www.ciwf.org.uk), fewer than half of them are even provided with straw, leaving them on bare concrete and slatted floors, which can cause health problems as well as preventing normal pig behaviour.

And **farrowing crates** – small stalls into which sows are put for a week or two either side of giving birth – are still the norm. The industry claims these are needed to protect the piglets from being crushed to death, but organic pig farmers have shown that with good husbandry this isn't necessary.

Besides welfare issues, food buffs are quick to point out that intensively farmed pork is nearly always floppy, watery and tasteless.

What can you do?
For a start, favour pig meat from the **UK** – a large proportion of what gets sold in Britain is imported from countries where welfare standards are lower. Secondly, look out for pork meat marked **free-range**. With a lack of legal definitions, this doesn't always mean the same thing – it's largely down to individual farmers – but in most cases it implies a considerable improvement to the prevailing standards. At

Two extremes of pig farming: the best of organic (left) and the worst of intensive (right)

minimum, you'll know the pigs aren't kept permanently indoors. Note that **outdoor-reared** is better than **outdoor-bred** – the latter ensures that the pig was *born* in free-range conditions (so no farrowing crates), but the former also implies that it was *raised* outdoors.

Organic pig meat – which is free-range but allows pigs to be kept indoors for a proportion of the time – offers further improvements. Farrowing crates are out; rooting and exercise areas are in; piglets are not removed from their mother so early; the diet is better; and medicines used must be approved by a certifying body. If you can't find free-range or organic pork in your supermarket, or if you want to buy directly from farmers, see pp.181–187 for pointers.

You might also see pork products marked with the **Little Red Tractor** or the RSPCA **Freedom Food** logos. These offer some basic animal welfare guarantees – especially Freedom Food – though fewer than organic.

BEEF & VEAL

Meat from cows ranges widely, both in terms of animal welfare and its wastefulness (as already discussed, intensive beef farming requires remarkable quantities of water and crops). Much of the UK's beef comes from **suckler herds**, which spend most of their lives moseying around in fields, the calves staying with their mothers for up to a year. Compared with beef from intensively raised cattle, this is more animal-friendly, wastes less energy and crops, and is generally much better quality, both because of the breeds favoured and the exercise the cows get. The animals' diets still leave a bit to be desired (despite post-BSE laws banning cows, sheep, pigs and other large animals in the feed, **waste poultry and fish** products are still permitted) and the animals suffer stress during transportation. But compared with pigs or dairy cows, these animals are treated reasonably well.

However, a growing proportion of our beef comes from **intensive farms**, usually stocked with excess calves from the dairy industry, mostly removed from their mothers on day one. (Old worn-out milkers were also once used for meat, though, post-BSE, their car-casses are burned instead.) In these farms, the cows are kept mostly or entirely indoors, usually in barren and over-crowded concrete sheds, with no chance to exercise or graze. As with most intensive farming, this increases the chance of many illnesses, which in turn increases the need for **antibiotics** and other drugs.

Veal

Eating veal is not inherently very different, ethically speaking, from eating lamb or any other young animal, but the way much of it is pro-duced is cause for serious concern. In the worst cases, veal calves are reared in **crates**, in which they can't even turn around, packed into dark sheds. They suffer great distress, are very susceptible to disease – hence preventative antibiotics are often used – and are fed a poor **all-liquid diet** deliberately lacking in certain nutrients, to help create a white-coloured meat. Though an EU ban should see an end to their use by 2007, veal crates are still used in many EU countries. The UK has already phased them out, marking a vast improvement in welfare standards. That said, the majority of our veal is still produced in all-indoor intensive or semi-intensive farms, similar to those used for many beef cows (see above).

What to buy

Suckler-herd or **free-range** beef obviously makes for a more ethical choice, and is very common, so look out for labels or ask your butcher. In the case of veal, suckler-herd meat from calves that have stayed with their mothers until slaughter is sometimes labelled using the French term *veau sous la mère*. Better still is buying **organic**, which ensures strict animal-welfare standards, rules out routine antibiotics and shuns animal and fish products in the feed. Organic beef is widely available and less expensive than many organic meats, and organic veal (which is often *sous la mère*) is also available, though less ubiquitous; for pointers to suppliers, see pp.181–187. Whatever you buy, favour UK over continental veal.

LAMB & MUTTON

In terms of animal welfare, sheep get a pretty good deal compared to most farm animals. The overwhelming majority spend their lives freely grazing over extensive pastures, being bought inside only when the weather demands it. This is largely because, as yet, no one has worked out a way to make intensive sheep farming viable. But that's not to say the situation is perfect. There are some serious problems with how many sheep and lambs are transported and slaughtered, and neglect by some farmers means that around 1 in 10 lambs die of **cold or hunger**. Many are also castrated without anaesthetic.

To ensure the best guarantee of animal welfare, as well as respect for the environment, go for **organic** lamb and mutton, or buy directly from local farmers whom you can question about welfare issues (see pp.181–187).

POULTRY & EGGS
Factory fowl

The chicken industry is perhaps the most extreme example of modern farming methods. Governed by technology and market forces, this is a whole sector of farming carried out almost entirely behind closed doors, and mostly by large firms. Amazingly, just three companies – Aviagen, Cobb-Vantress and Hybro – provide nearly all the world's chicks, both for meat and egg-laying birds, which, during the last half decade, have been engineered into completely separate creatures. The chick companies are proud of their scientific approach, and make no back-to-nature pretence. Visit one of their websites – such as www.aviagen.com – and you'll be invited to check out the "features and benefits" or a "technical data sheet" for each of their "products". And if this sounds more like marketing for cars than hens, the names of the breeds – such as the **Hybro PG+** and **Cobb 500** – won't convince you otherwise.

BROILERS – MEAT CHICKENS

Conditions for egg-laying hens are very gradually improving (see p.133), but the same cannot be said for meat chickens, or **broilers** as they're called. Like so many other foods, chicken meat was thought of as a luxury food until relatively recently, when intensive farming methods allowed prices to be slashed. Unfortunately this happened at the expense of animal welfare.

A brave new chicken

The whole idea of a chicken bred solely for meat is only around fifty years old, but today intensive broiler farms in the UK account for nearly all of the roughly 800 million chickens we consume each year (around fourteen for each person in the country). To achieve this remarkable turnover, farms use chicks that have been specially bred to grow in the shortest possible time: a modern broiler can get to slaughter weight in just over **forty days**, twice as quickly as a few decades ago. And the technology is still quite young – some industry visionaries expect thirty days to be realistic in the near future.

Regrettably for the birds, however, while their breasts grow unnaturally quickly, the rest of the body cannot keep up, and millions of broilers each year develop painful **leg disorders** or die of **heart failure**. Indeed, the genetic selection is so rigorous that chickens kept for breeding broilers have to be severely underfed; if they weren't, their super-efficient ability to put on weight would kill them before they reached egg-laying age. But animal welfare is never really going to be a priority while the leading chick suppliers make such proud claims as "output of meat per breeder placed is the ultimate measure of performance".

It's not just breeding process that focuses on a need for speed. Every other element of a broiler's life is controlled by the same bottom line, from their sleep patterns (total darkness is kept to an absolute minimum as a sleeping bird won't eat) to its feed: maximum weight-gain, minimum-excrement pellets.

Chickenshit

Most broilers live in flocks of tens of thousands in giant, windowless sheds, each bird getting about as much space as a piece of A4 paper. This is far less than either the EU or the British government recommend for basic levels of welfare, but there are no specific laws governing this industry. With such dense stocking, clearing out the **litter floor** is only possible once the birds are taken to slaughter, so the birds spend their short lives standing and sitting in their own filth, often leading to **ulcerous feet** and **skin disease**. Evidence of the latter was found in two percent of the chicken meat examined in a recent sample by *Which?* magazine.

When their days are up, the birds are transported by crowded truck to a slaughterhouse and processing plant, many of which can cope with more than 10,000 chickens per hour. After being hung upside-down by their feet, the birds have their head dipped into an electrified pool and their throats cut by a spinning blade. A couple of hours, miles of conveyor belt and numerous machines later, they'll come out plucked, gutted, wrapped and packed – perhaps even marinated (or, more accurately, injected) – and ready for the restaurant or supermarket shelf. For more information about broilers, see the campaign sites of Compassion in World Farming (www.livefastdieyoung.org) or the RSPCA (chickens.rspca.org.uk).

As well as animal welfare concerns, industrially produced chicken is said by those in the know to be disastrous for taste and quality. The lack of exercise, poor diet and absorption of water during processing creates, according to none other than Delia Smith, "a coarse-grained, watery, limp chicken that has no flavour".

How free is free range?

Various types of chicken – and other poultry – that guarantee better welfare standards (and taste) are now widely available in the UK, but the labelling isn't as simple or strict as you might expect. Here's a rundown of the various labels you'll come across:

▷ **Extensive indoor or barn-reared** The same as standard intensive systems but with lower stocking densities and a slaughter age of at least 56 days.

▷ **Free-range** Basically the same as above but the birds have continuous daytime access to open-air runs for at least half their lifetime.

▷ **Traditional free-range** As above but with smaller flock sizes, a minimum slaughter age of 81 days, and access to open-air runs from six weeks of age at the latest.

▷ **Free-range total freedom** As above but with "open-air runs of unlimited area".

▷ **Organic** Once again, this is the best option. Organics standards require welfare at least as good as traditional free-range, but have far smaller flock sizes, a better diet (mainly organic and free from animal protein), a slightly older minimum slaughter age and better pollution restrictions.

Even if free-range chicken isn't available, look out for the **RSPCA Freedom Food** label, and avoid fresh chickens with brown "hock burn" marks near the knee joints – these often imply that welfare standards have been low.

EGGS

The vast majority of laying hens in the UK – more than 20 million according to RSPCA estimates – are kept in cramped **battery cages**, stacked up high in vast buildings with little or no natural light. In most cases the hens have so little space they cannot even turn around or stretch their wings, let alone follow their instincts to preen properly and "dust-bathe". The cages lead not just to discomfort, but to **foot injury** and **weak bones**, so that by the end of their productive lives – usually about one year and a few hundred eggs – almost a third of the birds have broken bones, according to animal-welfare groups. And the other two-thirds are in such poor condition that after slaughter they are only used for processing and animal food.

An egg-layer's **diet** contains not only of grains, soya and nutrients, but often also fish products and even (in an odd twist on the chicken-and-egg question) waste chicken extracts. The hens are also given colorants, both artificial and natural, to ensure the consumer isn't faced with a perfectly harmless variety in yolk colour, and antibiotics are routinely administered. A study by the Soil Association showed that a large proportion of eggs contain traces of the toxic medicine lasalocid, known to be harmful to mammals but never tested on humans.

One advantage of cages is that it makes it harder for crowded birds to peck each other, meaning that they don't necessarily need to be **debeaked** (the trimming of chicks' beaks with a red-hot blade). However, many battery hens are debeaked anyway, and many claim that careful and minimal debeaking is less cruel than battery conditions. Either way, the practice isn't necessary with a small flock size in better conditions, as is typical of hens which produce organic eggs.

A good egg?

Battery farming still accounts for around two-thirds of UK egg production, but things are starting to change. There are now various non-battery options and some food manufacturers have committed to using free-range eggs – which offer some improvement – in their prepared products, the best known being Marks & Spencer and even MacDonald's. Also, the UK is implementing an EU directive to replace the worst cages, by 2012, with marginally more spacious "**enriched cages**", with a nest, perching space and scratching area. These developments are still a very long way from ruling out cruel practices, but they are at least a step in the right direction. In the mean time, a wide range of labels and descriptions are used. So here's how to read an egg box…

▷ **Farm, Fresh, Country, etc** take no notice of terms such as these, which often appear next to pictures of rural cottages with birds pecking happily around outside. They mean nothing at all, with the

Free-range may be better than battery or barn reared, but – as this image from a modern farm in Rotterdam shows – it's a long way from the traditional farmyard scene pictured on many egg boxes

exception of some descriptions like "Super Fresh", which relate simply to the delay between laying and packing.

▷ **The Lion Quality** mark appears on around 75% of UK eggs. The scheme was set up in the wake of the salmonella crisis, and it focuses on food safety rather than animal welfare or environmental practices.

▷ **Four-grain eggs** come from hens fed on natural (non-animal) food, but this doesn't reflect on the welfare of the birds.

▷ **Barn eggs** are produced in similar indoor conditions to battery eggs but without the cages. This allows the birds to move around, but conditions are usually still grossly overcrowded, leading to birds attacking (and sometimes killing) each other, and even eating each others' droppings. Debeaking is necessary.

▷ **Freedom Food, RSPCA approved** requires basic welfare standards to be in place. Rules out the battery cage, but not crowded barns, colorants or debeaking – and doesn't necessarily mean free-range.

▷ **Free-range** laying hens must have continuous access to outdoor runs "mainly covered with vegetation". However, the sheds are still usually overcrowded – less than one square foot per bird is permitted – and the colony sizes are large, resulting in unnatural behaviour from the birds (sometimes including, ironically, a fear of going outside). Debeaking is standard.

▷ **Organic free-range** eggs, which have become much easier to find in recent years, are the best option. Birds must have free access to organic pasture, be fed largely on organic food and be kept in smaller flocks; debeaking, routine antibiotics and colorants are banned. A new organic egg standard will be introduced in 2005; until then, eggs accredited by the Soil Association have to pass the most stringent criteria, with flocks sizes of less than 500 birds. However, note that organic hens are rarely bred on organic farms: they are delivered by one of the big chick rearing companies at a few weeks old.

NON-CHICKEN POULTRY & EGGS

Most poultry – including **turkey**, **duck**, **quail** and **guinea fowl** – are intensively farmed in a similar way to chicken, so look out for better alternatives: the same multilevel free-range labelling systems apply. One exception is **geese**, which (so far at least) have not been able to survive the rigours of industrial farming, so are necessarily free-range. As for eggs, those from quails are commercially produced, intensively, but duck and geese eggs are generally not, so will mostly be from small-scale farms where animal welfare conditions are likely to be relatively high.

DAIRY PRODUCTS
It's a cow's life

Vegetarians sometimes take the moral high ground on issues of animal welfare. But those who eat and drink dairy products are possibly speaking too soon. The milk trade not only props up the **veal industry** (see p.129), but is also sometimes responsible for animal suffering itself. Dairy cows could easily live for two decades, but such is the strain put on them by modern breeding and milk production techniques that most are slaughtered before they're five – exhausted, ill and, in the harsh light of profit margins, economically inefficient.

Modern dairy cows have been **intensively bred** to yield the maximum quantities of milk. While a calf would naturally suckle a few litres a day from its mother, milking machines now extract up to fifty litres. The cows often have oversized udders, which according to animal-rights groups creates spinal problems, lameness and other damage. A significant proportion of dairy cows also develop mastitis, a painful infection of the udder. Breeding (mainly through artificial insemination and embryo transfer) has been so intense in the last few decades that the cows have grown too big for older milking parlours.

As with beef farms, dairy farms range from "free-range" setups, where the cows spend most of their time eating grass in fields, and more intensive operations, where the herds are often kept inside for far more of the year than necessary, often in cramped and uncomfortable conditions. Besides the animal welfare issues, more intensive farms are also more ecologically problematic (for the reasons discussed on p.116–123) and more likely to rely on preventative antibiotics.

And as for the calves...

To keep them milking, dairy cows are usually made to have calves each year, so for most of the year they're both pregnant and lactating.

Newborn calves are taken from their mothers almost immediately – often within hours of birth – which is widely reported to cause great distress to both. Females wait in turn to replace their mothers, often spending their first few months in a cramped individual pen. Males are usually taken straight to the market to be sold for veal (see p.129) or are moved to intensive farms to be fattened up for low-quality beef.

Ethical dairy

The best way to guarantee your milk and cheese have been produced with a high standard of animal welfare, and have generated a minimum amount of pollution in the process, is to buy **organic**. In organic farms, cows get a better diet and living conditions, spend more time outside and have a lower incidence of lameness. Preventative antibiotics are banned. Calves stay with their mothers for longer, and aren't weaned off milk for at least three months, or removed from the farm before six months.

Organic dairy products are in no short supply. So much organic milk is now produced, in fact, that as much as half of it ends up being mixed with and sold as standard milk. But if you're having difficulty finding a specific organic dairy product, see the specialist directories listed on pp.181–187.

You may also see milk – organic or non-organic – marked **White & Wild**. This scheme aims to increase farmland wildlife and also give environmentally conscientious farmers a better deal. As intensive techniques have driven down the farm-gate, wholesale price of milk, many smaller, non-intensive farmers have been struggling to get a price for their milk that even covers the cost of production. The White & Wild scheme gives them a small premium in return for committing to conservation plans – designating a tenth of their farms to the sole aim of maintaining wildlife habitats. A premium also goes to The Wildlife Trusts. See:

White & Wild www.whiteandwild.co.uk

FISH & SEAFOOD
Plenty more in the sea?

The World Resources Institute estimates that fish consumption has risen by more than fivefold in the last half century. In some ways this is a positive thing: fish provide a very healthy and important protein source for hundreds of millions of people around the world, and – unlike livestock – they don't require vast areas of crop land for feed. However, the massive global increase in fish consumption, which shows no sign of slowing down, has been made possible by two developments – **industrial fishing** and intensive **fish farming**, or "aquaculture" – both of which have come with serious environmental, and in some cases social, costs. This section looks briefly at the issues surrounding caught and farmed fish, and then looks at the ethical options (see p.146).

SEA-CAUGHT FISH: TUNA, COD, SWORDFISH, ET AL

As fishing vessels have grown from small wooden boats to giant factory ships, the world's waters have been reaped so heavily that the proverb "plenty more fish in the sea" is starting to look distinctly tenuous. By the time industrial fishing came of age in the early 1980s, the global catch in two years was equivalent to all the fish caught in the nineteenth century. And today, according to UN figures, a quarter of the world's fisheries are either **over-exploited or depleted**, while another half are being fished to maximum safe levels. The best-known example is **cod** – which in some areas have gone from being richly plentiful to basically extinct – but this certainly isn't the only species to have suffered.

People have long argued about the extent and implications of overfishing, but a recent groundbreaking study published in *Nature* suggested that the problem may be far worse than was previously expected. By scrutinizing early fishing records, Canadian academics reached the staggering conclusion that in the last half century 90% of

"The one and only pure ocean machine, unflawed, navigating the waters of death",
wrote Pablo Neruda about the bluefin tuna. But, like nearly all the great carnivores
of the sea, its number have been decimated by high-tech fishing – both legal and
illegal – and it's now critically endangered. Bluefin is most widely used in sushi,
though it's also often served in steaks.

all large fish – including **halibut**, **marlin**, **swordfish**, **sharks** and **tuna** – have been wiped out. And those that are left are tiny compared with their relatively recent ancestors.

The implications could be far reaching, as over-fishing not only knocks out the target fish but also causes havoc in the wider food chain (partly indirectly, and partly because large numbers of non-target fish and other sea creatures are regularly also killed in the nets). If these trends continue, the effect could be a "complete re-organization of ocean ecosystems, with unknown global consequences", in the words of one of the *Nature* report's authors. And global warming may compound the problem, since changing sea temperatures are also starting to have an effect on marine eco-systems.

Currently, many of the most over-fished areas are around Europe and North America. Europe has implemented a quota system to limit the damage and allow replenishment. But even if this is sufficient (which many experts doubt) and the rules are implemented properly (which so far they haven't been, according to the EC), other areas are feeling the pressure in the meantime. The EU, for example, has already purchased fishing rights from a number of African countries. This may provide short-term income for countries that definitely need it, but many predict that a lack of regulation will soon see stocks in these regions depleted, resulting in dwindling catches for local people who actually rely on fishing to survive.

Bycatch and sea-bed damage

Fishermen have always hauled in a certain amount of "bycatch" – non-target fish and other marine life. But as fishing has become more industrial, the problem has become much more serious. The relationship between tuna fishing and dead **dolphins** is relatively common knowledge (see box overleaf), but the problem actually is much wider, with **turtles**, **sea birds**, **seals**, **whales** and **sharks** routinely getting caught, not to mention huge quantities of small fish, which are very often just thrown back dead. Driftnets, used to catch **tuna**, **swordfish**, **sardines**, **herring**, **albacore** and other species are one

TUNA AND DOLPHINS

The various species of tuna sold in the UK are all being very heavily fished, some – such as the giant **bluefin**, which is often used in sushi – near to the point of extinction. **Skipjack** and **yellowfin,** which dominate the tinned market, are not in such a bad way, but their catching sometimes involves the killing of **dolphins**. The controversy relates primarily to yellowfin, which live in the Eastern Pacific and swim in large schools underneath groups of dolphins. Since around 1950 fishermen have exploited this relationship: find a group of the easily visible dolphins, surround them with large purse-seine nets, and pull in the tuna underneath, usually along with the dolphins, which are thrown back dead. This practice is thought to have killed many millions of dolphins, seriously damaging their numbers, which have not recovered since. **Driftnets** and other tuna-fishing techniques are also responsible for killing dolphins.

The issue came to the US public eye in the 1980s, resulting in a consumer boycott, improved fishing techniques, tighter regulations (in some countries) and the **"Dolphin Safe"** label from the Earth Island Institute (www.earthisland.org). All this has made an enormous difference and, though dolphins continue to die in tuna nets, only a tiny amount of the tuna on the European market now comes from so-called "dolphin-deadly" fisheries. In the UK, there hasn't yet been a consistent, legally binding definition of Dolphin Safe or Dolphin Friendly, but most of the major retailers and processors are now affiliated with the Earth Island Institute, so in general the dolphin-friendly claims that consumers come across can be trusted.

Still, the issues aren't quite cut and dried, because some tuna-fishing methods that avoid dolphins altogether – attracting them with floating logs or using baited hooks hanging off mile-long floating lines – can be problematic in other ways. They may be better for dolphins but worse for **sharks**, **turtles** and **non-target fish**, and they may risk damaging tuna stocks by yielding younger fish that haven't yet reproduced. Further, some claim that the inspection system is very weak and the tuna supply chain so convoluted that it's almost impossible to know where your fish has actually come from.

While tuna has got most of the attention, other species such as sea bass and swordfish are also widely associated with dolphin deaths.

major culprit – despite recent legislation, these are often many miles long and have earned the nickname "walls of death" for good reason. But **bottom trawling**, which entails dragging a fine net over the sea bed, can be even worse. This technique – widely used for prawns, scallops, plaice, clam, snapper and other species – can result both in incomparably more bycatch than target, and can also cause serious damage to the sea bed. In biologically diverse underwater "seamounts", *New Scientist* recently reported, trawling is wiping out scores of species before they can even be identified.

FARMED FISH: SALMON, PLAICE, TROUT ET AL

With the seas suffering from depleted stocks, fish farming seems like the obvious solution. And, indeed, an increasing proportion of our fish is reared in farms – around a third of the global total – making aquaculture the **fastest growing of all food sectors**. For years the lochs of Scotland and the fjords of Norway have been gradually filling up with the **salmon** industry's giant plastic nets, with farms accounting for nearly 100% of the Scotch salmon on sale. **Trout** is also widely farmed and, with stock numbers low and financial potential high, the farming of **cod**, **sea bass** and **bream** is also on the rise.

Farms certainly get around the problem of bycatch and satisfy consumer demand for cheap fish, but instead of alleviating the over-exploitation of the sea they very often actually exacerbate it. After all, to farm carnivorous fish like salmon, cod and haddock, you need to catch a huge quantity of smaller fish to feed them. For each kilo of salmon you buy in a shop, for example, up to five kilos of fish will have been caught – sometimes on the other side of the world – transported and turned into fish food. By the end of this decade, some estimate, around 90% of the world's fish oil will be used to make aquaculture feed.

And the problems of fish farming can go beyond this wastefulness: green and anti-poverty groups claim the farms can also be problematic in terms of **pollution**, **animal welfare** and – in the case of tropical prawns (see box overleaf) – **human rights**.

Environmental impacts

Probably the most pressing of the accusations made against intensive fish farms is the environmental impact. Millions of fish churn out a lot of **mineral-rich faeces.** Scottish salmon, for example, excrete twice as much phosphorus as the country's human population according to the World Wildlife Fund.

This goes straight into the surrounding waters, suffocating sea-bed life and possibly creating the **toxic algal blooms** that have left much

THE PROBLEM WITH PRAWNS

Prawns fall into two categories. There are the small cold-water ones frequently used in sandwiches, and the larger tropical ones – also known as "tiger" or "king" prawns – which have become favourites in restaurants and supermarkets in the last decade or so. According to many environmental and anti-poverty groups, tiger prawns are about as unethical a crustacean as you can consume, their cultivation involving the very worst practices of both farmed and caught seafood, linked to terrible abuses of people and the environment.

The majority of the tigers that reach the UK have been intensively farmed in Asian countries such as **Bangladesh** and the **Philippines**. Tropical prawn farming has a long history as a sustainable aquaculture, but the large-scale modern methods – if campaign groups are to be believed – are an example of destructive and short-term food production at its worst. According to critics such as Christian Aid and the Environmental Justice Foundation, the prawn farms' man-made pools drain local water sources, requiring an estimated 50,000 litres of water for each kilo of prawns produced, and become a major source of pollution. **Salt** is added to the water in large quantities, as well as fishmeal food, antibiotics to limit the risks of overcrowding, growth stimulants to make the process faster, and lime to regulate the acidity. This saline cocktail inevitably filters back into nearby **agricultural land**, rendering it unproductive, and pollutes local drinking water sources.

Nearby fishing areas also get hit, both by direct pollution and by aggressive industrial fishing for potential prawn-feed: like salmon, prawns consume far more food than they produce. And, furthermore, the farms are responsible for massive destruction of **mangrove swamps**, which are

of Scotland closed to shellfishing. Besides minerals, the waste – not to mention the fish – also contains a cocktail of **antibiotics**, uneaten food and dyes (farmed salmon would be grey, not pink, if dye wasn't added). Various illegal chemicals and hormones, banned for their environmental and health impact, have also often shown up in spot checks.

Another potential affect of fish farms is a reduction in **wild stocks** near by. Sometimes this happens through the inevitable spreading of

essential to tropical coastal ecosystems. Amazingly, around 25% of the mangrove forest lost each year is due to prawn farming, according to the Marine Stewardship Council.

In many cases the ponds end up so toxic or virus-ridden that they have simply to be abandoned, the companies that own them moving on to new locations and leaving local people with impure water, a damaged ability to feed themselves and few, if any, real benefits. There have even been numerous reports of people being **violently displaced** from prospective pond sites, as well as murder and rape in some extreme cases. However, despite all these problems, intensive prawn farming makes quick and serious money – at least for some people. For this reason, the World Bank and other international agencies have encouraged the growth of the industry, and it is increasingly popping up around the coasts of Africa and South America.

Not all tiger prawns are farmed: other are **sea-caught**. But these aren't necessarily any better, since prawn trawlers are associated with as much environmental destruction as the farms. The technique used – dragging a fine net over the sea-bed – is as effective as it is unselective. As well as seriously damaging the sea-bed itself, the nets bring in, by weight, as much as **twenty times more bycatch than prawns**, endangering turtle and other sea life and diminishing the catch of subsistence fishermen. According to the Environmental Justice Foundation, prawn trawling accounts for a third of the world's bycatch but produces only a fiftieth of its seafood.

For more information on the tiger-prawn issue, see:

Christian Aid www.christianaid.org
Environmental Justice Foundation www.ejfoundation.org

the diseases and lice that thrive in intensive farms, but there may also be a more sinister mechanism at play. Farmed salmon, for example, regularly escape in huge numbers (the WWF estimates that 630,000 salmon escaped from Norwegian farms in 2002 alone) and if these fish, not adapted for life in the natural world, breed with wild salmon, a kind of **negative evolution** takes place, with wild fish becoming less and less able to cope with their natural conditions.

Finally there are the issues of animal welfare. Few people find it easy to empathize with fish, but keeping creatures that are naturally migratory and/or solitary in incredibly cramped spaces with 50,000 others is surely beyond the pale. And so are practices such as allowing fish to suffocate as a way of killing them, and stocking them in such high density that their fins are regularly damaged – two things reported to be common practice on trout farms.

ETHICAL FISH

The problems described above are serious, but they don't necessarily mean that we should stop eating fish and seafood. There are various measures you can take to minimize the negative impacts of what you buy. One option is to look out for the **Marine Stewardship Council logo** (see box opposite). However, as yet supplies aren't huge and the range is small – a good sign for the integrity of the scheme, perhaps, but not great for the shopper.

Another option is to **be picky** about which types of fish and seafood you choose. The quandaries of tropical prawns, farmed salmon and sea-caught cod have already been discussed, but there are many other species endangered by over-fishing or caught in destructive ways, and others still which are relatively unproblematic. For an in-depth view, get *The Good Fish Guide*, a book by Bernadette Clarke of the Marine Conservational Society. You can order it directly from them (www.mcsuk.org ▷ 01989 566017), but a taster is provided overleaf in the form of the Society's top species for consumers to avoid or eat with a clear conscience.

THE MARINE STEWARDSHIP COUNCIL

 Any seafood bearing this blue tick/fish label has been caught according to sustainable criteria set out by the **Marine Stewardship Council** (MSC). Initially set up by Unilever and the WWF, but now an independent organization, the MSC both promotes a responsible approach to fishing and monitors practices. To be awarded the mark, fisheries need to be able to demonstrate their commitment to:

▷ The maintenance and re-establishment of **healthy populations** of targeted species, and the integrity of ecosystems

▷ **Effective management systems**, considering biological, technological, economic, social, environmental and commercial aspects

▷ Following relevant local, national and international **laws, standards, understandings and agreements**

A small but growing number of fisheries are now accredited and stocked in the supermarket, including **Alaskan salmon**, **Burry Inlet cockles**, **New Zealand hoki**, **South West handline mackerel**, **Thames herring** and **Western Australian rock lobster** (pictured). For more information, including where to buy, visit: www.msc.org

FISH & SEAFOOD

Do eat...

Alaska or walleye pollock
Bib or pouting (line-caught)
Black bream or porgy or seabream (line-caught)
Clam (sustainably harvested)
Cockle (MSC certified or sustainably harvested)
Coley or saithe (from North sea)
Common dolphinfish (line-caught)
Cuttlefish (trap caught)
Dab (line-caught or seine netted)
Dover sole (from Eastern channel)
Dublin Bay prawn (MSC certified or pot- or creel-caught)
Flounder
Grey gurnard
Herring or sild (MSC certified or line-caught from North sea)
Hoki (MSC certified)
King scallop (sustainably harvested)
Lythe or pollack (line-caught)
Mackerel (MSC certified or line-caught)
Mussel (sustainably harvested)
Oyster (farmed Native & Pacific)
Pacific halibut (line-caught)
Pacific salmon (MSC certified)
Red gurnard
Red mullet
Salmon (from organic or Freedom Food-certified farms)
Spider crab
Sprat (from the North Sea, dolphin friendly)
Whiting (from the English Channel)
Winkle (sustainably harvested)
Witch (line-caught)

Don't eat...

Alfonsinos or golden eye perch
American plaice
Argentine or greater silver smelt
Atlantic cod (from overfished stocks)
Atlantic halibut
Atlantic salmon (wild-caught)
Blue ling
Chilean seabass or Patagonian toothfish
Dogfish (inc. catshark, nursehound)
European Hake
Greater forkbeard
Grouper
Haddock (except from North Sea, West of Scotland, Skaggerak, Kattegat and Iceland)
Ling
Marlin (blue, Indo-Pacific & white)
Monkfish
Orange roughy
Plaice (except from Irish Sea)
Rat or rabbit fish
Red or blackspot seabream
Redfish or ocean perch
Roundnose grenadier
Seabass (trawl-caught only)
Shark
Skates & rays
Snapper
Sturgeon
Swordfish
Tiger prawn (except organically farmed)
Tuna (except dolphin-friendly, pole- and line-caught yellowfin and skip-jack)
Tusk

For more information on the fish in these lists, see the MCS's FishOnline site:

FishOnline www.fishonline.org

Also, as a rule, try to avoid young, undersized fish, as catching these can exacerbate pressure on stocks.

A final option is to buy organic fish. These are, by default, farmed (nothing caught in the wild can qualify as organic, since you don't know where it has been or what it has eaten), but in much less intensive conditions, with no antibiotics or colorants and better protection for the environ-

MSC-certified New Zealand Hoki

ment. Devotees also swear the organic fish taste much better, as their diet is superior and the lower density of stocks allow them to exercise properly. If your local shops don't sell organic fish, try looking online. A number of suppliers do quick delivery, one example being:

Hawkshead Organic Fish www.organicfish.com ▷ 01539 436541

For more, try the delivery services and directories listed on p.183–184.

Bear in mind, though, that even organic salmon, trout and other carnivorous fish are nonetheless fed on fishmeal from sea-caught fish, so you're not entirely sidestepping the problem of the oceans' ever-depleting fish stocks (or avoiding the sea-borne toxins your fish has been fed on).

FRUIT & VEGETABLES
What to buy, where to buy

The ethical considerations involved in buying fruit and vegetables relate to many of the issues discussed at the beginning of this chapter and the first section of this book. First there's the effect of the growing techniques on the **environment** – everything from the impact on wildlife of pesticides running off into streams, to soil erosion caused by over-industrial techniques. There's also the environmental question of **food miles** (see p.100): can it ever be ethically sound to buy fruit and veg from the other side of the world when equivalent products are available from local sources? As already discussed, our fresh produce is travelling further than ever, and the fuel used in food transport is an ever-growing source of the greenhouse gases that are already thought to be killing tens of thousands people every year (see p.43).

Another consideration is whether the workers are receiving decent **pay and conditions**. Are they being subjected to exploitative terms, denied union bargaining power, or being exposed to dangerous agrochemicals and other risks? The "sweatshop" issues of inhumanly long hours, and other types of labour abuse, are just as common, if not more so, in the agricultural sector.

The most shocking labour abuse in the fruit and veg sector has occurred in the developing world, such as on the **banana plantations** of Central and South America (see pp.152–153). However, a number of recent exposés – such as those in Felicity Lawrence's book, *Not On The Label* – have shown that many European farms, including those in Britain, rely on temporary, non-resident workers subcontracted through "gangmasters" and paid sub-minimum-wage rates.

Then there's the question of where we should buy our fruit and vegetables. The **supermarkets** (see p.175), which have become the unrivalled superpowers of the fresh-produce supply chain, are regularly accused of using their size to squeeze suppliers – both at home and abroad – so hard that it becomes almost impossible for them to stick to any serious labour and environmental standards. In the case of fruit and veg, they are also resented for causing so much waste, and increased agrochemical use, by refusing to accept anything that doesn't fulfil their infamously strict specifications of size, shape and colour. The degree of conformity required – with carrot length, for example, specified in millimetres – would be entertaining were it not so disturbing (see p.178).

Another matter that often crops up in discussions about the ethics of the fruit and veg industry is the dwindling number of varieties on offer. Though we're now offered star-fruit and guava at every turn, green commentators often lament the loss – some permanently – of the literally thousands of varieties of apples, potatoes, squashes and other produce which once flourished in Britain. As Andrew Kimbrell wrote in *The Ecologist*, "monoculture industrial agriculture not only limits what we can eat today, it also reduces the choices of future generations ... the UN Food and Agriculture Organisation (FAO) estimates that more than three quarters of agricultural genetic diversity was lost in this past century". Again, the blame for this is usually jointly pinned onto industrial farming and the supermarkets, which farmers and the green movement accuse of favouring shelf life and profit margins over and above everything else.

ETHICAL FRUIT & VEG

For all the above reasons, the most common ethical advice is, first, to favour **organic** produce, which offers a range of environmental benefits (see p.86). And, second, to avoid supermarkets and use **seasonal**, **locally produced** fruit and veg from alternative outlets such as **box schemes** and **farmers' markets** – for more on these, see pp.181–187.

Conversely, however, the supermarkets are just about the only place you're likely to find fresh produce bearing the **Fairtrade Mark**...

BANANAS: GLOBALIZATION IN A SLIPPERY SKIN

The world's most widely consumed fruit provides a perfect illustration of many of the most pressing and heated debates about world trade and intensive farming. There are hundreds of varieties of banana grown around the world, most of them in India and other countries where they are cultivated for domestic consumption. But the export market, almost entirely driven by the US and Europe, is largely dominated by just one variety and a handful of giant companies. Roughly 60% of banana exports are controlled by just three multinationals – **Chiquita**, **Dole Food** and **Del Monte** – which produce primarily in Central and South America, the world of the so-called "dollar banana".

Banana farming has always been a big-business sector. It was once dominated by the **United Fruit Company**, which controlled much of Central America and was instrumental in bringing about the 1954 CIA-orchestrated coup in Guatemala, which overthrew the country's elected government and led to half a century of conflict and bloodshed. Today, the big banana firms don't stand accused of starting "real" wars, but they were behind the trade war which saw the US, Ecuador and various American countries battling with the EU at the World Trade Organization in the late 1990s. The point in question was the legality of EU's banana import policy, which to a certain extent shunned "dollar bananas" in favour of those grown in ex-European colonies in the so-called **ACP** (African, Caribbean and Pacific) countries.

Pro-free-trade commentators claimed that Ecuador and other poor dollar-banana countries were suffering due to their restricted access to European markets. But the EU claimed that small ACP family farms – and in some cases whole countries' economies – would be unable to survive without preferential treatment, so the human consequences of leaving everything to the free market would be huge. Anti-globalization protesters agreed, describing the situation as a classic case of big companies trying to use global trade rules to profit from a "race to the bottom". They pointed out that the Latin American producers were only able to undercut small farmers in the ACP countries because their plantations depended on terrible exploitation of workers and the environment.

It's certainly true that the big banana producers have long been dogged by allegations about their lack of ethical standards. First, there's the question of wages – in the dollar-banana plantations, the workers who actually grow the bananas receive only 1–3% of the final price, or, put another way, as little as a dollar a day, in return for twelve or more hours of hard labour (according to figures from the Fairtrade Foundation). But that's only one issue. Child labour has been shown to be widespread, as has the **intimidation, firing** or even **murder** of would-be union organizers. And health and safety has often been seriously compromised by the use of **agrochemicals**.

Required in vast quantities due to the single-crop nature of the plantations, fungicides and other pesticides are often sprayed from planes, and though there are theoretically rules to ensure that workers are not put in danger, these have not always been observed. As well as directly breathing in the chemicals, the workers, many of whom live on or next to the plantations, have often ended up drinking and bathing in contaminated water, with sometimes catastrophic results. In the last few decades thousand of workers have died, been made seriously ill or given birth to deformed babies. According to a Fairtrade Foundation report from 2000, "some 20% of the male banana workers in Costa Rica were left sterile after handling toxic chemicals", while women working in the pack houses had twice the normal incidence of leukemia. The ecological damage of the big plantations has also been severe, including soil degradation, lost biodiversity, toxic run-off and forest clearance. None of this was deemed relevant to the WTO case, however, since international trade rules don't currently take social and environmental issues into account.

Partly as a result of the "banana wars" – which the EU eventually lost – two things happened. The first was the extension of the **Fairtrade labelling scheme** to bananas. Sourced from small-producer co-operatives in the ACP countries, Fairtrade bananas provide all the standard ethical guarantees of the Fairtrade Mark (see p.18), including improved health and safety and a higher proportion of the price going to the farmers.

The second was that the big banana firms started trying to redefine themselves as "socially responsible" companies, publishing codes of conduct relating to health and safety, pesticide use, and union representation. Chiquita even joined the UK's Ethical Trading Initiative (see box on pp.68–69) and launched a partnership with the Rainforest Alliance. As with all such big-business initiatives, however, the degree to which these aims are benefiting the workers on the ground is an open, and much-debated, question.

Where Fairtrade bananas aren't available, go for bananas from the ex-British colonies in the Caribbean – usually given a Windward Isles label – as they are generally grown by smaller-scale farms with better workers' rights, fewer chemicals and a slightly higher percentage of the profits heading back to the workers. For more on the banana trade, see:

Banana Link www.bananalink.org.uk

FRUIT & VEGETABLES

Fairtrade fresh produce

The success of the Fairtrade banana has led to an ever-growing range of Fairtrade fruit and veg. Like all products bearing the Fairtrade Mark, these are sourced from the developing world, according to rules which guarantee that the producers receive a higher proportion of the price we pay for their crops, a premium for social and environmental improvement, advance payments opportunities, and reliable long-term trading relationships. For more on how the Fairtrade scheme works, see p.18.

At the time of going to press, the Fairtrade range includes apples, bananas, grapes, lemons, mangoes, oranges, pineapples, pears, plums, green beans and peppers. But each item is only available from certain supermarkets and some independents (see below), according to **market availability** and **seasonality**. For the most up-to-date list of products and suppliers, see:

Fairtrade Foundation www.fairtrade.org.uk

FAIRTRADE FRUIT AND VEG – AND WHERE TO GET IT	Asda	Booths	Budgens	Co-op	Morrisons	Safeway	Sainsbury's	Somerfield	Tesco	Waitrose	Independents
Apples				✓					✓		
Avocados	✓			✓	✓	✓	✓		✓	✓	✓
Bananas	✓	✓	✓	✓	✓	✓	✓	✓	✓	✓	
Clementines		✓	✓						✓	✓	✓
Grapes				✓					✓		
Lemons			✓	✓					✓	✓	
Mangoes				✓			✓		✓	✓	✓
Oranges				✓					✓	✓	
Pineapples				✓			✓		✓	✓	
Pears				✓							
Plums				✓					✓		
Satsumas		✓	✓						✓	✓	

Sorting mangoes in a Fairtrade-certified plantation in Chacras, Ecuador

Fairtrade versus local

The first Fairtrade fruit and vegetables were tropical fruits such as bananas and pineapples. But as the range expands to include products that can also be grown at home – such as South African apples, which were added in 2003 – a slight tension is emerging between the Fairtrade movement, on the one hand, and environmentalists, "localists", and UK farmers on the other. Surely it's crazy, the latter argue, regardless of the good intentions, to fly in apples from the Southern Hemisphere when the bumper crops from Britain's own famously good orchards are rotting in the fields, their owners unable to match the price of imports. As well as the significant environmental costs of flying or shipping the goods 10,000 miles, they argue, imports are leading to poverty and depression at home, where orchards – and ways of life – are being abandoned every week.

PESTICIDE RESIDUES

With thousands of farm workers killed every year by poisoning, and wildlife and the environment suffering in numerous ways, pesticides unequivocally pose certain threats to people and planet. But what about the residues on our fruit and veg? Green campaigners link pesticide residues to skin and eye irritation, mental and nervous problems, breast cancer and other conditions, and point out that little is known about the long-term effects of many of these substances (some of which are hormone disrupters), especially their combined "cocktail effect".

But most toxicologists seem less convinced that the quantities in question are big enough to be a worry. A major government study published in 1998 tested more than 2000 fruit and vegetable samples and found that around 73% were residue-free, 26% had residues below the MRL ("maximum recommended limit") and 1.3% contained residues above the limit. Some people were up in arms about the 1.3%, yet the report's authors concluded that – even in the case of those foods that slightly exceeded the limits – "food is safe from the point of view of pesticide residues".

Still, those who are concerned about pesticide residues – especially those who don't feel that they can justify the expense of buying organic for all their fresh produce – may be interested to know which fruit and veg tend to contain higher residues than others. The following lists of the fruit and veg at the top and bottom of the pesticide residue scales were prepared by the US's Environmental Working Group. They relate specifically to the levels of residues found in food as typically prepared – *not the amount used in growing*. So banana, for example, because of its thick, inedible skin, comes on the low-residues list despite being associated with massive pesticide use and worker exploitation. These lists, then, are not equivalent to the "most ethical" fruit and veg.

Highest levels Apple ▷ Bell Pepper ▷ Celery ▷ Cherry ▷ Grapes ▷ Nectarines ▷ Peach ▷ Pear ▷ Potato ▷ Raspberry ▷ Spinach ▷ Strawberry

Lowest levels Asparagus ▷ Avocado ▷ Banana ▷ Broccoli ▷ Cauliflower ▷ Sweet corn ▷ Kiwi ▷ Mango ▷ Onion ▷ Papaya ▷ Pea ▷ Pineapple

For more information, and methodology, see www.foodnews.org. Or to read more about the pesticide issue, see:

Pesticide Action Network www.pan-uk.org

On the other hand, the apples from South Africa not only support the poor (and grinding poverty is undoubtedly a more pressing issue in Southern Africa than it is in the UK), but also support a number of positive initiatives and "empowerment projects", including creating opportunities for landless workers to "become co-owners of fruit farms", a scheme recently praised by Nelson Mandela among others. Once again, there's no obvious answer for the ethically minded shopper; a similar choice sometimes has to be made between organic and Fairtrade foods, and organic and local foods.

Soil Association Ethical Trade

For a brief while it looked as if the Fairtrade scheme was going to start being applied to certain British-grown organic foods, in an attempt to deal with the fact that, even in comparatively wealthy countries such as the UK, growers frequently struggle to cover the cost of production. In the event, the idea was dropped, because Fairtrade consumers tended to believe the scheme should prioritize the extreme poverty of the developing world. In its place, however, the Soil Association has launched its own **Ethical Trade** label. The scheme aims to introduce similar criteria to those of the Fairtrade Mark – based around "fairness, mutual respect and transparency" – into the UK organic market, with separate rules and certification required for participating farmers. The key principles are:

▷ A fair price for the farmer and others in the supply chain
▷ Fair treatment of workers
▷ Involvement in the local community

However, at the time of writing the scheme is still in its very early stages, and isn't likely to appear on a wide range of products until at least the middle of 2005. For the latest information, including more details on the criteria, contact:

Soil Association www.soilassociation.org.uk ▷ 0117 314 5000

COFFEE & TEA
... and other Fairtrade products

COFFEE

The ethics of the coffee trade are perhaps more widely discussed than those of any other sector. And it's not hard to understand why. First, there's the sheer scale of the industry. Literally billions of cups of coffee are consumed around the world every day, a colossal demand that has made coffee, in terms of total value, the **most traded commodity in the world after oil and illegal drugs**. It's thought that around 100 million people work in the coffee trade – more than double the entire working population of the UK – including more than 20 million farmers, the vast majority of whom are small-scale growers with less than 10 acres of land.

The second reason we hear so much about coffee is that the world is in the midst of a so-called "**coffee crisis**", with the prices received by

GROWING COFFEE

The coffee "tree" is an evergreen tropical shrub that only flourishes within a couple of thousand miles of the Equator. Especially in the case of the high-quality **Arabica** species – as opposed to the **Robusta** or **Liberica** used for lower quality and instant coffees – it's an incredibly high-maintenance crop. After an initial four or five years bearing no fruit, each bush produces a few thousand "beans" (actually the seeds of the cherry-like fruit) – enough for only around one kilo of roasted coffee. The plants require constant attention, and the cherries usually have to be picked by hand, as they ripen at different times. Much highland coffee is grown on slopes so steep and remote that horses or mules, let alone motor vehicles, cannot be used.

farmers having dropped to their lowest levels in decades. Coffee farmers have never been a wealthy bunch. For reasons ranging from their lack of capital to Western trade rules that slap huge import tariffs on processed goods, the vast majority of the profits from each jar of coffee we buy goes to the retailers and packagers – with the farmers receiving as little as two percent.

But as farm-gate prices have plummeted, millions have been pushed into desperate poverty. This has resulted in massive suffering in many areas, and has been especially catastrophic in countries such as Ethiopia and Burundi, where coffee is central to the wider economy. As wages have dropped many farmers have had to take their children out of school, forego medical treatment, or accumulate unpayable debt just to keep things ticking over. Others have abandoned coffee growing completely, in some cases finding themselves with no viable option but to turn to the production of illegal crops such as **coca** and **marijuana**. In some countries, such as Nicaragua, thousands of children are **starving** as a result of the crisis, according to the United Nations World Food Programme.

The coffee crisis – what happened?

The main cause of the price crisis faced by millions of coffee growers is massive **oversupply**: there's simply far more coffee being produced than consumers want to drink. On and off until 1989, coffee production and prices were regulated by quotas set by the **International Coffee Organisation** – a group of producer and consumer countries that aimed to keep supply and demand in line with each other.

However, at the end of the 1980s, disagreement between producer and consumer countries, and a prevailing economic ethos of trade liberalization, led to the dismantling of the quota system. Production patterns soon started to change, with **Vietnam** – following advice from the World Bank – investing heavily in the coffee sector and becoming a major new supplier. Vietnam certainly needed the income and jobs, but its emergence as a major player in the coffee market, along with other factors such as new processing technologies that allowed lower quality beans to be substantially improved, soon led to a massive rise in the production of useable coffee. As the basic laws of supply and demand dictate, this was accompanied by a concurrent drop in the price that farmers could get for their crops.

The crisis soon spiralled into a vicious circle. Since many coffee farmers lack the experience, circumstances or capital to produce other crops, many have tried to deal with the price drop by working as hard as possible to produce even more coffee. But this, of course, only helps to build up the stockpiles and drive prices down even further.

The shifting dynamics of the coffee industry are also having **environmental impacts**, with traditional "shaded coffee", grown under a native tree canopy, giving way to "sun coffee". Sun coffee yields more coffee more quickly, but the bushes last for only 10–15 years, as opposed to the 50 years of a shaded bush. They typically also require far more fertilizers and pesticides, which, combined with the forest clearance required to plant the bushes, hugely endangers the delicate ecological balances of highland tropical areas. According to groups such as Conservation International (www.conservation.org), these farming methods are threatening whole ecosystems, from Latin America to Indonesia.

The coffee giants

Even greater than the supermarkets' stranglehold over food retail is the domination of the coffee market by a handful of giant roasters and packagers: **Nestlé** (producers of Nescafé), **Kraft** (owned by tobacco giant Philip Morris and behind Kenco, Maxwell House and Carte Noire), **Sara Lee Corp** (who own Douwe Egberts) and **Procter & Gamble** (who mainly sell in the US).

Since these firms make their money buying, processing and reselling coffee, the drop in farm-gate prices has been to their advantage. Hence Nestlé's Annual Management Report for 2000, in explaining their good profits for that year, pointed to "favourable commodity prices" – business terminology that obscures the people behind the product. The idea of giant companies getting richer while farmers suffer – and

STARBUCKS AND OTHER CAFÉS: AN ETHICINO?

Some independent cafés have been offering Fairtrade coffee for some time, but recently the trend has been boosted – ironically enough – by the kind of chain cafés which have themselves often been the target of campaigner anger. **Costa Coffee** was the first big player to get involved, offering any drink with CaféDirect Fairtrade coffee for 10p extra. Then **Starbucks** caught on, adopting Fairtrade in the UK for filter coffee and – once a month – as "coffee of the day", so you can slurp a responsible latté. The Organic Consumers Association, accused Starbucks of making only a "token" gesture, pointing out that only a tiny fraction of the company's coffees were Fairtrade, but, more recently, the company has been praised by none other than Oxfam, who wrote "It is a welcome relief ... to see Starbucks taking a lead amongst the major coffee companies in addressing the crisis in the coffee market ... it is paying its suppliers around double the open market price and it has independent checks done to see that it carries out its own purchasing guidelines."

This leaves ethical consumers with yet another conundrum. The company's coffee buying policies are clearly progressive, but writers such as Naomi Klein have criticized Starbucks' aggressive expansion policies (forcing out local cafés), its questionable employment practices (keeping employees as temporary workers to avoid benefit and pension obligations), and its contribution to the homogenization of high-streets globally (with everything from the design to the music prescribed by the Seattle HQ).

Similarly, **Pret A Manger** offers Fairtrade coffee as an option, though the fact that they're owned by McDonald's means that many consumers make it a no-go area.

One option, of course, is to ask your local independent cafés to start stocking Fairtrade. Or look out for **Progreso** – a forthcoming café chain set up, and jointly owned by, two Honduran coffee co-operatives, Oxfam and the UK's leading independent coffee roaster. The plan is to open twenty branches over the next few years, with "targeted sites" including London, Glasgow, Edinburgh, Brighton, Bristol, Bath, Oxford and Cambridge. For more information, see:

Progreso www.progreso.org.uk

in some cases literally starve – has led to a huge amount of resentment.

In a sense, the big coffee firms are simply doing what companies always do: buying their raw products from the cheapest seller with the aim of maximizing shareholder value. And it's true that they can't really be blamed for the oversupply. Still, campaigners accuse the Big Four of failing even to acknowledge the extent of the problem, and of ignoring the plight of the very families from whom they have profited for years.

There are signs that one or two of the big companies are starting to change their ways. Procter & Gamble and Kraft have both recently launched a Fairtrade range in the US, and at the time of going to press there are rumours of Nestlé considering doing the same – something which will doubtless raise a few eyebrows, considering the ongoing boycott of Nestlé for its stance on baby milk products (see p.172).

Oxfam recently assessed the policies of each of the Big Four, in terms of the prices paid to farmers and other efforts made to deal with the crisis, and gave them each a score out of 100 according to the efforts they've made to improve things for the coffee farmers worse affected by the crisis:

▷ **P&G:** 49% – "needs to expand its Fairtrade coffee range"
▷ **Nestlé:** 43% – "a failure to grasp the depth of the crisis"
▷ **Kraft:** 38% – "miserable failure in addressing the issues"
▷ **Sara Lee:** 27% – "failed in almost every aspect of dealing with the crisis"

Fairtrade coffee

Like all products marked bearing the label, Fairtrade coffee is sourced directly from the grower according to ethical trading principles. This gives the farmers a number of advantages (see p.18 for more details), but probably the most important in this case is a **minimum price guarantee**. No matter what happens on the commodity markets, the Fairtrade coffee price will never go lower than a certain level. At the time of writing, for example, despite the fact that Fairtrade coffee is only marginally more expensive than the conventionally traded equivalent, the price received by coffee farmers under the Fairtrade scheme is three times the international price for robustas and double the international price for arabicas.

Despite the clear benefits of Fairtrade coffee, the organizers of the scheme are well aware that, on its own, it doesn't provide a long-term answer to the problems caused by coffee oversupply. Other than every consumer increasing their caffeine intake, a structural solution would have to involve drastic measures such as destroying the coffee stock-piles and returning to a quota system. Since this seems relatively unlikely to happen, some right-wing commentators have taken the rather extreme attitude that Fairtrade may be more of a hindrance than a blessing (dragging the problem out and giving "conventional" coffee a bad name) and that the problem would be better left to the free market. For more on this debate, see pp.22–23.

Fairtrade coffees are very widely available in supermarkets and health-food shops – and via the Net. The selection includes instants, beans and ground ranging from Kilimanjaro Mountain Special and Ethiopia Djimma to Sumatra Mandheling and Italian-style espresso blend.

Of the many coffee brands whose products carry the Fairtrade Mark, one that deserves a special mention is **CaféDirect**, which has been central in bringing Fairtrade into the mainstream since being founded by Oxfam, Traidcraft, Equal Exchange and Twin Trading in 1991. The company exceeds the basic Fairtrade standards, feeding a percentage of its gross profits each year back to the farmer groups that supply it. For more information, see:

CaféDirect www.cafedirect.co.uk

Or for a full list of Fairtrade coffe brands, and where to buy them, try:

Fairtrade Coffee www.fairtrade.org.uk/products_coffee_buy.htm

And for background info about the coffee trade and crisis, visit:
ICP www.ico.org
Oxfam www.maketradefair.com

TEA

Whereas coffee is grown mainly by small-scale independent farmers, tea is primarily a **plantation** crop. There are some small tea producers, but the sector is dominated by large estates, many of which include a factory in which the teas are processed and packed. As such, the most pressing issues are those of **workers' rights** – pay, hours, conditions, etc. As with many areas, unions are often discouraged, or disallowed, on tea plantations, leaving the pickers and packers, most of them women, with little bargaining power to demand better conditions. Health and safety is also important, especially the issue of pesticides, which are widely use on (non-organic) tea plantations, in some cases leading to health problems among the workers.

Fairtrade & organic tea

Tea bearing the Fairtrade Mark (see p.18) ensures decent minimum standards of pay, conditions and labour rights for tea workers. Its strictures also include some environmental policies, but tea that is both organic *and* Fairtrade ensures even stricter standards.

In the last few years, the range of Fairtrade teas has grown enormously, so even connoisseurs and fans of obscure flavours are likely to find something to their taste:

▷ **Clipper** (available from supermarkets and independents, but for full range buy online at www.clipper-teas.com): Standard; Organic: Camomile, Peppermint, Black Chai, Green Chai, Earl Grey, English Breakfast, Irish Breakfast, Lapsang Souchong, Darjeeling, Assam, Ceylon; Sri Lanka Gold; Nilgiri Blue Mountain; Green Tea with Aloe Vera/Lemon/Echinacea/Ginkgo/Ginseng.

▷ **Equal Exchange** (available at health food and independent shops): Organic: Standard; Assam; Breakfast; Earl Grey Tea Bags; Darjeeling; Green; Earl Grey; Lemon Green; Masala Chai; Mint Green; Rooibos

▷ **Hampstead Tea & Coffee Company** (available at heath food and independent shops): Organic Biochai Masala; First Flush; Makaibari

Darjeeling; Green; Oolong Leaf; Earl Grey; Ginger Green; Green
Verveine; White Leaf

▷ **Suma** (available at health food and independent shops): Assam;
Earl Grey; Darjeeling; Breakfast

▷ **Teadirect** (available at most supermarkets and independents):
Standard; Earl Grey; Lemongrass; Cinnamon

▷ **Traidcraft** (available at health food and independent shops)
Standard; Indian Ocean; Earl Grey; East African; Tanzanian

▷ **Supermarket own brands:** Morrisons, Sainsbury's, Somerfield,
Tesco

As for the household-name tea brands, most of them – from **Tetley**
to **Taylors** to **Twinings** – have signed up to an initiative called the **Tea
Sourcing Partnership**, which aims to monitor and improve ethical
standards across in the supply chains of the participating companies.
Very much a corporate affair (with PricewaterhouseCoopers responsible for the monitoring), the scheme is itself a member of the Ethical
Trading Initiative (see box on pp.68–69). It's certainly a welcome
development – and unusual in the extent of its industry coverage –
but doesn't offer anything like the same guarantees as Fairtrade.

Tea Sourcing Partnership www.teasourcingpartnership.org.uk

OTHER FAIRTRADE FOODS & DRINK

Though the Fairtrade Mark is primarily associated with coffee and
tea, it can be found on a much wider range of products. A few of these
– such as **mexican honey** – raise the question discussed on p.155: is it
more ethical to buy Fairtrade or to favour the locally produced equivalent on environmental grounds? Others, however, pose no such
dilemmas. Fairtrade **chocolate**, for instance, is not only giving a living
wage to small farmers who desperately need it. It's also helping to
inject transparency and other ethical standards into an industry

which is being increasingly associated with serious human rights abuses. Nearly half of the world's chocolate is grown in Cote d'Ivoire in West Africa, where, according to US government estimates, more than 100,000 child labourers work in hazardous conditions on cocoa farms. Many of these are slave labourers, taken from neighbouring Mali. To make matters worse, cocoa farmers – like coffee producers – are currently suffering a low market price for their crop.

Fairtrade **sugar**, on the other hand, allows consumers to support the more conscientious growers in the developing world – which may help them overcome the crippling effect of Europe's farm subsidies (see p.18).

Here's a list of all the Fairtrade foods and drinks available at the time of writing. These can be found in some supermarkets, but also try the the Fairtrade specialist suppliers listed on pp.185–186. For the most up-to-date range, see www.fairtrade.org.uk/products.htm

▷ **Chocolate and chocolates** by Chocaid, Co-op, The Day Chocolate Company, Green & Black's, Starbucks, Tesco Own Brand, Traidcraft

▷ **Cocoa and drinking chocalate** from Caley's, Clipper, Cocodirect, Day Chocolate, Equal Exchange, Green & Black's, Traidcraft

▷ **Fresh fruit and veg** (see p.154)

▷ **Fruit juice**, including orange juice, breakfast juice and tropical juice by Fruit Passion, JP Juices and Tesco

▷ **Honey**, including set and clear, by Cotswold Speciality Foods, Equal Exchange, Rowse and Traidcraft

▷ **Muesli**, by Alara, the Co-op, Tesco

▷ **Preserves and condiments**, including strawberry jam, marmalade, mango chutney and chocolate hazelnut spread, by Traidcraft, Duerr's and Venture Foods

▷ **Snack bars, biscuits, cookies and cakes** by the Co-op, Doves, Equal Exchange, Tesco, Traidcraft, Tropical Wholefoods and Village Bakery

▷ **Sugar**, including white, golden, raw cane and Demerara, by the Co-op, Equal Exchange, Traidcraft, Whitworths

▷ **Wine**, including chardonnay, cabernet sauvignon and pinot noir, by Vinfruco

The Dubble from Day Chocolate company is the first "ethical" product to enter the market alongside Mars, Snickers and the like. Made from cacao from the "Kuapa Kokoo" Fairtrade-certified co-operative in Ghana, it's widely available in supermarkets, newsagents and other outlets.

FAIRLY TRADED FOODS & DRINKS WITHOUT THE MARK

It's quite common to see foods which don't bear the Fairtrade Mark, but which – according to the packaging or retailer – have been "fairly traded". Sometimes these are products that aren't yet covered by the Fairtrade scheme, such as **rice** and **pasta**, but which have been imported and packaged by long-established ethical trading organizations, such as Traidcraft. Many such foods can be found via online fairtrade specialists (see pp.185–186) or at organic supermarkets and health-food shops. In other cases, however, you might comes across "unofficially" fairly traded foods – especially coffees – in product areas that the Fairtrade scheme does cover. Such claims are most commonly added in good faith by small firms that consider themselves to be responsible businesses. However, they don't offer any official guarantees, and arguably serve to harm the credibility of the Fairtrade system.

FOOD & DRINK: THE BIG BRANDS
Nestlé et al: who owns whom?

Food is an increasingly branded world. In the UK every day brings, on average, nearly thirty new "food products". That's 10,000 new crisp flavours, fizzy drinks – and, indeed, organic chutneys – each year. Of these, only around 10% will last twelve months, the other 90% – with all the ad campaigns, press releases and packaging that went with them – will be junked in the bulging trash can of food-marketing history.

Despite this extraordinary turnover of new products, however, the more popular and widely known food brands – such as Coca-Cola, Nescafé and Flora – are remarkably enduring. There are hundreds of such household names, but the number of major companies actually producing them is surprisingly small. Just as food retail is increasingly controlled by just a few giant supermarkets, and pesticides by a few huge agrochemicals firms, branded, packaged food and drink is increasingly dominated by a handful of multinational corporations, each the result of many mergers and takeovers.

These big firms are a highly controversial bunch. Besides specific accusations such as Nestlé's alleged promotion of formula milk in the third world (see p.172) and Pepsi's financial support for George Bush, the sector as a whole is associated with the unethical promotion – including advertising to children – of salty, fatty and otherwise harmful foods that are leading to a massive rise in obesity, diabetes and other nutrition-related diseases.

Whether these problems are the fault of the companies or cultural shifts, such as people doing less exercise, is an open question. But the situation is looking increasingly extreme – in both rich and poor countries alike. In the UK, according to a 2004 House of Commons Health Committee report, "obesity has grown by almost 400% in the last 25 years", and in the future, "the sight of amputees will become much more familiar … There will be many more blind people. There will be huge demand for kidney dialysis … Indeed, this will be the first generation where children die before their parents as a consequence of childhood obesity."

The big "snack and pop" companies certainly aren't entirely to blame for the obesity boom, yet the firms do spend an astonishing amount of time and money each year lobbying governments against legislation that might do something to solve these problems – banning fizzy drinks in schools, or sweets at supermarket checkouts, for example, or enforcing compulsory health warnings on the packaging of certain products. Indeed, the major American food brands are A-list political donors, while in the UK – according to documents obtained by *The Guardian* in 2004 – "the food manufacturers' lobbying group, the Food and Drink Federation, on its own had over 2,000 contacts with ministers, MPs, lords, MEPs, MSPs and special advisers last year".

The big companies consistently describe themselves as being socially responsible "corporate citizens", and yet their trade associations have a tendency simply to refuse to admit that unhealthy foods and drinks cause health problems. For example, the "Heath and Diet" section of the British Soft Drinks Association website (www.britishsoftdrinks.com), with no hint of irony, claims that: "All soft drinks are healthy because they provide the vital fluids our bodies need with some also providing contributions to the various vitamins and minerals we need every day." Hmmm.

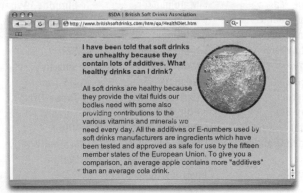

The industry line on fizzy drinks and fresh fruit

A FEW OF THE BIG PLAYERS

It's well beyond the scope of this book to examine the ethical standards of every major food brand. But following is a quick summary of a few of the most controversial members of Big Food, with a list of the best-known brands owned by each. To find out more, try the online resources listed on p.360, seek out the *Good Shopping Guide* (see p.364) or subscribe to *Ethical Consumer* magazine (see p.362).

Nestlé

With more than 230,000 employees and control of more than half of the international coffee market, Nestlé is easily the world's largest food company. The company's brands have been marred by two and a half decades of boycotting relating to their marketing of formula milk in the developing world (see box overleaf). And it came under fire in 2003 when it attempted to claim millions of dollars from the the government of Ethiopia for assets seized by that country's military regime way back in the 1970s. Eleven million Ethiopians were

Nestlé brands

▷ Aero
▷ After Eight
▷ Black Magic
▷ Blue Riband
▷ Breakaway
▷ Buitoni
▷ Buxton
▷ Carnation
▷ Cheerios
▷ Dairy Box
▷ Drifter
▷ Golden Grahams
▷ Herta
▷ Jellytots

▷ Kit Kat
▷ Lion Bar
▷ Matchmakers
▷ Milkybar
▷ Minties
▷ Munch Bunch
▷ Munchies
▷ Nesquik
▷ Perrier
▷ Polo
▷ Quality Street
▷ Rolo
▷ Rowntree Fruit
Pastilles/Gums

▷ San Pellegrino
▷ Santa Maria
▷ Shredded Wheat
▷ Shreddies
▷ Simply Double
▷ Ski
▷ Smarties
▷ Tip Top
▷ Toffee Crisp
▷ Valvert
▷ Vittel
▷ Walnut Whip
▷ Yorkie

facing starvation at the time, but Nestlé still saw fit to call it a "matter of principle", only dropping the claim after a public outcry. Nestlé has also recently been criticized by Oxfam for failing to act to help the farmers hit by the coffee crisis (see p.162). However, rumours that the food giant may launch a Fairtrade range in the near future may soften views on this.

Altria (Philip Morris)

Tobacco giant Philip Morris is best known for its Marlboro cigarettes Less well known is the fact that the same corporation – recently renamed Altria – is among the world's biggest food companies, owning the majority of Kraft foods, among other things. Philip Morris's ethical record includes such highpoints as denying that smoking is addictive, being fined for failing to disclose political donations, and coming close to the top of the table of George Bush campaign contributors (see pp.80–81).

Altria brands

▷ Bird's	▷ Kaffee HAG	▷ Philadelphia
▷ Carte Noire	▷ Kenco	▷ RITZ
▷ Dairylea	▷ Kraft	▷ Suchard
▷ Dime	▷ Lunchables	▷ Terry's
▷ Jacobs	▷ Maxwell House	▷ Toblerone

Coca-Cola and PepsiCo

When the World Health Organization launched an offensive on the global health effects of sugary foods in 2003, fizzy drinks were at the top of their hit-list. To defend themselves against such attacks, and ensure that no one restricts their capability to sell fizzy drinks to kids, the market leaders of this sector – Coca-Cola and PepsiCo – have got the US government on their side through proactive lobbying and political donations (both are major George Bush sponsors, according, again, to www.opensecrets.org).

NESTLÉ & INFANT FORMULA

Since 1977, Nestlé, the world's largest food company, has been the target of the most global, long-standing and highly publicized of all consumer boycotts. The food giant has scores of brands (see p.170), but the controversy focuses on the product that launched the company right back in the 1860s: **infant formula**, also called breastmilk substitute, baby milk or bottle milk.

Where breastfeeding is impossible or impractical – as is often the case – infant formula can be a lifesaver, but it also comes with certain health risks. Even in rich countries, babies fed on formula milk during the first few months are more likely to suffer certain health problems, since breastmilk provides a perfect combination of nutrients and antibodies. But in **developing countries** the dangers are more acute. Formula milk needs to be prepared with water and served in sterilized bottles, which can be problematic if pure water or fuel are in short supply. And if parents find themselves stuck with it but unable to afford sufficient quantities (a real possibility, because moving back to breastfeeding is often impossible once formula milk has been used) they may over-dilute it, mix it with unsuitable solids or substitute it for cheaper but completely unsuitable alternatives, such as cows' milk or tea.

These risks have been known for decades. Right back in the 1930s pioneering pediatrician Dr Cicely Williams published and spoke about the hazards of inappropriate bottle feeding. But for much of the twentieth century the formula milk manufacturers – of which Nestlé was and is the biggest – aggressively promoted their products around the world. Pictures of plump "first-world" babies were used on tins and posters and free samples (sometimes given out by marketing "nurses") were provided for hospitals and given out to new mothers, often making breastfeeding impossible and forcing mothers into months of purchasing. The result was a huge decline in the exclusive use of breastfeeding and the completely avoidable deaths of hundreds of thousands of babies each year around the world.

Things came to a head in the early 1970s, after exposés by *New Internationalist* magazine and War on Want. The latter's article was translated into German as "Nestlé Tötet Babies" (**Nestlé Kills Babies**) and Nestlé sued for libel. It won the court case on the grounds of this title, but it generated massive negative publicity for itself in the process. Things didn't really improve, so a few years later a consumer boycott began – first in the US and then internationally – co-ordinated by the International Baby Food Action Network (IBFAN).

In 1981, the World Health Assembly drew up the **International Code of Marketing of Breastmilk Substitutes**, a set of recommended minimum standards relating to the promotion (or non-promotion) of formula milk. A few years later,

Nestlé agreed to implement the Code voluntarily and the boycott was lifted. But four years after that, the campaign was revived, as IBFAN determined that Nestlé hadn't lived up to its promises and was still supplying cheap or free formula milk to hospitals.

A decade and a half on, the situation is still dire: in 2001 the World Health Organization reported that "some 1.5 million children still die every year because they are inappropriately fed ... less than 35% of infants worldwide are exclusively breastfed for the first four months of life". And though there have been many positive developments – explicit formula milk marketing has been almost stamped out, and breastfeeding rates in the developing world are rising – the question remains as to whether Nestlé, who have gone to great lengths to promote themselves as an ethical company, are acting responsibly.

According to IBFAN, the answer is unquestionably no, since Nestlé and other firms are "continuing their unethical promotional activities whilst claiming to abide by the International Code". The campaigners continue to document some direct violations of the Code – which they display on their website – though their main accusations today relate to more subtle things such as Nestlé lobbying against regulation relating to infant formula, and refusing to accept that the Code should apply to *all* "breastmilk substitutes" – including those aimed at older babies – not just "infant formula".

Nestlé denies such allegations, pointing to its widespread promotion of breastfeeding, its regular audits, and its internal ombudsman for reporting bad practice. Peter Brabeck-Letmathe, the CEO, even claims to look personally into each reported breach of the Code, while acknowledging that – in a company of nearly a quarter of a million staff – slip-ups are bound to happen occasionally. Nestlé also claims that formula milk products are "legitimate and useful", allowing mothers in poor countries the option of returning to work instead of staying at home – something which women in the West take for granted. And they claim that the only reason why they receive all the negative publicity is because they're the easiest target: while their food and drink brands are household names, the other baby milk firms are pharmaceutical companies, so couldn't easily really be boycotted.

However, criticism of Nestlé's formula milk activities – albeit less fierce than it once was – keeps coming from sources as wide ranging as UNICEF and, in 2003, the *British Medical Journal*. And the boycott continues. For both sides of the story, and more background on the breastfeeding issue, visit:

IBFAN www.ibfan.org ▷ **Nestlé** www.babymilk.nestle.com ▷ **UNICEF** www.unicef.org

Coca-Cola, especially, has also courted controversy on many other levels. During the months in which this chapter was written, for example, they have been faced with public and shareholder criticism regarding their failure to address the murder of trade unionists in a Colombian bottling plant, and also for their factory in Kerala, India, where farmers have complained of their water reserves being bled dry and their fields polluted by dangerous waste which the factory allegedly sold to them as fertilizer.

Coca-Cola brands	PepsiCo brands	
▷ Capri-Sun	▷ Doritos	▷ Walkers
▷ Dr Pepper	▷ Pepsi	▷ Wotsits
▷ Fanta	▷ Quaker	
▷ Kia Ora	▷ 7UP	
▷ Lilt	▷ Smith's	
▷ Sprite	▷ Tropicana	

Unilever

Though often described as among the more benevolent of the food giants, Unilever have also faced heavy criticism. Besides standard transnational behaviour – massive fat-cat pay, tax dodging through havens, etc – the company has been accused of working hard to keep tea prices to a minimum, testing on animals, buying crops harvested by child labour, harming people and the environment at its thermometer factory in India, and actively lobbying for GM in Europe while claiming to be "listening to our customers".

Unilever brands

▷ Becel	▷ I Can't Believe it's	▷ Ragú,
▷ Ben & Jerry's	not Butter	▷ Red Label
▷ Bertolli	▷ Knorr	▷ Slim-Fast
▷ Birds Eye	▷ Lipton	▷ Solero
▷ Findus	▷ Magnum	▷ Walls
▷ Flora	▷ PG Tips	
▷ Hellmann's	▷ Pro-activ	

SUPERMARKETS & ALTERNATIVES
Where to shop?

The explosive growth of **supermarkets** in the last half century has completely revolutionized the food sector. If Britain ever was a nation of shopkeepers, it's certainly not any more. With the recent takeover of Safeway by Morisons, just four companies – **Tesco**, **Sainsbury's**, **Asda** and **Morisons** – sell more than three-quarters of our food. Along with a handful of smaller players, including Marks & Spencer, Waitrose, the Co-op, Iceland and Budgens, the supermarkets – or "multiples" as they're known in the trade – account for the overwhelming majority of grocery sales. And it's not just retailing they've taken over: they've also displaced a huge number of businesses in the import, distribution and wholesale sectors.

Despite the supermarket stranglehold, however, some markets and local shops survive. And a number of alternatives with a distinctly ethical slant – such as **farmers' markets**, **organic box schemes** and **specialists** in Fairtrade products, free-range meat and so on – are starting to gain popularity across the country. Following is a brief look at the morals of supermarket shopping, followed by small directory of these alternatives (from p.181).

SUPERMARKETS

Perhaps more than any country in the world, the UK is addicted to supermarkets. Maybe it's their special offers or their dazzling choice. Or perhaps it's their all-under-one-roof convenience. But, whatever the reasons, few Britons buy food anywhere else.

Compared with most giant companies, the big supermarkets have quite a lot on their ethical CVs. ASDA, Marks & Spencer, Safeway, Sainsbury's, Somerfield and Tesco have all signed up the **Ethical Trading Initiative**, which aims to improve labour standards among suppliers (see box on pp.68–89). They quickly responded to consumer fears about **GM foods** by removing them from their stores. And they've been central in bringing certain "ethical foods" – such as **organic** and **Fairtrade** products – into the mainstream. Arguably, the supermarkets also have a very worthwhile aim: making a wide selection of foods available to the public at prices that people can afford.

But despite all this the supermarket sector is the subject of more resentment than almost any other, with criticism coming from consumers, environmentalists and farmers alike. Some of the objections are standard complaints about big businesses – **political lobbying** (which the supermarkets are famously good at), executive pay, and so on. And some relate to **quality**: food writers and gourmands accuse the big retailers of replacing the UK's base of knowledgeable fishmongers, butchers and greengrocers, and countless vareties of local fruit and veg, with a food non-culture devoid of expertise and variety (see p.151). But there are also a number of more specific accusations, which fall into three categories…

#1 Damaging communities and small businesses

The era of the supermarket has been the era of the **decline of the local shop**. According to a study published by the New Economics Foundation (www.neweconomics.org), in the five years to 2002 alone, "50 specialised stores like butchers, bakers, fishmongers and newsagents closed every week". That's 13,000 in total, before you add in milkmen and other food service providers who have been forced out of business.

Apart from obvious negative effects on town centres – and on people who for whatever reason are unable to drive to the supermarket – this has also led to a loss of decent **jobs**. Even according to research funded by the supermarkets, each new out-of-town store causes a net loss of 276 jobs. And those jobs which do get created are usually pretty unsatisfying: working as a check-out assistant can't exactly compare with running a greengrocers'.

One way in which the supermarkets have undercut local bakers, milkmen and grocers is by treating basics like milk, bread and tinned tomatoes as "**loss leaders**", selling them at less than the wholesale cost and making up the profits from other products. On one level, this seems like good news, meaning that even people on very low incomes – if they can get to a supermarket – shouldn't struggle to afford the basics. However, since the supermarkets then overprice more healthy foods – and numerous reports have shown that they are around 30% more expensive than greengrocers for many fruit and vegetables – then the overall effect may be negative. Indeed, loss leaders are illegal in many countries and the recent publication by the UK's Competition Commission declared these tactics as working against the public interest, but failed to suggest any rules to stop it. Some have linked this to the industry's extraordinary connections in government.

Commentators who worry about the effect of supermarkets on local communities also point out that the money spent in, say, a Tesco or Sainsbury's, bypasses, rather than filters through, the **local economy**. The New Economics Foundation calculated that a pound spent on an organic box scheme generates nearly twice as much money for the local economy as a pound spent in the supermarket.

#2 Exploiting farmers

With just a few big players in the market, the supermarkets have extraordinary **power over their suppliers**. Indeed, as farmer's groups have said for years – and as food writer Joanna Blythman documented in her recent book, *Shopped: The Shocking Power of British Supermarkets* – the big chains are in a position to completely dictate farm-gate prices and terms of trade. One result of this is that prices have been driven so low that many small farmers have gone out of business, and bigger ones have been forced to cut corners on labour and environmental standards. According to NFU figures, from a food basket costing £37 in the supermarket, farmers today receive only £11, while campaign group Corporate Watch noted in 2003 that "Tesco's profits, at £1.4 billion, are more than half the entire UK income from farming, £2.36 billion."

But it's not just prices. Farmers claim that the supermakets' buying power has allowed them to get away with **avoiding long-term buying contracts** (hence shifting much of their business risk onto their suppliers), **delaying payments**, refusing perfectly good fruit and veg on minor cosmetic grounds, and even making farmers absorb the cost of **special offers** such as two-for-the-price-of-one promotions.

Despite all this, however, farmers find it very difficult to complain, for fear that the supermarket will simply refuse to continue stocking their products – something that, in many cases, would be enough to spell financial ruin. According to Joanna Blythman's investigations, many farmers "lay awake at night, dreading that phonecall from supermarket HQ saying 'Sorry, but we're going to de-list you'".

#3 Harming the environment

Though the supermarkets claim to be committed to the environment, there's no escaping the fact that they create a number of environmental burdens. They contribute to global warming, for example, by increasing the distance from "plough to plate" on three different levels: locally (by encouraging out-of-town-centre shopping), nationally (since product gets delivered to stores via few-and-far-between centralized distribution centres) and internationally (by sourcing goods from abroad when British produce is available).

The supermarkets are also notorious for refusing to accept fruit and veg on pernickety cosmetic grounds, something that leads to a great deal of waste, and also to farmers increasing their agrochemical inputs to ensure that their carrots, for example, have "crowns" with diameters of within the specificed range of millimetres. Joanna Blythman examined supermarket specifications and compiled a list of "faults" that would "almost certainly" cause a consignment of tomatoes to be rejected:

▷ More that five percent of the tomatoes not uniform in size (to within 5mm circumference)
▷ Light scarring or blemishes

▷ Ribbed, angular or misshapen tomatoes
▷ A colour of 0, 1, 2 or 7 on the supermarket's colour chart
▷ Slightly chewy skin
▷ Soft, tender tomatoes
▷ Tomatoes at different colour stages in the same box

Furthermore, organic exponents have accused the supermarkets of profiteering from their movement while flagrantly ignoring its eco principles, wrapping organic fruit and veg in unnecessary plastic packaging and failing to favour local growers.

Which supermarkets are the most responsible?

By now, it *ought* to be easier to compare the ethical performance of the supermarkets than those of businesses in other sectors, since 2000 saw the launch of "**Race to the Top**". Organized by the International Institute for Environment and Development, the scheme set out to work with the top ten supermarkets, measuring their ethical policies and practices and helping them to improve their standards in everything from labour and animal welfare, to their impacts on the environment and local economics. Three years later, however, the project was wound up, the closing press release headed: "How ethical are our supermarkets? We can't tell you." All the big players had jumped ship after Tesco and Asda refused to participate.

It's not too surprising that it was these two supermarkets who put a spanner in the works. **Asda**, after all, is owned by the world's biggest and arguably least popular company: Wal-Mart. If the whole concept of the modern supermarket is problematic, then Wal-Mart must be the best example, a famously anti-union, political-lobbying, sweat-shop-exploiting, gun-selling multinational whose predatory, expansionist policies are the stuff of corporate legend, and whose considerable donations to the Republican party helped lubricate George Bush's journey to the White House. China's *People Daily* once looked into why no unions were recognized among Wal-Mart's Chinese suppliers, but the company soon cleared up the confusion:

SUPERMARKETS AND ANIMAL WELFARE

When it comes to animal welfare, the rule seems to be pretty simple: the posher the supermarket, the better the policies. Hence in one recent survey the RSPCA congratulated "Marks & Spencer, Selfridges and Harvey Nichols" as the only supermarkets to ban battery eggs completely. However, it's not quite that straightforward. The best research into supermarkets and animal welfare is done by Compassion in World Farming (www.ciwf.org.uk), which compares the big retailers on the full range of relevant issues each year. The 2003 report ranked the main supermarkets as follows, out of a possible 63 points:

▷ Waitrose 53.5　　　　　　▷ Safeway 31.7
▷ Marks & Spencer 47.6　　　▷ Morrisons 29.6
▷ The Co-op 41.6　　　　　　▷ Somerfield 27.3
▷ Tesco 33.5　　　　　　　　▷ Asda 22.7

Sainsbury's and Iceland "declined to participate". For more information, download the full report from:
www.ciwf.org.uk/publications/reports/Supmart2003.pdf

"A Wal-Mart spokesman explained that there are no trade unions in its branches in other parts of the world either."

Tesco, the UK market leader, is not in the same league as Wal-Mart. It doesn't suppress unions, and it recently even launched an extensive Fairtrade range – including the UK's first Fairtrade flowers. But with its aggressive, global-expansion business model, it's come in for more criticism than the rest of Britain's supermarkets. Even as this chapter is being written, Tesco's green claims have been marred twice: the company was named as a "significant repeat offender" by the Environmental Agency and was kicked out of a WWF initiative to stop sourcing endangered hardwood (used for the supermarket's garden furniture).

Sainsbury's fares slightly better – and has been praised for its extensive environmental reporting by Innovest and others in the corporate social responsibility circles – while **Somerfield** and **Safeway** at least demonstrated transparency by staying involved in the Race to the Top scheme when others had dropped out. But, in most respects, all three trail behind the more up-market players such as **Waitrose** and **Marks & Spencer** – both of which have progressive policies on animal welfare, chemicals and more. These are far from beyond criticism, however. M&S was branded "irresponsible" by Greenpeace for selling garden furniture made from "trashed rainforest timber" in June 2004 – the same month that animal-rights group Viva! exposed terrible factory-farm conditions at the supermarket's duck supplier (see www.viva.org.uk).

Overall, probably the most ethical supermarket (unsurprisingly enough) is the democratically run **Co-op**. Also the UK's biggest farmer, the Co-op shows how much room for improvement there is among its competitors. It's open about who manufactures each of its own-brand products (most of the rest won't reveal such facts). It has thrown an incomparable weight behind Fairtrade – all its own-brand coffee and chocolate, for example, now bears the Mark. Its labour-rights audits are verified by an external company. It's started voluntarily phasing out certain pesticides. It's cleaning products are certified as animal-testing free. The list goes on.

FARMERS' MARKETS

Though they still only account for a fraction of a percent of UK food sales, farmers' markets are on the up. The concept is simple: buy produce straight from the growers or producers, giving them a better deal than they would get via a retailer, cutting down on environmentally harmful food transport, getting fresher and better quality food, cutting the big-business machine out of the equation and getting the chance to ask questions directly to the producers.

According to the National Association of Farmers' Markets, "it is generally accepted ... that stall holders must have grown, bred, caught, pickled, brewed or baked the goods themselves" and that the main emphasis of the markets is "to help local producers and processors to sell their goods direct to the public, near their source of origin, creating benefits to them, the environment and the local community". To ensure these aims are kept pure, the Association has developed a set of standards which "genuine" certified farmers' markets must adhere to:

▷ **Local produce** "Primary produce" sold must be grown, reared or caught by the stall holder within the defined local area: usually a 30 mile radius around the market, though up to 50 miles is acceptable

Reconnecting field and city: a farmers' market in central London

for larger cities and coastal or remote towns and villages. "Secondary" (prepared) produce must be brewed, pickled, baked, smoked or processed by the stall holder using at least one ingredient of origin from within the defined local area.

▷ **The principal producer** or a representative directly involved in the production process must attend the stall.

▷ **Information** should be available to customers at each market about farmers' markets standards and the production methods of the producers.

Farmers' markets are increasingly springing up all over the country: to find out more, or locate your nearest one, visit:

Farmers' Markets www.farmersmarkets.net ▷ 01225 787914
London Farmers' Markets www.lfm.org.uk

ORGANIC DELIVERY & FARM SHOPS

Even if there weren't other arguments against the supermarkets, they're not an ideal place to buy organic food. In most supermarkets, organic produce is overpriced, over-packaged in plastic, often poor quality and – in some cases – imported by environmentally burdensome air freight. Because of this, many people prefer to get their weekly shop from a **box scheme**.

For a weekly fee, you'll get a mixed box or bag of local and seasonal fruit and veg – perhaps bolstered by foreign goods imported by ship – either delivered to your door or left somewhere ready for you to pick up. Most box-scheme companies also offer all sorts of other foods and goods, from bread to washing up liquid, so it's perfectly possible to save yourself ever going to the supermarket. Even when you factor in the delivery van, the overall pollution and energy use will in most cases be much smaller than driving to the supermarket.

Farm shops can also be good and fairer sources of organic veg, and even where there is no actual shop, many organic (and other) growers offer "farm-gate sales".

The Soil Association is the best source of information about all these organic retailers. Their annual *Organic Directory* lists thousands, as well as everything from restaurants to organic textile suppliers to fish delivery. The guide is available both in paper form (order by phone) and on their website (you have to register before accessing it, but it's free, quick and easy):

Soil Association www.soilassociation.org ▷ 0117 914 2446

You could also try the smaller but more user-friendly lists at:

A Lot of Organics www.alotoforganics.co.uk
About Organics www.aboutorganics.co.uk
Links Organic www.linksorganic.com

If you can't find any local schemes, or if those you've tried aren't very good, you could try one of the bigger box scheme companies, some of which will deliver to nearly anywhere in the UK. For example:

Fresh Food www.freshfood.co.uk ▷ 020 8749 8778
Simply Organics www.simplyorganic.net ▷ 0870 760 6001

The South East is also well served by Organic Delivery (London only) and Abel & Cole, who won the Organic Retailer of the Year prize in 2004.

Organic Delivery www.organicdelivery.co.uk ▷ 020 7739 8181
Abel & Cole www.abel-cole.co.uk ▷ 020 7737 3648

Or, for fresh **organic meats**, including beef, pork, chicken and lamb, try Graig Farm Organics. And for fish, probably the best option is Hawkshead, which sells salmon, trout, sea bass, prawns and mixed cases. Order in bulk and it doesn't work out as too expensive.

Graig Farm Organics www.graigfarm.co.uk ▷ 01597 851 655
Hawkshead Organic Fish www.organicfish.com ▷ 01539 436 541

A typical mixed box from Abel & Cole. Like most organic delivery services, they offer a wide range of fruit and veg options – from the Farmer's Choice Combi Bag (£7.50) to the Large Mixed Organic Box (£22) – as well as bread, fish, meat and store-cupboard goods.

Finally, a number of suppliers offer **organic booze**, including a huge range of wines – some produced in the UK – and scores of traditional ales. Organic booze is usually also vegetarian friendly (hardline veggies avoid many beers and most wines since fish derivatives are often used in their preparation). Three of the best suppliers are:

Organic Wine Company www.ecowine.com
Vinceremos www.vinceremos.co.uk
Vintage Roots www.vintageroots.co.uk

FAIRTRADE SPECIALISTS

The Fairtrade Foundation's website – www.fairtrade.org.uk – lists all the certified Fairtrade products available in the UK, along with contact details for each of the suppliers. Some of these sell directly and others can tell you where to find their products.

You'll often find the best range in a specialist fair-trade shop – such as those listed in chapter nine (see p.349). Many organic or health food shops also have a decent selection, but in terms of price you might be best buying online (or by phone). Among the best sites are:

Fairtrade Online

www.fairtradeonline.com ▷ 0191 491 0591

This joint Oxfam–Traidcraft project sells a good range of food at reasonable prices. On offer are basics such as sugar, rice, pasta, nuts, jam and honey; a wide selection of teas and coffees; and a mouthwateringly rich list of sweets that deliciously exploits every combination of the words praline, chocolate, almond, ginger and cappuccino. Things tend to come in bulk packs of six or ten (some things initially look a bit pricey until you notice this).

Goodness Direct

www.goodnessdirect.co.uk ▷ 0871 871 6611

Offers a large range including more than fifty fairly traded products, though it caters mainly to veggie, vegan and specialist concerns. As well as the usual biscuits, sweets, grains, cereals, pasta and coffee there's also chilled food and drink, a "Deli Counter" and pet food on offer. They even have a convenience food section, so the time-strapped can eat on the go with Organic Tofu Smoked Almond & Sesame Slices or No Chicken Nuggets.

Ethical Shopper

www.ethicalshopper.co.uk ▷ 0845 456 2429

A wide selection of organic and Fairtrade foods, as well as other ethically traded odds and sods such as cards, bags and shirts. Their "Pantry" section stocks cooking spices, chillis and peppercorns, and we impatiently await their "Not Yet Available" Organic Chanterelle Mushrooms, "fairly traded from Zambia".

Clipper Store

www.clipperteasshop.com ▷ 01308 863344

Choose from Clipper's excellent range of Fairtrade and organic coffee, tea and chocolate, that stretches to "White Tea" and "Ayurvedic Teas". Or join their "Tea Club" online – free membership includes their magazine *Teapot Times* four times a year, which is apparently "packed full of information about teas from around the world, up to date news on Fairtrade developments, as well as exclusive offers, including tea samples, recipes ... plus rare varieties of tea you won't find elsewhere".

OTHER LOCAL, SPECIALIST FOODS AND WHOLEFOODS

Following are a few other sites and organizations that sell food relevant to the issues discussed in this chapter.

Big Barn

www.bigbarn.co.uk

A portal allowing you to search for your nearest local-food suppliers, find deliverers and order online. As they put it, it's a website that "gives consumers the opportunity to buy meat, game, fish, fruit and vegetables, cheese and dairy products, drink, bakers' products and even nursery plants direct from the people who produce them". The site has recipes which use seasonal ingredients, and has an interactive "Recipe Search" box – enter an ingredient and it'll try to come up with a suggestion or two for lunch.

Food UK and UK Food Online

www.fooduk.com
www.ukfoodonline.co.uk

Though geared towards high-quality food, rather than ethical issues, both those sites include large lists of relevant suppliers, for example for free-range veal and the like. Also, since they don't limit themselves to organic producers, they include many suppliers not found in the Soil Association list.

Farmgate Direct

www.farmgatedirect.com ▷ 0870 754 0014

Owned by the RSPCA, Farmgate Direct supply fresh chicken, beef, lamb, veal and salmon accredited under the Freedom Food scheme (see p.124). They aim to deliver "within 72 hours of confirming receipt of your order".

Suma Wholefoods

www.suma.co.uk ▷ 0845 458 2295

Though they primarily supply to shops, this large wholesaler of green, organic and fairly traded foods (as well as other products) will deliver directly to customers who don't have access to a local retailer, subject to minimum orders. Suma is a workers' co-operative with an equal-pay-for-all policy and it describes its ethos as "a political statement that workers can successfully manage their own businesses without an owner/manager elite". One of its initiatives is RSPB rice: an organic, "bird friendly" rice, for which the RSPB (Royal Society for the Protection of Birds) receive 10p per pack of rice sold.

HDRA Grow Your Own Organics

www.hdra.org.uk/gyo.htm

A superb resource for anyone wanting to go organic in their own back yard. It's regularly updated, so it can give gardening and growing advice specific to whichever month it is. The site assures you that you don't need to have a huge garden to grow organic herbs, fruit or vegetables (athough if there was advice on things to do with a windowbox there, as one of the pages implies, it was impossible to find). Mushroom-heads should also see: www.fungi.com

05

CLOTHES, COSMETICS & JEWELLERY

Beauty may be only skin deep, but our clothes, make-up and jewellery raise issues that are less superficial. Besides garment sweatshops, the clothes and shoes industries are associated with certain environmental and (in the case of leather and fur) animal rights issues. Cosmetics, meanwhile, are all too often also the result of animal experiments, and the jewellery trade is only just starting to come to terms with the moral problems that accompany it such as child labour and conflicts funded by the illicit sales of diamonds. This chapter takes a quick look at these three industries, and lists the most ethical – and, in some cases, the not so ethical – companies in each.

CLOTHES & SHOES
Fashion victims

Mention "ethical shopping" and the first thing many people think of is the boycotting of exploitative Asian sweatshops producing branded clothes for the West. It's certainly true that labour standards in the apparel sector are bad. But the factory isn't the first step in the making of clothes – and it's not the only one associated with social and environmental problems. First of all, the raw material needs to be grown, killed or manufactured, and dyed the right colour.

Cotton

Cultivated by humans for more than 5000 years, and the basis of products ranging from T-shirts to US dollar bills, **cotton** is something of a natural wonder. But much has changed since the ancient Greek historian Herodotus first documented the existence of Indian "tree wool … exceeding in beauty and goodness". Today, cotton lies at the heart of global debates on **agrochemicals**, **GM** and **organic production**, as well as unfair **international trade rules** and **child labour** (see box).

The first three of these issues relate to the fact that "conventional" modern cotton growing relies on a huge quantity of chemical inputs. More **pesticides** are used on cotton than on any other crop: despite covering only a few percent of the world's cultivable soils, cotton farms account for roughly 10% of all herbicide use and an astonishing 20–25% of insecticide use.

People can and do argue about whether or not these chemicals – which include strongly carcinogenic and otherwise nasty substances such as carbamates and organochlorines – harm the eventual wearer of the cotton. But the effect on farmers and the environment is much more pressing. There are no accurate global measures but, according to pesticide campaigners, thousands of cotton-farm workers are killed by agrochemicals each year. Research by Pesticide Action Network, for example, showed that one region of the small West

US COTTON SUBSIDIES

Though it's not exactly a "consumer issue", any discussion of the ethics of the cotton trade should mention the single biggest problem faced by farmers in the developing world: the massive subsidies given to giant cotton farms in wealthy countries. In the US, partly for historical reasons, and partly due to effective political lobbying from farm groups, around 25,000 cotton farmers receive around $4 billion support from the government – an average of £160,000 each. This allows them to sell below the cost of production, driving down international prices and making it extremely difficult for growers in poor countries to compete. In the words of Oxfam's Celine Charvariat, "American and European taxpayers are financing the destruction of the livelihoods of millions of cotton farmers in Africa … the cotton barons of Texas and Alabama are getting huge subsidies … and driving more efficient African farmers out of business."

Though they certainly haven't caused the problem, these subsidies have also been linked to child labour, as they hinder the economic growth of poor cotton-growing countries. According to a study by the India Committee of the Netherlands (www.indianet.nl) 90% of all labour in the Indian cottonseed market is carried out by nearly half a million children, mostly girls aged between six and fourteen.

At the time of going to press, the World Trade Organization had just ruled in favour of a complaint by Brazil, who complained that US cotton subsidies are illegal. But the US government has promised to appeal, and "defend US agriculture in every forum we need to". To email them in protest, and for more information, see:

Oxfam www.maketradefair.com

African state of Benin alone saw "at least 61 men, women and children" killed by cotton pesticides between 1999 and 2001. And, of course, for every one person who dies, hundreds of others have to put up with the effects of polluted air and water on their health.

Some commentators also worry that the chemicals are entering the food chain, as the vast quantities of cottonseed harvested are fed to animals and made into cottonseed oil for human consumption.

So what's the solution to this chemical overload? According to biotechnologists, it's GM, which is already widely used among cotton growers (see box below). According to greens, on the other hand, consumers should opt out both of the pesticides and biotechnology by choosing **organic cotton** and favouring alternatives such as **hemp** (see p.194). Just as with food, organic fibres can be grown using chemical-free alternatives to pesticides. In Uganda, for example, black ants are collected and set on the cotton fields to eat the pests.

Organic fabrics are also more eco-friendly in terms of processing. In the manufacture of conventional cotton cloth thousands of synthetic substances are used: chlorine **bleaches**, heavy-metal **dyes**, formaldehyde to lessen creaseability and anti-shrinking treatments. Many of these are highly toxic, and can cause environmental and health problems if not handled and disposed of correctly.

The market for organic cotton is rocketing, thanks to orders from

GM COTTON: IMMORAL FIBRE?

As with other areas of agriculture, the organic brigade are not alone in claiming they have the solution to the pesticide problem. The biotech companies – mainly Monsanto – have produced GM cotton engineered to be resistant to insects (with Bt toxin built into their leaves) and/or resistant to a powerful herbicide (which in theory allows less of other herbicides to be used). The technology is probably the most successful application of a GM crop, and has, according to the UN, allowed farmers in China, India and elsewhere to reduce their pesticide use substantially and increase yields. Critics aren't convinced, however, claiming that Bt-resistant insects will inevitably appear (though this has yet to happen) and that GM crops may prove damaging to biodiversity by killing non-target insects. They also point out that, as with any GM crop, releasing it into the environment could have any number of unforeseeable implications.

More than half of the cotton on sale is now estimated to be GM; anyone with an ideological problem with the technology – or, indeed, with the biotech companies – should buy organic.

specialists and from a few big companies – including Nike and Levi – who have started buying a small proportion of their cotton from organic sources. The US used to be the biggest producer, but increasingly organic production is spreading to developing countries, which can undercut the West when it comes to low-chemical, labour-intensive production methods. Organic products aren't necessarily fair-trade, of course, but there are now a number of manufacturers and suppliers selling clothes that are both.

For a list of organic clothes sellers, see p.213.

Silk: sericulture slavery

Silk thread is made by unravelling the cocoon of silk worms, each of which wraps itself up in a single continuous strand of up to a kilometre in length. Known as **sericulture**, the process of harvesting silk – cultivating the worms, harvesting the threads and winding them into thicker strands for making material – is a big industry in Asia, with China and India by far the biggest suppliers.

Millions of economically marginalized people make a living out of the silk trade but, in some regions including parts of India, the industry is rife with **child workers**, many as young as five and in "bonded" positions: essentially slaves paying off a family debt. A report from 2000 available from the Indian wing of UNDP, the UN's global development network (hdrc.undp.org.in), makes for grim reading:

> Children are employed in almost all processes of the sericulture industry making it almost a child-based economy … They are required to work in filature units that are cramped, damp, dark, poorly ventilated … the handling of dead worms with bare hands, and the unbearable stench is also a cause for spreading infection and illness. Standing for 12–16 hours a day with hardly any break, concentrating on reeling the fine threads, leads to other health disorders. Vapours from the boiling cocoons and the diesel fumes from the machines also contribute to the poor conditions in the units … found responsible for retardation of the child's normal growth and development.

TIME FOR A HEMP REVIVAL?

While some people advocate organic or GM cotton as the best fabric for the environment and the health of farmers, others are singing the praises of hemp – not the King Size Rizla variety, but its non-psychoactive industrial counterpart. The fact that most of hemp's rather evangelical advocates also seem to be keen smokers of their favourite plant doesn't do the campaign many favours. But with increasing numbers of governments and farmers examining its benefits, it seems they may have a point.

Cannabis sativa has a long and distinguished history, taking in at least 5000 years of use as a source of food, cloth, nets and countless other items. Many products have started out life as hemp, from proper paper – first created in Tibet at roughly the time of Christ – to Levis jeans. Until the twentieth century, the plant was also the main source for ropes and sails (the word canvas is derived from the Latin *cannabis*), which made it so central to naval success that both Britain and the US once had laws requiring all farmers to dedicate a proportion of their land to it.

Yet a couple of centuries after George Washington advised Americans to "make the most of hempseed and sow it everywhere", the wonderplant was on the decline, gradually being replaced by cotton for clothes, wood for paper and nylon for rope. Once the first round of the war on drugs got under way, things got even worse, with hemp officially or effectively banned in many countries.

Hemp fans claim that now is the time for a revival. Farmers would gain because the plant is unusually easy, quick, inexpensive and safe to grow, requiring very few agrochemicals (compare that with cotton, see p.190). Consumers would benefit because hemp products, once produced in large quantities, would be cheaper than current materials, and because hemp cloth is many times stronger and more durable than cotton. The environment would benefit through reduced use of chemicals, improved soil structures due to the plant's deep roots, and reduced felling of trees for paper and board, since hemp fibre is far quicker to produce at a sustainable rate than wood fibre and requires less energy input and chemical treatment. The plant could also potentially contribute to reduced fossil fuel use, as it's an ideal bio-fuel and can be used to make biodegradable alternatives to plastics and metals (in the 1940s Henry Ford famously produced a partly hemp-resin car powered by hemp fuel). To cap all this off, the plant's seeds are unusually nutritious, with a blend of amino acids close to perfect for humans.

Not everyone is entirely convinced of all hemp's supposed advantages, and fibre-processing technology will need to be developed before it becomes commercially advantageous. Still, few deny that the plant could offer some real long-term ecological benefits. So it's no wonder that "ethical clothes" suppliers often sell hemp clothes, sometimes sourced and produced according to some fair-trade principles (though, it's worth pointing out that the world's biggest hemp producer is China, a "category A" oppressive regime).

If you fancy supporting the hemp movement and clothing yourself in cannabis, check out the selection at the following stores. If you really catch

Harvesting the hemp in Russia, 1956

the hemp bug, a Google search will also reveal everything from ropes to varnishes and paints produced from the the very same plant.

Hemp Store www.thehempstore.co.uk ▷ 01223 309993 ▷ 90 Windsor Rd, Cambridge
Stocks a wide range of hemp clothes, plus bags and wallets – the owners also claim to be committed to fair-trade, sourcing most of their own-brand goods from a trusted Nepalese importer.

INBI Hemp www.inbi-hemp.co.uk ▷ 0870 333 1858
Though the strapline "clothing for the inner you" suggests relaxation tapes and didgeridoos, the hemp range at this Brighton-based supplier is actually rather sharp.

Other reports describe endemic bronchial ailments, coughs, back pains, asthma and TB among the child silk workers, as well as seriously damaged hands from checking the boiling cocoons.

This isn't true of all countries – nor the whole of India – and a blanket boycott of the sector would hurt millions of impoverished silk producers who don't exploit bonded child labour. Also, a real solution can probably only come from the relevant governments: "the problem", according to a 2003 Human Rights Watch study on bonded labour in the Indian silk industry, "is political will".

Still, consumers can opt for **fairly traded** silk products, which are available from companies such as Silken Dalliance and Traidcraft (see pp.219 and 220). These not only have policies governing silk thread manufacture, but they also aim to ensure that more of the profits head back to the people weaving the cloth and sewing the garments.

The West, curiously, pays much less attention to the children and adults working in the silk industry than to the **silk worms** themselves, though admittedly they do get a rather rough deal. If a worm eats its way out of its cocoon, the thread is broken, so the cocoons are boiled or baked while the worms are still inside (in some countries the worms are eaten afterwards). It is possible to make 'raw'-style silk without killing the worm, and you may occasionally see this sold, usually labelled as vegetarian or vegan friendly.

Leather vs veggie alternatives

Vegetarians object to leather for obvious reasons: though it might be only a *by-product* of the meat industry, the hide of an animal adds substantially to its slaughterhouse value, and so subsidizes the **meat industry**, including intensive farms.

But leather – whether it be from cow, pig, sheep or goat – also raises another question: its **environmental impact**. Indeed, though animal skin may be a "natural" material, modern leather is the result of intensive chemical processing, including toxic carcinogenic substances such as salts of **chromium**. This not only makes it surprisingly energy-inefficient to produce but means that it generates massive quantities of waste: treating a ton of raw hide can result in 75,000 litres of waste water and 100 kg of dried sludge. And anyone who has been within smelling range of a tannery will be unsurprised to learn that this waste, when not treated properly, can be extremely dangerous.

As environmental regulation has tightened up in the West, developing-world tanneries have seen their businesses expanding. This provides much-needed jobs and income, but the human and environmental costs can be high. A study by the Tokyo Institute of Technology found that 62% of the 2.4 million people in Kasur, Pakistan, are suffering from serious ailments – including cancer, tuberculosis and blindness – caused by industrial waste, with tanneries the major contributor. Similarly, in the Bangladeshi capital Dhaka, according to a report cited in the World Health Organization Bulletin, half a million residents are at risk of serious illness due to tannery pollution, with tannery workers there 50% more likely than their peers to die before the age of fifty. In other areas, large areas of agricultural land have been rendered unusable by tannery pollution. Farmers in Tamil Nadu in southern India have recently been compensated for the ruin of their land, but not everyone has been so lucky.

Besides all the chemicals, leather is also very often treated with palm oil, a product linked to widespread destruction of rainforests in Indonesia (see p.224).

You may occasionally come across leathers tanned and dyed with natural substances, but this has yet to catch on. Instead, some people advocate "vegetarian" **leather substitutes**. Being made of polyurethane and other plastics, these aren't exactly the most green products in the world, but they're arguably a more ethical choice – especially if you don't want to support the meat industry. The best-known suppliers include the following, all of which sell online or via phone/mail order:

Ethical Wares

www.ethicalwares.com ▷ 01570 471 155
Leather-substitute footwear – from Black Cat stilettos to steel-toe-cap boots – as well as some fair-trade clothes, bags and jewellery (in a rather hippyish style).

Freerangers

www.freerangers.co.uk ▷ 01207 565 957
English-made non-animal Birkenstock-esque shoes, plus bags, briefcases, belts, wallets and even cases for your palm pilot.

Vegan Store

www.veganstore.co.uk ▷ 01273 302 979
Sells a range of "fabulously fake jackets" (very realistic and good value, too) as well as shoes, belts and other vegan essentials (such as non-animal-derived marshmallows).

Vegetarian Shoes

www.vegetarian-shoes.co.uk ▷ 01273 691 913 ▷ 12 Gardner Street, Brighton
A wide range of stylish non-animal footwear including boots, smart shoes, trainers and Camper-style day-to-day wear – some of them produced in Britain's oldest co-operative (established 1881).

FUR

Compared with most ethical shopping campaigns, the anti-fur movement of the 1980s and 1990s was hugely successful. The majority of fur specialists shut down, and high-street shops phased out fur trims. But recently fur has bounced back, with sales rising as much as 35% per year in the UK, and claims from the industry that fur isn't as cruel as people think. The International Fur Trade Federation, for example, suggests that the farmed foxes and mink that supply around 85% of the world's pelts are "among the world's best cared for farm animals".

Animal rights campaigners aren't convinced, claiming that the fur farms (which are now banned in the UK) keep their minks and foxes in small cages equivalent to those used for battery chickens. And, for all the claims of respect for animal welfare, there is plenty of very disturbing footage – such as that filmed by PETA (People for the Ethical Treatment of Animals; www.petatv.com) – showing caged fur animals apparently driven mad by their captivity, knawing their own legs and running insanely round and round. Slaughtering methods – designed to protect the fur – are also contentious, in some cases allegedly including genital electrocution.

Trapping still provides some furs, and is often described as less cruel since animals get to live natural lives until capture. But most traps – such as the leghold models described as "inhumane" by the American Veterinary Medical Association – cause enormous suffering, with animals desperately trying to escape at first and being left exposed and in pain for anything from hours to days. Inevitably, non-target animals are also caught in the traps, which add to the death count for each coat – which even in the case of bigger farmed animals is around 30–40 minks or foxes.

PETA
www.furisdead.com

International Fur Trade Federation
www.iftf.com

Garment factories

The garment trade has long been associated with sweatshops. Way back in 1895, the *Standard Dictionary of the English Language* defined a "sweater" as an exploitative employer, "especially a contractor for piecework in the tailoring trade". There are various reasons for the link between clothes manufacture and labour abuse. One is the fact that the infrastructure costs of setting up a garment factory, or "shop", are relatively low, and the training needed to work there is minimal. So middlemen can afford to set up factories and compete for the business of clothes designers and retailers. Unlike the car sector, say, in which the big companies tend to own their factories, and are therefore accountable to their own workers, the various layers of sub-contracting in the garment trade tends to diffuse and dissolve responsibility for workers' rights.

The subcontracted garment sweatshop was invented and first flourished in nineteenth-century Europe and America, but in the era of **globalization** the garment sector was one of the first to relocate to the developing world. It's not difficult to understand why. Clothes are big business, with British consumers spending on average around £400 per year on them – that's more than £23 billion in total. Yet, aside from materials, the only major production cost is **labour**, which is required in large quantities: taken together, the apparel and textile industries are the biggest industrial employers in the world, with a workforce of around 25 million.

For a UK firm, sourcing from a factory in Asia, Africa or Latin America doesn't just reduce this labour cost – it decimates it. For example, as Seumas Milne wrote in *The Guardian*, the women who make Littlewoods clothes at the Dressmen factory in Bangladesh get "less than a fiftieth of the hourly rate earned by their relatively low-paid British counterparts". Some of the savings the firms make on labour costs are offset by the fact that the UK imposes high tariffs on clothes imports, but these are due to be dropped at the beginning of 2005, paving the way for more of our garments to be produced in developing countries.

The collapse of the garment trade in the UK – where, according to some estimates, more than three-quarters of sewing jobs have disappeared in the last 25 years – has undoubtedly caused pain for many individuals who have found themselves out of work. But there's also no doubt that these kinds of jobs are desperately needed in poor countries, where millions have been created. The developing world now accounts for close to three-quarters of the world's clothing exports, with some economies relying almost entirely on the sector. In 2000, for example, textiles and clothing accounted for 84% of exports from Bangladesh (where around two million workers produce more than a billion garments for export each year) and 72% of Pakistan's.

This is all good news, many people argue. And, indeed, you might even see the transfer of European garment jobs to Asia just deserts for Britain's having systematically destroyed India's textile trade back in the Colonial days (which it did with the aim of creating a bigger

HOME-GROWN SWEAT

While the majority of the garment factories that deserve the "sweatshop" label are in the developing world, they certainly haven't vanished in the West. According to the Smithsonian Institute, conditions for garment workers in rich countries improved during the mid-twentieth century, but almost universally fell in the 1980s. By 1996, the US government estimated that at least half of the country's 22,000 garment factories were in "serious violation of wage and safety laws". The UK is not quite as bad, though serious violations – especially in London's East End – are not uncommon.

While the term sweatshop usually refers to factories, exploitative subcontracting is just as big an issue in the homeworking sector, which is also important to the rag trade. The National Group on Homeworking (www.homeworking.gn.apc.org) estimates that there are around one million homeworkers sewing, packing, assembling and manufacturing in the UK. Many of them earn significantly less than the minimum wage, and some – usually those from ethnic minorities – receive less than 50p per hour.

market for British textiles). However, as Western clothing companies shop around for the best deal from suppliers (just as we do on the high street), countries and factories end up competing to offer the cheapest, most "flexible" workforce. Combine this with individual factory owners hell-bent on extracting every last drop of profit at the expense of their workers, and the result in all too many cases, is abysmal working conditions.

Regardless of whether you see these conditions as a never ending race to the bottom, or the first mile of a poor country's road to greater prosperity (for more on this debate, see p.51), there's little doubt that conditions are often extreme. True, some campaigners simplify or exaggerate the situation: jobs in export garment factories are clearly in demand and, with the exception of some cases where workers are locked into their positions through debt to their employer, they're clearly seen as a better option than the alternatives. Yet a range of sources – from workers' accounts to audits commissioned by the clothes companies themselves – have shown that, in return for the privilege of having a position, the mostly female workforce has to put up with inhumanely long hours, widespread suppression of unions, abusive managers and demeaning treatment.

Perhaps the biggest issue in most people's eyes is **child labour** – many Western shoppers have an image in their heads of rooms full of eight-year-olds sewing our branded clothes and trainers. The problem does exist, often with young teenagers being considered to be "apprentices" or "helpers" and earning even less than the adults, but arguably this problem is slightly exaggerated. In countries associated with bad sweatshops, such as China, there is little documented child labour in export manufacturing. Child workers are much more common in less-discussed areas, such as silk production (see p.193) than in clothes factories.

A more obvious problem is **health and safety**, both in terms of workers getting injured by machines (due to lack of training or unsafe equipment) and the risk of **fires**. Despite minimal coverage in the mainstream media, hundreds of garment workers have been killed by fires in factories producing for export to the UK. In late 2000, for example, around fifty died in a garment factory near Dhaka, Bangladesh, where most clothes factories are rented properties not designed for the purpose. Most were killed by fumes and flames, but some were impaled on a fence when they tried to jump from fourth-floor windows: it was reported by local journalists that the exits were locked. Two years later, in an almost identical incident, forty died in a fire at the Shree Jee footwear plant in Agra, India, allegedly contracted via an agent to make shoes for British firms such as Stylo (Barratts), Peacocks, Stead & Simpson and Jacobson. Again, doors and windows were said to be locked. These are many such examples.

Fumes and dust are another serious health and safety issue. Many workers have been made seriously ill in clothes and shoe factories through exposure to **toxic glues** (for shoe soles), while **air-borne fibres** can lead to lung damage when proper masks and ventilation aren't used. In a report on Gap factories produced by the UNITE union, for example, one African worker is quoted complaining that "we can't escape breathing in the fibres and particles from the air. When we cough, if the T-shirt we were working on was made of blue fabric, then our mucous would be full of blue fibres." But the fact that it was Gap was immaterial: according to a "provincial task force" report quoted in the *Washington Post*, 96% of businesses in China's Guangdong province – a centre of clothes manufacturing – were in violation of health standards. The number of workers getting sick is rising 70% per year, with more than 2500 deaths from people having died of occupational illnesses since 1989.

But perhaps the most pressing issue of all is the **suppression of unions**. A report on Asian garment industry by CAFOD (the Catholic Agency for Overseas Development) pointed out that efforts by local workers, NGOs and trade unions, "are the most important factor in trying to improve wages and working conditions in Asia". The report noted that "In some countries, such as the Philippines and Sri Lanka, a history of active trade unionism, and state support for some degree of labour rights, have established expectations about acceptable

NIKE AND GAP: DEMONS OR DEMONIZED?

In the UK, the sweatshop issue is associated almost exclusively with trainers by **Nike** and clothes by **Gap**. Both companies have been linked to some extremely exploitative factories and bad practice, from Nike allegedly petitioning the Indonesian government for exemption from the minimum wage and lying about labour conditions at its contractor factories (see box on p.207) to Gap's exploits at Saipan (see box on p.209). And the comparison between what Nike spends on advertising and what it spends on workers is a frightening and depressing indictment both of world inequality and the power of advertising in modern Western society. According to Sweatshop Watch, an average Nike worker would need to put in no fewer than 72,000 years of work to receive what Tiger Woods got for one five-year sponsorship contract (if he or she had worked a seven day week since homo sapiens first arrived in East Asia, they might be nearly finished today).

But are these companies qualitatively different from the industry as a whole in terms of labour and environmental standards? According to most people working to improve garment sweatshops, the answer is no. In fact, due to the threat of campaigns and boycotts, these two major brands have probably done more to improve things than many of the less-high-profile retailers. They still won't reveal the names and addresses of the factories where most of their good are made, but at least Gap has started to be honest about the fact that problems are rife in many of its supplier factories, and Nike has at least signed up to the FLA (see p.208) and improved health and safety by phasing out dangerous solvent-based glue (as well as environmentally problematic PVC).

So why the focus on Nike and Gap? Part of the reason is that they're both huge companies which were early adopters of the outsourcing model. And part of the reason is that they're very much marketing-led firms, whose lifestyle advertising clashes sharply with the daily life of the people who actually cut, stitch and glue their products. But part of the reason is simply that, as major US firms, they've been subjected to the scrutiny of that country's unusually big and tireless anti-sweatshop movement. Many other American clothes manufacturers, from Wal-Mart to Liz Claiborne, have also felt the pressure, but they don't make the headlines in the UK, since they're not familiar high-street names.

labour standards. In others, such as China, Vietnam, and Bangladesh, the floor is often set by physical endurance; how many hours a day, over how many years, can one ill-nourished human body continue to function." And yet many Western clothes and shoes firms have been slow to demand union recognition in the factories they source from, and organizers continue to be harassed or assaulted. One Bangladeshi women interviewed by CAFOD, for example, had been attacked and slashed with razor blades for being a union activist at a clothes factory. Sadly, this kind of assault and intimidation seems to be relatively common.

CLOTHES & SHOES: THE BIG-NAME SHOPS & BRANDS

With such poor conditions in developing-world garment factories, the most pressing issue for ethical shoppers is what efforts each company has made to ensure their suppliers are sticking to decent minimum standards. Despite the focus on Gap and Nike (see box opposite), this is a question that applies to all clothes and shoe companies.

Due to increasing pressure from consumers, most of the big brands have at least considered this matter – and certain environmental issues, too. Usually this has meant drawing up a **code of conduct**, which the clothes companies request their suppliers adhere to. They've been a long time coming, but today most high-street names have a code based on key labour standards, including the **right to organize** (join a union).

Worker groups and sweatshop campaigners agree that these codes are very useful: they can help inform workers of their rights, make it more difficult for factory owners to claim they didn't know the rules and provide a yardstick by which to measure a company's progress and failings. But they also shouldn't be taken at face value: as discussed in chapter three, voluntary codes of conduct are not necessarily enforced. And it's often very difficult to tell, because the mainstream companies treat the names and addresses of their supplier factories as a closely guarded corporate secret. If the case of Nike vs Kasky (see box opposite) is anything to go by, the big companies also simply lie about their commitment to ethical standards.

The gap between professed policy and enforced action leads many commentators to conclude that the big firms are still all basically the same. **War on Want**, for example, interviewed Bangladeshi garment workers and concluded: "it didn't matter which factory they worked in, who owned it, or whom they supplied – the conditions were always bad". Likewise, according to pressure group Labour Behind the Label: "Much as we would like to recommend good companies over bad ones, we have not come across a single company which we feel comfortable recommending."

Young women applying glue to sport shoes at a Reebok Factory in Zhongshan, China. Companies like Reebok – which today is one of the slightly more progressive of the big sportwear firms – have helped created massive economic growth in China. But many people question whether it can ever be ethical to source from a country with an appalling human rights record, widespread labour abuse and no recognition of independent trade unions.

CLOTHES, COSMETICS & JEWELLERY

DON'T BELIEVE ALL YOU READ: NIKE VS KASKY

In 1998, Californian activist Marc Kasky filed a law suit in the US, claiming that Nike had made misleading claims in response to accusations regarding conditions at one of its Vietnamese factories (accusations partly based on Nike's own research). Instead of defending its statements as true – presumably because it couldn't – Nike argued it could claim whatever it liked under US free speech law. In 2003, after various rounds of appeals, the state's supreme court decided, as Kasky contended, that free speech didn't apply, as Nike's statements were "commercial speech", intended to increase sales. The case was sent back to the lower courts, to try and determine whether the statements were lies, which are illegal in commercial speech. But Nike finally settled out of court by agreeing to contribute $2 million to the Fair Labor Association and worker education initiatives.

The folks at Reebok, meanwhile, have gone beyond claiming to be a reasonable employer and reinvented themselves as defenders of human rights, instigating the annual Reebok Human Rights Awards. The view that this was a cynical effort to cash in on the bad publicity surrounding Nike was bolstered in 2002 when prominent labour-rights activist Dita Indah Sari rejected the $50,000 prize in protest at the "low pay and exploitation" of Reebok employees in Indonesia and elsewhere.

This seems like pretty good grounds for avoiding the high-street names wherever possible and favouring fair-trade specialists such as those listed from p.213. In reality, however, the range of fairly traded clothes is still pretty small. So what efforts have the individual brands made?

One level up from drawing up a code of conduct is joining an ethical trade group, such as the UK's Ethical Trading Initiative (see p.68), which serves as a forum for working towards the implementation of a wide-ranging "base code". Membership certainly doesn't guarantee best practice, but it's a start. Littlewoods controversially dropped out in 2003, but a large number clothes companies are still involved. The big-name members include:

207

▷ Debenhams   ▷ Mothercare   Ellesse, KangaROOS,
▷ Levi Strauss   ▷ NEXT   Kickers, Lacoste,
▷ Marks & Spencer   ▷ Pentland Group: Mitre, Red or Dead,
▷ Monsoon   Berghaus, Brasher,   Speedo, Ted Baker

For sports brands, the main equivalent is the US-based **Fair Labor Association**, or FLA, initially set up by Bill Clinton's administration in response to growing concern about sweatshops among US consumers. The FLA focuses exclusively on garment companies, with the aim of enforcing an "industry-wide Workplace Code of Conduct … based on the core labor standards of the International Labour Organization". In 2003, the FLA broke ground by making the results of company factory audits – code-breaches, warts and all – available to the public (see www.fairlabor.org). However, questions have been raised regarding the number and quality of the factory audits. One insider told Rough Guides that some of the FLA auditing firms had no significant experience of interviewing workers, and had a financial interest in not offending the company whose factory they are examining. Still, the initiative is certainly much better than nothing. Members include:

▷ **adidas-Salomon**   ▷ **Patagonia**   ▷ **Reebok**
▷ **Nike**   ▷ **Puma**   ▷ **Van Heusen**

So what about the rest? Many of the remaining UK retailers are controlled by entrepreneur **Philip Green**, who owns **BHS** as well as the giant Arcadia Group, which includes **Burton**, **Dorothy Perkins**, **Evans**, **Miss Selfridge**, **Outfit**, **Top Shop**, **Top Man** and **Wallis**. Green, a famously fast-living Monaco-based billionaire, is described by the T&G union's textile division as "extremely ruthless" in his dealings with suppliers, and has been criticized for paying no tax in the UK. Arcadia has a code of conduct but hasn't ignored requests to join the Ethical Trading Initiative and was the subject of a damning report in mid 2004 by Labour Behind the Label, which documented numerous examples of bad treatment of workers during the same period in which company profits doubled, adding an "estimated … £1 billion to the personal fortune of owner Philip Green".

Then there's **Gap**, of course. Sourcing from 3000 factories in more than 50 countries, the company has long been the bête noir of sweat-shops campaigners. But it was recently lauded by some of its long-standing critics for releasing an unusually frank assessment of its supply chain. Its *Social Responsibility Report 2003* admitted that the

MADE IN THE USA? THE SAIPAN DEBACLE

Saipan is part of the Northern Mariana Islands in the western Pacific Ocean. Having been previously held by Spain, Germany and Japan, it was captured by the US in World War II and later given US territorial status. That makes it basically part of the States – so items produced there for the US market are free from import tariffs and quotas. And yet the minimum wage is lower, customs duties are said to be slacker and foreign workers can be granted renewable one-year work permits. Companies soon realized that they could benefit from these favourable conditions and still write "Made in the USA" on their labels. Trade soared and before long the temporary foreign workers – mainly from East Asia – outnumbered the locals by around fifty percent.

However, alleged labour abuse in the islands' many garment factories didn't take long to surface. There were reports of effective indentured labour (with workers unable to leave their jobs due to debts imposed by their employers), withheld wages, workers being forced to "donate" unpaid hours on top of their normal shifts, and union organizers facing sacking and deportation.

Finally, in 1999, a collection of workers, human rights groups and others sued some factory owners and more than twenty major retailers and manufacturers, including **Abercrombie & Fitch**, **Calvin Klein**, **Gap**, **Polo Ralph Lauren** and **Tommy Hilfiger USA**, over the alleged labour abuses. Eventually, all the companies except **Levi Strauss** (which claimed the allegations against them were false) were part of a $20 million settlement to pay withheld wages and set up a monitoring organization co-ordinated with the International Labour Organization.

majority of its factories were not in full compliance with its code of conduct, and detailed the way in which it has encouraged factories to improve and dropped those that have refused. However, Gap is still criticized for keeping its factory list secret, and rarely uses independent auditors. The company claims this is because independent monitors "cannot currently replace the work of our experienced and fully dedicated internal team". But probably more important is the fact that independent auditing has proved to be "an extremely resource-intensive process". And, despite the sweatshop campaigns, a Gap spokesman recently told the *New York Times* that the company thought it was unclear whether the consumer would "care at all" whether or not they spent millions on expanding their monitoring operations.

Upmarketness doesn't necessarily correlate with better or worse behaviour. Of the smaller, classier retailers, **Timberland** is often cited as something of a shining example, fully committed to improving standards and auditing not only its factories but also leather tanneries and other suppliers. **French Connection**, on the other hand, has what campaigners describe as a feeble code, with no reference to monitoring. Labour Behind the Label wrote with reasonable indignation in 2002 that the company "has never, in the course of five years of letter-writing by consumers and LBL, acknowledged our letters and concerns". Fcukers.

Out-of-town specialist **Matalan** is under fire at the time of writing for not mentioning the right to unionize in its code of conduct; **H&M**, conversely, has a decent code of conduct but is currently under attack from campaign groups for not cracking down on union busting in its factories.

Shoes

Compared with clothes production, shoe manufacture tends to be more industrial and hi-tech – something that usually means longer-term contracts and more leverage over labour conditions for brands and retailers. However, aside from the trainer companies discussed above, the shoe sector has shown very little interest in ethical issues.

There is still not a single shoe company in the Ethical Trading Initiative, and in a recent survey of fourteen high-street shoe shops by *Ethical Consumer* magazine (see p.362), only **Clarks** and **Ecco** responded to the request for a code of conduct – and even those didn't make any reference to external monitoring of factories. So this industry clearly has a long way to go. Right now, just about the only shoe shops that seem concerned with ethical matters are specialists producing non-leather shoes (see p.198).

One contentious shoe company is **CAT**, whose bulldozers have become a favourite tool of the Israeli army. As the *Business Respect* newsletter noted in November 2003, the company "celebrated its inclusion for the third year in the Dow Jones Sustainability World Index, just as protesters in Iowa slammed the company for selling equipment to Israel that would allegedly be used 'to bulldoze Palestinian homes'".

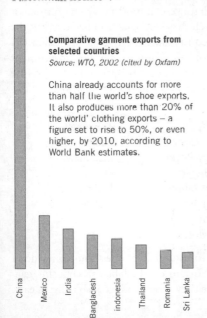

Comparative garment exports from selected countries
Source: WTO, 2002 (cited by Oxfam)

China already accounts for more than half the world's shoe exports. It also produces more than 20% of the world' clothing exports – a figure set to rise to 50%, or even higher, by 2010, according to World Bank estimates.

China | Mexico | India | Bangladesh | Indonesia | Thailand | Romania | Sri Lanka

China and Burma

Regardless of the codes and promises of clothes companies, another ethical question is *where* they do business. The international trade in shoes and clothes in increasingly dominated by just one country: China. Usually defined as an oppressive regime, China has no recognition of independent trade unions and its sweatshops are notorious. Yet nearly every clothes company is shifting its production to China – "to stay competitive", in the words of Gap.

China already accounts for more than 50% of shoes exports and 20% of clothes exports. And from the first day of 2005, when a complex set of Western textile import tariffs will be removed, China will almost certainly soak up the garment market share of countries such as Bagladesh, Cambodia and Sri Lanka. This is because, under the tariff system, these countries have been given preferential access to Western markets, and garment exports have become absolutely central to their economies. So, with the end of this favoured status, the inevitable exodus of orders to China is expected to cause massive job loss and suffering. Some people have suggest that this – combined with the Chinese government's appaling human rights record and its occupation of Tibet – makes a very strong ethical case for avoiding "made in China" clothes and shoes.

A more extreme case, however, is Burma (p.399), whose abhorrent military dictatorship directly profits from the clothes export industry. Most of the major brands that were importing from Burma, or Myanmar as it may appear on clothes labels, have pulled out, but the following companies have failed to assure the Burma Campaign UK that they don't still import from the country (the UK government knows which of them are still sourcing from Burma but they refuse to reveal this information). For the most up-to-date list, see: www.burmacampaign.org.uk

- ▷ Animal
- ▷ Bay Trading
- ▷ By Design Plc
- ▷ Ciro Citterio
- ▷ Etam
- ▷ First Sport
- ▷ Harrods
- ▷ Hobbs
- ▷ Intersport
- ▷ Jane Norman
- ▷ Jeffrey Rogers
- ▷ Joe Bloggs
- ▷ Karen Millen
- ▷ La Coste
- ▷ Liberty
- ▷ Lillywhites
- ▷ LK Bennett
- ▷ Mambo
- ▷ Miss Sixty
- ▷ MK One
- ▷ Pied à terre
- ▷ Shellys

Unfortunately, recent EU law means that clothes companies don't have to specify the country of origin on the label, so choosing garments on the grounds of where they were produced isn't always easy.

More info

To keep abreast of the issues surrounding brands and workers' rights in the rag trade, visit:

Clean Clothes Campaign www.cleanclothes.org
Sweatshop Watch www.sweatshopwatch.org

FAIR-TRADE & ORGANIC CLOTHES

As the issues covered in this chapter become more widely discussed, a growing numbers of **fairly traded** and **organic** clothes are appearing on the market. Traditionally, this section of the clothes industry tends towards flowing dresses, flowery patterns and "ethnic" styles. There's still quite a lot of that around, but there are now also many stylish and modern options, such as the T-shirts and tops from HUG and Gossypium, and the women's clothes from Ethically Me and Eco clothWORKS (all listed below).

Standards for organic materials are precise and legally binding, just as with food (see p.86). But no clothes will bear the official Fairtrade stamp at least until 2005. In the meantime, the labour standards of the "fair-trade" suppliers have to be taken on trust. Most of the companies listed here are widely respected in the field, so you shouldn't worry too much that you're being taken for a ride. But, conversely, most of them acknowledge that their trading standards are neither perfect nor comprehensive. In some cases their relationships with suppliers are also based on trust, and they don't have unlimited time and resources for auditing. Still, at the very least, you can be confident that non-exploitative and environmentally sustainable sourcing is more central to the business of these companies than to any of the high-street names.

All of the following (except Traid) sell online and/or via a catalogue. They're listed alphabetically, but with a few of our favourites first. All of these top picks will let you go fair-trade or organic without a hint of "flower child". Also see the veggie-leather list on p.198.

Rough Guides top picks: fair-trade

Ganesha

www.ganesha.co.uk ▷ 020 7928 3444 ▷ 3 Gabriel's Wharf, 56 Upper Ground, South Bank, London

Stylish skirts, kurtars (for both men and women), scarves, T-shirts and more, mainly in colourful Indian materials and produced by members of IFAT (see p.26). Ganesha also stock designer flip-flops from West Bengal (made by a multinational company, but from a factory certified to the ISO 9002 standard for employer and environmental safety) and four categories of cool bags: "street India", "kitsch", "leather" and the very stylish "a bit fancy".

From Ganesha: handloom cotton shirt with handworked mother of pearl buttons (£25) from a small IFAT-registered Bagladeshi company, and a pink floral bag (£15) from a social enterprise in south India.

Gossypium

www.gossypium.co.uk ▷ 0800 085 6549 ▷ Abinger Place, Lewes

Elegant, simple T-shirts, tops, night-wear and knickers – plus yoga and kids' clothes – in fairly traded organic cotton from India. Their kimono-style hoody is one of the more stylish items you'll find in the world of fair-trade threads. Gossypium (who take their name from the Latin term for the cotton-plant genus) are fully transparent about their products' origins, from field to shop.

HUG

www.hug.co.uk ▷ 08451 301 525

Nicely cut T-shirts and tops ("Hugs") for men, women and children. The style is quite similar to what you might find at Gap, but these garments are made with fairly traded, organic Peruvian cotton – the long-staple tanguis "used by leading Italian design houses" – and high-tech, eco-friendly dyes. Order online and your item will arrive in a letter-box-friendly parcel; if you don't like it, simply send it back freepost.

People Tree

www.ptree.co.uk ▷ 0845 450 4595

Selling via the Web, phone, fax or their catalogue/magazine, People Tree offers one of the bigger fair-trade clothes ranges, with a wide selection of everyday basics – mostly in organic cotton. Not every item is a beauty, but there are some nice clothes as well as bags, baskets and other accessories. Besides its fair-trade policy, the company uses its profits to support a school in Bangladesh.

Traid

www.traid.org.uk ▷ 020 8733 2580

London 61 Westbourne Grove, W2
69–71 Kilburn High Road, NW6
2 Acre Lane, London SW2
119 King Street, W6
375 Holloway Road, N7
Brighton 39 Duke Street
Wembley Unit 12–13 Central Square

OK, it's not exactly "fair-trade", but Traid ("Textile Recycling for Aid and International Development") definitely warrants a mention here. Launched in 1999, with the twin aim of raising money while promoting recycling and waste reduction, it's like a cross between a charity shop and an exclusive boutique. Unwanted clothes are donated to the shops, and then "redesigned and reconstructed" by Traid designers to make unique and fashionable garments. Prices are similar to high-street stores, but the garments are one-offs and the profits go to charity.

Rough Guides top picks: eco and organic

Eco clothWORKS

www.clothworks.co.uk ▷ 01225 309 218

Prices aren't low – the pintucked pure silk shirt, dyed with madder and oak galls, is a cool £160 – but the Eco clothWORKS range of organic cotton, silk and hemp clothes is as designer as ethical fashion gets. It currently only offers clothing for women and children, but does so in a variety of stylish and sometimes slightly retro looks.

Epona

www.eponasport.com ▷ 0191 415 1201

A small range of reasonably priced, "fairer trade" sportswear items made from organic cotton in factories that are certified to the SA8000 benchmark (a strict set of labour-focused standards set by Social Accountability International). Aerobics tops, shorts, T-shirts and zip-tops are among the offerings.

Howies

www.howies.co.uk ▷ 01239 615 988

Fashionable extreme sports and skater clothes with a difference. The fabrics are organic, the T-shirt messages subversive and their well-designed, interactive website full of "truths" – facts and stats – on everything from fish farms to food packaging.

Howies girl's jumper, in 100% recycled cotton

Patagonia

www.patagonia.com/europe ▷ 01629 583 800

High-quality fleeces, jackets and other outdoor pursuits gear made from organic cotton by a company with good environmental credentials. Use the details above to find your nearest stockist or order a catalogue.

Other suppliers

Bishopston Trading Company

www.bishopstontrading.co.uk
Bristol 0117 924 5598 ▷ 193 Gloucester Road, Bishopston
Stroud 0145 376 6355 ▷ 33 High Street
Bradford-on-Avon 0122 586 7485 ▷ 33 Silver Street
Glastonbury 0145 883 5386 ▷ 8A High Street
Totnes 0180 386 8488 ▷ 79 High Street

This workers' co-operative provides above-average wages, secure employment, health care and various other benefits to more than 400 weavers and tailors in South India. It mainly offers flowing organic cotton clothes for women and children, though does stock some men's shirts and trousers. Available via mail order, in various fair-trade shops and in their own five stores in the west of England. Any profits go to the company's own charity, the South Indian Rural Development Trust.

Chandni Chowk

www.chandnichowk.co.uk
Barnstaple 01225 483 541 ▷ 102 Boutport Street
Bath 01271 374 714 ▷ 6 New Bond Street Place
Bristol 0117 930 0059 ▷ 66 Park Street
Exeter 01392 410 201 ▷ 1 Harlequins, Paul Street
Taunton 01823 32737 ▷ 14a, The Bridge, Riverside Place

A mainly female range of vibrant Indian-influenced clothes with an emphasis on artisan-style manufacture: hand-loomed materials, hand-block prints, and natural fibres. Committed to a people-friendly scale of production and eco-friendlier techniques. Available in many fair-trade shops (see p.349) and Chandni Chowk's five west-country shops.

Ethically Me

www.ethicallyme.co.uk ▷ 0870 005 7080

Though the name sounds a bit like an anger management course, Ethically Me sell some beautiful clothes (again, mainly women's – decent men's clothing is an ethical niche crying out to be filled), including both casual and some relatively formal items – a rarity in this sector. Their code of conduct isn't altogether different from those of the big brands, but their small scale allows them to be in "direct contact" with all their producers and they're committed to transparency, providing social and environmental info on the label in each garment. Worryingly, at the time of writing, their website isn't being updated and their phone's not being answered...

Greenfibres

www.greenfibres.com ▷ 01803 868001 ▷ 99 High Street, Totnes
Among the best-known organic textile companies, Greenfibres sell clothes for men, women and children – underwear, casual wear and even suits – as well as towels and sheets, etc. It describes itself as "non exploitative", though not explicitly fair-trade.

Natural Collection

www.naturalcollection.com ▷ 0870 331 3333
Natural Collection sell a full range of men's and women's clothes – casual wear, sportswear, knitwear, underwear and more – in organic cotton and hemp. The selection includes that rare thing in the ethical world: a nicely cut men's shirt (Italian-designed and in hemp).

One World is Enough

www.one-world-is-enough.net ▷ 0845 166 1212
This fair-trade organization only buys from small manufacturers and workers co-operatives. They have a few modern designs, but much of the range is reminiscent of a Glastonbury stall, with dolphin T-shirts and yin-yang jumpers.

Ralper

www.ralper.co.uk
Launched in mid-2004, Ralper aims to become "the brand that gave the young fashionable dresser the ability to buy ethical clothes". Their range – which includes T-shirts with and without screenprints – is designed in Britain and branded to appeal to a trendy market. But the clothes are made by developing-world producer groups registered with IFAT (see p.26).

ORGANIC WOOL

There may not be much organic leather available, but there's no shortage of organic wool. Though sheep aren't the worst-treated of farm animals, buying organic wool supports small-scale, ecologically friendly farms. Suppliers include:

Ford Barton 01398 351 139 ▷ www.fordbarton.co.uk ▷ Stoodleigh, Tiverton, Devon
Hebridean Woolhouse www.hebrideanwoolhouse.com ▷ 01932 25485
Lower Turley Farm 01884 32234 ▷ Cullompton, Devon
Organic Pure Wool www.organicpurewool.co.uk ▷ 01570 493 374 ▷ Ceredigion, Wales
Organic Wool Company www.organicwool.co.uk ▷ 01239 821 171
Rosuick Organic www.oatesorganic.co.uk ▷ 01326 231 302 ▷ Heleston, Cornwall

Ralper, which currently sells exclusively online, is a member of the British Association of Fair Trade Shops (see p.349).

Siesta

www.siestacrafts.co.uk ▷ 01227 464 614 ▷ 1 Palace Street, Canterbury
Fairly traded Latin American clothes of a hippyish nature (they also sell didgeridoos and wind chimes).

Silken Dalliance

01993 810008 ▷ 25 Oxford St, Woodstock
A specialist retailer of fair-trade silk products, mostly sourced from Vietnam, Thailand and Bangladesh. Stocks dresses, skirts, tops, shirts, trousers and suits as well as beaded bags, scarves, hats and silver jewellery.

Spirit of Nature

www.spiritofnature.co.uk ▷ 0870 725 9885
Despite a patronizing strapline ("Natural living is fun"), this company sells an extensive range of organic cotton and hemp clothes for adults and children, including jeans.

Traidcraft

www.traidcraft.co.uk ▷ 0191 491 1001

Traidcraft offer a very varied, though not enormous, range of fair-trade clothes, from silk ties, shawls and dressy tops to alpaca scarves and jumpers. Available via their mail order catalogue, their joint website with Oxfam (www.fairtradeonline.com) and some fair-trade shops (see p.349).

More alt.clothes...

We've covered the main "alternative" suppliers above, but there are some others, including some specialists – such as **Pachacuti**, who make, of all things, fairly traded panama hats (www.panamas.co.uk ▷ 01335 300 485). The high fashion world, if you can afford it, has at least one designer with a social and environmental conscience in **Katherine Hamnett**, and there are also a few companies producing fairly traded merchandise such as T-shirts for bands: look out for the **Ethical Threads** label, spearheaded by Billy Bragg, which sources from unionized shops and co-operatives.

Even **AdBusters**, the ultimate anti-consumerists famed for tweaking billboard ads to reverse their meaning, have started selling their own non-sweatshop trainers. Sold at www.blackspotsneaker.org, they're been designed specifically with Nike founder Phil Knight in

mind: "Phil Knight had a dream. He'd sell shoes. He'd sell dreams. He'd get rich. He'd use sweatshops if he had to. Then along came a new shoe. Plain. Simple. Cheap. Fair. Designed for only one thing: kicking Phil's ass." It's unclear whether the garment workers of the developing world would be impressed by AdBusters helping their plight by producing trainers in

Portugal, but the idea of a trainer from an "anti-corporation" undoubtedly has a certain appeal.

In the US – perhaps because of the sheer extent of non-unionized garment factories – another type of company has evolved, mainly selling clothes made domestically but under guaranteed union conditions. These include **No Sweat Apparel** (www.nosweatapparel.com), **American Apparel** (www.americanapparel.net) and **Sweat-X** (www.sweatx.net), the latter a brainchild of Ben Cohen of Ben & Jerry's ice cream. As yet, they don't sell in the UK, but that may change in the near future.

For a near-comprehensive list of organic clothes suppliers, check out the directory at the Soil Association website: www.soilassociation.org

NAPPIES & BABY CLOTHES
For principled parents

Babies may account for a small percentage of family biomass, but when kitted out with **disposable nappies** they generate roughly half the contents of a household's bins. A typical baby gets through around 5000 disposables during its nappy days; across the UK, this adds up to 8 million each day and an astonishing 3 billion each year. Most of these end up in landfills where, according to environmentalists, the plastic will take hundreds of years to break down, the superabsorbent granules will soak up groundwater needed for the decomposition of other waste, and the excrement and urine may pose a health hazard.

Even if these worries are overcautious, nappies are still enormously wasteful to make (each one requiring considerable quantities of oil for plastic and wood for pulp, as well as gels and other chemicals) and therefore also to buy (parents spend on average a total of £700 per baby on disposables, according to Market Intelligence). However, both the environmental and financial footprint can be reduced by around 80% by opting for **reusable cloth nappies**, which are increasingly being promoted by local councils, who are keen to cut down on the costs of dealing with used disposables.

Cloth nappies are very widely available, though you may prefer to look into fair-trade and organic options at specialists such as the following, most of which sell online and also offer **clothes** for babies and young children:

Bao-Bab
www.bao-bab.co.uk ▷ 01223 894 158 ▷ 210 Parkers House, 48 Regent Street, Cambridge

Beaming Baby
www.beamingbaby.com ▷ 0800 034 5672 ▷ 25 Ellerhayes, Hele, Exeter

Born
www.borndirect.com ▷ 0117 924 5080 ▷ 64 Gloucester Road, Bishopston, Bristol & 134 Walcot Street, St. Swithins Yard, Bath

Eco-babes
www.eco-babes.co.uk ▷ 01833 640 400

Green Baby
www.greenbaby.co.uk ▷ 020 7226 9244 ▷ 345 Upper Street, Islington, London

Greensleeves Clothing
www.greensleevesclothing.com ▷ 020 8458 1559 ▷ 61 Oakwood Road, London NW11

Flushable paper liners make cloth nappies very easy to use, though if you're intimidated by the prospect of washing the dirties, look into nappy **washing services**. You dump the used nappies in a bin provided, someone arrives in a van and swaps them for fresh ones. Even taking into account the delivery van, this system has the lowest environmental footprint of all due to the efficiency of washing in bulk. Unsurprisingly, though, it's also the most expensive option.

Try your local council for recommended services, browse the Yellow Pages (www.yell.com) or phone the UK Nappy Helpline: 01983 401 959.

COSMETICS & TOILETRIES
Because you (and the bunny) are worth it

When it comes to cosmetics, toiletries and perfumes, the major worry for most consumers is **animal testing**. We cover this below, but first it's worth running through a few less-discussed issues. One is the ethical standards of the giant businesses that dominate the "health and beauty" market. There isn't room here for a proper profile of each, but suffice to say that they're very politically active. According to Open Secrets (www.opensecrets.org), George Bush's Republican party has received substantial cash donations from **Bristol Myers Squibb** and **Revlon**. And **Procter & Gamble**, **Colgate-Palmolive** and **Johnson & Johnson** are, among other things, on the board of the National Foreign Trade Council, a lobby group which has actively opposed legislation to stop trade with Burma (and whose website opens with a quote of gratitude and approval from none other than Dick Cheney). To see the many brands these companies own, see the box on pp.226–227.

Another issue is the degree to which cosmetics manufacturers use needlessly risky chemicals, such as **persistent toxins** that may accumulate in the human body or the wider environment, posing risks to health and wildlife. As with household cleaning products (see p.285), there is very little evidence to suggest that standard exposure to cosmetics chemicals causes anything more serious than occasional allergic reactions, though intensive long-term exposure does seem to present risks. In 2002, for instance, researchers from Lund University, Sweden, found that female hairdressers were one-third more likely than a selected control group to give birth to babies with malformations or other serious physical defects (especially heart defects). Extended exposure to everyday hair sprays, dyes and the like seems to be the most likely cause.

There are environmental concerns about the use of **"natural" products**, too. According to the World Wildlife Foundation, between four and ten thousand plant species are threatened with extinction due to the demand for herbal remedies, and the natural ingredients used in certain toiletries and cosmetics inevitably pose similar threats. For example, rainforest campaigners worry about the growing demand for **palm oil**, derivatives of which are widely used in soaps, lipsticks and perfumes, among other products. According to environmental groups such as the World Rainforest Movement (see www.wrm.org.uy) these are helping to wipe out biodiversity and tacitly supporting the forced displacement of forest-based peoples in Indonesia and elsewhere.

Similarly, in 2003, a joint investigation by the Environmental Investigation Agency and Friends of the Earth revealed the extensive damage being done by illegal mining of soapstone for talcum power (used in everything from lipstick to deodorant) in the nature reserves of Rajasthan, India. Subjecting workers to appalling health and safety risks, causing serious pollution, lowering the water table and generally causing environmental wipe-out, these mines have been identified as the single most serious threat to the survival of the endangered Indian tiger (for more, see www.eia-international.org). Several multinationals were shown to be purchasing this talc: Revlon, Johnson & Johnson, Cussons, Avon and Unilever. However, to be fair, many smaller companies were probably also benefiting from this destruction.

Other issues surrounding cosmetics include the human rights standards of developing-world make-up factories – *New York Times* columnist Joseph Kahn recently reported slave labour conditions in a Chinese false-eyelash plant – and the question of whether ingredients such as cocoa butter are traded according to Fairtrade principles. Finally, vegans and strict vegetarians should be aware that many cosmetic items contain animal-derived products.

Animal testing

Animal testing for cosmetic and their ingredients has been heavily cut back in the last two decades, and the UK has banned such tests outright. However, testing does continue and the ban makes little difference since most of what's on sale in the UK is imported from, or contains ingredients imported from, abroad. According to animal rights campaigners, around 40,000 animals in Europe and millions globally are subjected to tests each year, for products ranging from hair dyes to toothpastes. These include notorious experiments such as the **Lethal Dose 50% Test** (animals are gradually poisoned with increasing doses of a substance until half of them die) and the **Draize Eye Test** (chemicals added to animals' eyes and the damage recorded over several days).

After persistent public and campaigner pressure, an **EU-wide ban** on the sale of animal-tested cosmetics was finally agreed in 2003. However, it's not due to become effective until 2009 and there have already been at least two legal actions to try and have it overturned: one directly from a coalition of cosmetics companies, which refuse to reveal their identities, and one from the government of France, home to industry giants associated with animal testing such as L'Oréal. So it remains to be seen whether the legislation will survive.

In the meantime, tests are gradually being developed that don't require animals – often funded, it has to be said, by the same companies that are still actively conducting animal experiments. And, in the EU at least, once an alternative test exists, it has to be used instead of the animal version. But until non-animal tests exist for all products and ingredients – which, as *New Scientist* has pointed out, is a matter less of ethics and more of governments deciding "how much tax-payers money should be spent" – the argument really comes down to whether you believe intense animal suffering is a reasonable price to pay for the development of new make-up ingredients.

CLEAN COSMETICS

According to survey after survey, nearly all consumers feel strongly that animal testing for cosmetics should be stopped. But the same people continue to give their support to companies that aren't on the animal-testing clean list. According to animal rights groups, this is partly because many statements on the sides of bottles and tubes are misleading. "Against animal testing", for example, means basically

WHO DOES AND DOESN'T TEST ON ANIMALS?

At the time of writing, according to the British Union for the Abolition of Vivisection, the following companies continue to conduct and/or commission animals tests for cosmetics, toiletries or ingredients:

▷ **Unilever** All Clear, Cutex Denim, cK cosmetics, Cerutto 1881, Chloe, Escape, Eternity, Jean Louis Scherrer, Karl Lagerfeld, Narcisse, Obsession, Valentino; Procter & Gamble: Hugo Boss, Max Factor, Oil of Olay, Crest, Head & Shoulders, Pantene Pro-V, Clairol Herbal Essence, Nice n Easy, Aussie hair products, Camay soap, Cover Girl, Giorgio Beverly Hills, Old Spice, Sure, Vidal Sassoon, Clarion, Colorfast, Mary Quant, Maxi, Noxell, Noxzema, Outdoor Girl, SK-11, Biactol, Clearsil

▷ **Colgate Palmolive** Colgate, Palmolive, Soft Soap, Lady and Mennen Speed Sticks, Vel Beauty Bar; L'Oreal: Elvive, Elnett, Studio Line, Plenitude, Feria, Recital, L'Oreal, Colour Cosmetics, Garnier Fructis, Garnier Ambre Solaire, Garnier Nutralia, Garnier Belle Colour, Maybelline, Freestyle, Excellence, Castings, Anais Anais, La vie en rose, Biotherm, Giorgio Armani, Helena Rubenstein, Lancome, Ralph Lauren, Cacharel, Redken, Vichy, Matrix

▷ **Lever Faberge (a Unilever subsidiary)** Mentadent, Signal, Ponds, Vaseline Intensive Care skin products, Pears, Sure, Impulse, Addiction, Sunsilk, Timotei, Organics, Lynx, Brut, Aquatonic, Shield, Lux, Dove, Knights Castile, Salon Selectives, Physio Sport, Lifebuoy, Harmony

▷ **Bristol-Myers** Clairol Nice 'n' Easy, Natural Instincts, Glints, Herbal Essences, Lasting Colour, Loving Care, Born Blonde, Mum, Mum Botanicals, Hydrience

▷ **Schwarzkopf & Henkel** Gliss, Mont Saint Michel, Scorpio, La Perla, Sergio Tacchini, Krizia, Fiorucci

▷ **Bourjois Limited:** Bourjois

▷ **Wella** Vivality, Vosine, Shock Waves, Silvikrin

▷ **COTY** Rimmel, Adidas, Sensiq, Cutex

▷ **Beiersdorf** Nivia, La Prairie, Atrixo

The following claim not to conduct or commission animal tests but do buy newly animal tested ingredients:

▷ **Boots** Botanics, 17, no. 7, Summer Sun, Soltan

▷ **Estee Lauder** Aramis, Clinique, Prescriptives, Origins, M.A.C, Aveda, La Mer, Stila, Jo Malone, Bumble & Bumble, Bobby Brown

▷ **Gillette** Mach3, Venus, Sensor, Right Guard, Oral-B

▷ **Yves Rocher** Yves Rocher Revlon: Revlon, Ultima II, Almay, Charlie

And the following are animal-testing free, having signed up for the HCS scheme (see p.228), which means they've agreed not to use any new animal-tested ingredients from a fixed cut-off point.

▷ American Formulating
▷ Arbonne International
▷ Auromere Ayurvedic
▷ Avalon Natural Products
▷ Better Botanicals
▷ Biorganics Hair Therapy
▷ Body & Face St Cyrus Ltd (Naroma, Body & Face Place)
▷ The Body Shop
▷ Calder Valley Soap Co
▷ California North
▷ Caswell Massey Co Ltd
▷ Christine Valmy Inc
▷ Conscience Cosmetics
▷ Co-op
▷ Dolma Vegan Perfumes
▷ Dr Bronner's Magic Soaps
▷ Earth Science
▷ Earth Solutions
▷ English Ideas

▷ The Essential Oil Company Ltd
▷ Faith Products (Faith In Nature)
▷ Glad Rags
▷ Good Earth
▷ Greenridge Herbals
▷ Honesty Cosmetics
▷ J&D Black Ltd (Hollytrees)
▷ JR Liggett
▷ Jason Natural Cosmetics
▷ Joe Blasco Cosmetics
▷ Kingfisher Natural Toothpaste
▷ Kiss My Face
▷ Kobashi Essential Oils
▷ Life in the Woods
▷ Liz Earle Naturally Active Skincare
▷ Make-Up International (Face To Face)

▷ Meadowsweet
▷ Mia Rose Products
▷ Montagne Jeunesse (Chantelle, Fab Face Food, Model Secrets)
▷ Moor Spa International Ltd (Moor)
▷ Natural By Nature Oils
▷ Nature's Soap Dish
▷ Neal's Yard Remedies
▷ Osea International
▷ Para Laboratories/ Queen Helene
▷ Paul Mitchell Systems
▷ Quinessence Aromatherapy
▷ Red Star Hand Crafted Soaps
▷ Rejuvi
▷ Sainsbury's
▷ Studio Magic
▷ Tara Personal Care
▷ Tom's of Maine

nothing at all. Others, such as "we have not carried out animal testing since 1990", could mean that the manufacturers simply commissioned the animal testing from other companies. For the strictest standards, look out for the white-rabbit logo of the **Humane Cosmetics Standard** (HCS), a scheme supported by many animal rights groups and administered in the UK by **BUAV** (the British Union for the Abolition of Vivisection).

To use the HCS logo, the company must exclude all ingredients tested on animals after a fixed **cut-off point** (usually a year in the 1980s or 90s) and prove this via independent audits. We've listed all the companies currently approved below, but for an up-to-the-minute list, or to request the wallet-sized *Little Book of Cruelty Free*, visit:

BUAV www.buav.org/gocrueltyfree

The fact that a company isn't HCS-endorsed doesn't necessarily mean it uses or commissions animal testing. Handmade soap specialist **Lush**, for example, doesn't buy from any companies that currently test on animals, but they don't have a fixed cut-off point. Such policies, according to the likes of BUAV, are a step in the right direction, but since they don't eliminate all long- and short-term incentives for developing ingredients that require animal testing, they remain insufficient.

Alternative suppliers

Leaving aside the animal-testing question, there are a number of manufacturers trying to be ethical operators on a more broad level. Often this doesn't go much further than shunning the plethora of

THE BODY SHOP

Founded by **Anita Roddick** in Brighton, 1976, the **Body Shop** is now a true multinational company, with nearly two thousand shops in fifty countries and shares on the London Stock Exchange. But it claims to be unlike other big companies, placing human rights, environmental sustainability and animal welfare at the very core of its operations. Dame Roddick, or "Queen of Green" as she is sometimes dubbed, has certainly been a tireless campaigner on a wide range of social justice and environmental issues, using her position at the Body Shop to bring numerous issues to the public's attention, from Amazonian rainforest destruction to Shell's activities in Nigeria. And the company has initiated various progressive projects, working with the likes of Amnesty International and creating a **fair-trade** scheme, called "community trade", for some items, including various beauty-product ingredients.

However, the chain has on occasion been tarnished by accusations of being less ethical than it claims. Sometimes the objections, such as those from **London Greenpeace**, have focused on general chain-store complaints: the company's near-identical shops leading to ever-more homogenization of public spaces, and its promotion of a "buy more" lifestyle fuelling the consumerism that's ravaging the planet. But others have been far more specific and cutting, and none more so than those made by American journalist **Jon Entine**, who throughout the 1990s made it a personal mission to expose Roddick and the Body Shop as an ethical fraud, which promotes itself as being far more socially and environmentally responsible than it actually is. His allegations – which have touched on the "theft" of the Body Shop name, the use of petrochemicals, low environmental standards, exploited franchisees, animal testing and the failure of the community trade scheme – were comprehensively laid out in his 25,000-word "social audit" of the company (still available at www.jonentine.com).

These attacks had lasting effect, but Roddick and the Body Shop have suggested that the vast majority of Entine's attacks were unfounded and spiteful. And it's certainly true that Entine is a controversial figure. An "adjunct fellow" with the influential right-wing think-tank, the American Enterprise Institute, he's a keen defender of resented big businesses and critic of many "green" movements. According to US activist and presidential candidate Ralph Nader, he recently gave a speech warning that "reasonable people should be concerned about the growing influence of the social investment community, and its emerging partnership with NGOs, most of which share a knee-jerk demonization of corporations and free markets. Its leaders are products of the activist community, yet they are different and more dangerous."

More recently, criticism of the Body Shop has come from a less likely source: Roddick herself, who these days has less direct management input. In 2001 she described the firms as a "dysfunctional coffin" driven too much by soulless market forces and shareholder profits.

So where does all this leave the only "ethical" company most people could name? Tarnished, perhaps. Yet the Body Shop remains far more progressive than its high-street neighbours. It has expanded its fair-trade efforts to 37 suppliers; it's HCS-approved for being animal-testing free; its been praised by Friends of the Earth for its policy on dangerous chemicals and by the WWF on sustainable wood; it has published far-reaching codes of conduct and done much social and environmental reporting; and it uses its stores to raise awareness of green electricity and other issues.

For more information, or to buy online, see:

Body Shop www.bodyshop.com

synthetic chemicals used by the big firms. But many of these companies also use organic ingredients and recycleable plastic bottles, and shun animal-based ingredients. And, unlike the big boys, they are small businesses far removed from the ugly world of corporate lobbying and political donations.

Green People

www.greenpeople.co.uk ▷ 08702 401 444
Established in 1997, Green People sell more than one hundred organic (and veggie-friendly) toiletries and skin products, from sun creams to organic Jojoba, hemp and rosehip oils. The website includes a useful questions and answers section, and the company donates 10% of its net profits to environmental charities.

Honesty Cosmetics

www.honestycosmetics.co.uk ▷ 01629 814 888

Admirably marketing their products "without unrealistic claims of emo-
tional or physical benefit", Honesty Cosmetics sell a wide range of reasonably priced toiletries and cosmetics, including own-brands products that
are non-animal-tested, petrochemical-free, vegan-friendly and made with
with natural oils sourced with an eye to environmental sustainability.
Available online or via a catalogue, the range also includes organic tam-
pons, lipsticks and nail varnishes by cosmetics by Beauty Without Cruelty,
and green household cleaning products.

Neal's Yard

www.nealsyardremedies.com ▷ 020 7627 1949

You may need to take out a small second mortgage to become a regular, but
Neal's Yard products – some organic, all non-petrochemical and minimally
packaged – are as good as toiletries get. Available in many specialist stores
(call for a local stockist) as well as online or via a catalogue.

And more...

CulPepper www.culpeper.co.uk ▷ 0870 950 9001
Faith In Nature www.faithinnature.com ▷ 0161 764 2555
Weleda www.weleda.co.uk

JEWELLERY
How bad is your bling?

Compared with clothes, say, the ethics of the jewellery industry are
rarely discussed – perhaps partly because, unlike T-shirts and jeans,
jewellery tends to be non-branded, so there are no household-name
corporations to hold to account. Yet both in terms of extraction of
materials and manufacture, the production of jewellery is associated
with a number of problems, including poverty wages, widespread

child labour, dangerous working conditions, environmental degradation and even wars.

In some cases, there are obvious things that consumers can do. If you happen to be buying **diamonds**, for example, you can demand assurances that the stones haven't come from conflict zones (see box

CONFLICT DIAMONDS

Granted, diamonds aren't an everyday purchase. But if you're going to spend a fortune on a wedding ring, or treat yourself to a once-in-a-lifetime gift, it's worth bearing in mind that they're directly associated with large-scale human rights abuses. The problem is that, like all valuable natural resources, diamonds have the potential to cause fuel corruption, land appropriation and even full-scale conflict in the countries in which they're found. Only a minority of diamonds come from war zones (an estimated 2%) but that minority has contributed to the drawing out of wars in which millions of innocent people have been murdered, mutilated or tortured. In the last decade alone, at least three brutal African conflicts – in **Sierra Leone**, **Angola** and the **Democratic Republic of Congo** (which has cost more civilian lives than any conflict since World War II) – have been party driven or funded by the exploitation of diamond mines by armed groups.

The victims aren't necessarily limited to those in the countries where diamonds are mined, however. According to Action Aid, the last couple of years have seen a boom in diamond sales – in part because the 9/11 terrorist attacks have reduced the demand for travel, leaving the affluent with more disposable income. But this is sadly ironic considering that **Al Qaeda** – believed to be behind the 9/11 attacks – are thought to have been partly funded by conflict diamonds.

After years of tireless campaigning from groups like Global Witness (www.globalwitness.org), the international community has started to address the conflict-diamond problem through an international initiative called the **Kimberly Process** (www.kimberleyprocess.com). Involving governments, NGOs and the diamond companies, it aims to "Stop conflict diamonds, Promote prosperity diamonds" by imposing a certification scheme that tracks all rough (uncut) stones from mining to cutting. Seventy countries, including producers, exporters and importers, have now signed up. And

below). And **coral** jewellery is a no-no: coral reefs are among the world's most fragile eco-systems, and they're already taking a severe beating from global warming, farm effluent and other pollution. Direct harvesting of coral for pendants can only make things worse.

For the more common materials, however, it's not immediately

while some of the organizations involved have expressed concerns about the lack of monitoring, the recent expulsion of Congo from the scheme (in response to its government's failure to combat conflict diamonds properly) has renewed faith in its legitimacy.

For all its positive impacts, however, the Kimberly Process only tracks diamonds to the cutting stage, so it's doesn't help jewellery shoppers to be sure about what they're buying. As such, some people have suggested avoiding African diamonds and opting instead, where possible, for Canadian stones, which are distinguishable through a minute etched hallmark of a polar bear. After all, even developing-world diamonds that *don't* come from war zones raise ethical problems: the expulsion of the Gwi and Gana Bushmen from their lands in the Botswanan **Kalahari**, for example, is seem by many as inseparable from diamond prospecting.

But a boycott of African diamonds would hurt some very poor countries that are economically reliant on these precious stones — in Botswana, for example, diamonds contribute 33% of GDP. So probably a better option is to quiz your jewellers as to where their diamonds are from, and whether their suppliers offer a warrantee that their stones are Kimberly certified. If they give you a blank look (which is highly likely) suggest that they get up to speed on the issue and shop elsewhere. And if they show you some paperwork, check that it isn't a simple gemmological certificate, which relates purely to the diamond's authenticity, not its origins.

By the end of 2004, things may be clearer, since a number of NGOs and big players in the diamond industry are in the process of developing a "**fifth C**" label that *will* appear in the shops. The idea is that conflict and child labour certification is added along with the "four Cs" by which diamonds are currently measured: carat, colour, clarity and cut. Bigger stones may even come with a microchip tracing their origin back to the mine.

For more information on conflict diamonds, see: www.conflictdiamonds.com

obvious how ethical shopping can improve standards. For instance, the majority of precious and semi-**precious stones** (though not diamonds) come from small-scale mines in remote regions of poor countries such as Brazil, Madagascar, Mali and India. These mines are associated with desperate and dangerous conditions – with women and children "literally scratching for a living", in the words of campaigner and fair-trade jewellery retailer Greg Valerio – as well as serious, and often avoidable, environmental impacts. But jewellery shops and importers aren't directly associated with the mines or their workers, so it's unlikely that consumer pressure will result in direct improvements. And, since the mines are very often the only source of employment in a region, simply avoiding precious stones is not going to help.

Similarly, the more industrial mines from which most of our **gold** and **silver** come are linked to environmental hazards such as the contamination of groundwater through "acid-rock drainage" – a phenomenon that takes place when air reacts with sulphide minerals in the rocks. Yet, in most cases, there's no way to know the green credentials of the specific mines from which a bracelet, say, originated.

Then, of course, there's the question of the conditions under which the jewellery is manufactured. Much of the cheaper, mass-produced stuff is made in **sweatshop** conditions in East Asia. As ever, jobs in these factories are in much demand, but the mostly non-unionized workforce is often exposed to serious health and safety risks. Many migrant workers in China, for example, have been left crippled by **silicosis** – also known as "dust lung" – after drilling beads or cutting semi-precious stones such as opal and topaz into hearts and other shapes for use in Western bangles, necklaces and earrings. And child labour is common throughout the smaller developing-world workshops that produce many of the higher-quality pieces on sale.

Ethical jewellery suppliers

A number of companies are now offering jewellery sourced according to fair-trade principles. As with all uncertified fair-trade, there are no rules and regulations governing exactly what this means, but in general it refers to the retailers working directly with manufacturers, ensuring they get decent working conditions, a decent slice of the profits and long-term trading agreements. Obviously, a few ethical jewellery suppliers can't immediately solve all the problems mentioned above, but in at least one case – **CRED** (see below) – the fairtraders are also doing their utmost to inject a dose of ethical awareness into the jewellery industry at large.

The main online/mail-order suppliers are listed below. Many fairtrade shops also sell some jewellery; see p.349 to find your nearest.

CRED

www.cred.tv ▷ 01243 839 249

CRED, which is a charity as well as a business, sells silver chains, bangles, bracelets and rings – some plain, some with stones – traded according to their primary goal: "justice for the poor". Shop online or by phone, or visit their stockists in Chichester (01243 536 638), London's Wood Green (020 8888 4462) or Bradford-upon-Avon (01225 868 888). Besides their own ethical sourcing efforts, CRED are causing something of a stir in the wider jewellery industry. They were recently behind the first major study on the ethics of jewellery supply chains, and they're currently in the process of setting up an Ethical Jewellery Initiative (a bit like a more specific version of the Ethical Trading Initiative; see p.68). They're also looking into officially certifying small-scale mining activities in the developing world, and exposing illegal large-scale mining operations that are harming local communities and their environments.

© Chichester Observer

People Tree

www.ptree.co.uk ▷ 0845 450 4595

Though it focuses on clothes, the People Tree website/catalogue includes some delicate silver earrings and necklaces, as well as a wide selection of bead-based piece from Thailand, Indonesia, India and elsewhere. Though it may not sound very pretty, the chain made from silver rings and recycled ring-pulls is surprisingly effective.

Silver Chilli

www.silverchilli.com

Online supplier of silver jewellery from Mexico, with much of the profits going back to local projects and communities and a fair-trade policy seeking to overcome the "mafia-style" Mexican silver business, in which wealthy shop owners reap most of the rewards. The selection ranges from the chunky Tejida Plata Bangle (£33) to delicate necklaces, earrings and bracelets made with silver-grey freshwater pearls (£6–24)

Tearcraft

www.tearcraft.org ▷ 020 8977 9144

Some people may have misgivings about supporting an overtly evangelical Christian organization, but Tearcraft's fair-trade catalogue and online shop includes a wide range of fairly traded necklaces, earrings, pendant, broaches and rings, most in silver but many pieces with semi-precious stones.

Traidcraft

www.traidcraft.co.uk ▷ 0191 491 1001

Traidcraft's trusty fair-trade catalogue and website includes a selection of inexpensive jewellery, mainly sourced from South East Asia and India. Other than the East Timor Bangle (£28), most pieces are less than a tenner.

06

FINANCE

Apart from stashes in biscuit tins and under mattresses, we generally trust our money to institutions which attempt to increase its worth – both for our gain and their own. They do this by investing the money in shares, bonds and property, loaning it at interest to companies, countries or individuals, or gambling it on currency or commodity values. This goes not only for the cash in our bank accounts, but also for our pension contributions and our investments, as well as the essentially collective pools of money in the power of insurance companies.

So what's wrong with that? Well, that depends whether you care who your money is invested in or loaned to. And unless the financial institution has a transparent investment policy stating otherwise, the companies your cash will be supporting may include those linked to oppressive governments, arms sales, deforestation, animal testing for cosmetics and the rest of the sin list. As for currency speculation, it's a way of making money that can wield economic chaos in developing countries (see box on pp.250–251).

All these issues are particularly pertinent because financial institutions are so powerful. Indeed, if there's any truth to the maxim "money talks", then these organizations are the most verbal on the planet: pension funds and insurance companies alone control around 70% of the UK stock market. And the political influence of financial companies is also immense. One director at the World Trade Organization, for example, claimed that the hugely controversial GATS agreement – which aims to open up global "trade" in services such as teaching and medical provision – would never have been created "without the tremendous pressure exerted by the American financial services industry, particularly by companies like American Express and Citicorp".

In response to a gradually increasing public awareness of these kinds of issues, more and more financial service providers – banks, pension funds, investment agencies, insurers and others – are offering "ethical" financial services. But how does it all work? And does it have any effect? This chapter deals with these questions, and then gives more specific background and recommendations for **banks** (p.248), **pensions** (see p.257), **insurance** (see p.262), **mortgages** (see p.265), **investments and financial advisers** (see p.267).

ETHICAL FINANCE BASICS
How does it work? *Does* it work?

In the world of money, as in any sector, the term "ethical" has no fixed meaning as such. But most commonly it refers to **socially responsible investment** (SRI): the practice of considering social and environmental factors when deciding which shares to buy and who to loan money to. This concept is nothing new – it's often traced back to

Quakers and Methodists boycotting certain sections of the stock market around a hundred years ago. But in the last decade it has become a booming sector. Indeed, there are now a number of banks, many pensions and more than fifty UK investment funds driven by SRI policies, plus numerous financial advisers specializing in the field. However, ethical investment policies vary widely, from the highly strict – usually dubbed "dark green" in the ethical finance world – to the more flexible, or "light green".

THE GREEN SPECTRUM

Dark green investment policies are traditionally based on **negative screening**. This involves drawing up a list of unacceptable practices deemed to be harmful to people, the environment, or animals and excluding any company found to be involved in these practices. An investment organization might decide upon its own criteria, or it could get some pointers from an external body such as EIRIS (see p.246) but either way the approach involves excluding *entire indus-tries* – nuclear power, arms manufacture and tobacco being a few common examples – as well as any individual company associated with unethical behaviour.

Another dark green approach is so-called "**caused-based**" invest-ment (also known as alternative investment, mission-based invest-ment and socially directed investment). Practised by the more specialist ethical organizations such as Triodos Bank (see p.254), this involves investing directly in projects and companies deemed to have social and environmental worth, usually completely avoiding loans to big companies and investments on the stock market. Typical benefi-ciaries are charities, organic farms and community housing projects – the kinds of organizations that struggle to find the credit they need at affordable rates elsewhere.

Light-green investors take a different approach. They may rule out a few industries, such as arms manufacture, but generally they prefer "**positive screening**": any company can qualify for investment as long as it fulfils a certain number of positive criteria, which may range from recycling waste to reporting openly on its own environmental impact – whatever that impact may be.

A variation on this approach is "**best-of-sector**" screening: investing only in the most ethical company in each sector. The logic is simple: if you accept that, say, nuclear power companies are inevitably going to exist, giving them all an incentive to be the best in the field may make a bigger difference than boycotting the whole sector.

COMMON SCREENING CRITERIA

Here are the kinds of pluses and minuses that an ethical finance organization would be looking out for:

NEGATIVE

▷ **Industries** The blacklist often includes alcohol, animal experiments, arms, fur, gambling, genetic engineering, intensive farming, nuclear power, oil, pornography and tobacco.
▷ **Environment** Association with specific problems such as chemical pollution, CO_2 emissions or deforestation; or a straightforward lack of any kind of environmental policy.
▷ **Human rights** Lack of a code of conduct on workers' rights; association with human rights abuses of any kind; or links to oppressive governments.
▷ **Management** Excessive directors' pay; lack of financial transparency; political donations; conflicts of interest; use of tax havens.

POSITIVE

▷ **Charity & community** Charitable donations; participation in and support for local events; sensitivity to the business's effect on local people.
▷ **Environment** Clear environmental policies; environmental auditing and reporting; recycling; minimizing pollution and avoidable energy use.
▷ **Staff** Clear codes of conduct on pay and labour conditions, equal opportunities, and staff "development".
▷ **Management** Disclosure of payments to foreign governments; compliance with "corporate governance" protocols.

But screening is typically only one half of a light-green policy, the other being an "**engagement**" strategy, with lenders and investors using their insider influence to push for better ethical standards. A bank might say, for example, "OK, we'll lend you the cash for your oil platform, but only if you fit robust environmental protection." Or a pension fund which owns shares in a supermarket chain may threaten to cause a fuss at the firm's annual general meeting unless it agrees to audit labour standards in the developing-world farms that supply it.

Dark green vs light green

The dark green vs light green argument largely comes down to the same old question of idealism vs pragmatism. Advocates of the dark-green approach think that it's morally unacceptable to profit from companies or industries whose activities may cause harm to others – regardless of whether the link is obvious (as with arms manufacturing) or more convoluted (oil consumption contributing towards global warming, for example). And they claim that the lighter-green banks and investment funds may actually do harm – by giving the thumbs up to dodgy firms, and in the process helping them create a veneer of "social responsibility".

On the other hand, the pragmatists argue that working *with* companies – through engagement and positive screening – is far more likely to make a difference than simply avoiding their whole sector. It's better to have progressive bankers and investors involved in every industry, they claim, than to leave the most unscrupulous financial backers and most dodgy businesses to get on with wrecking the planet. After all, dark-green ethical banks, pensions and investment funds have a tiny market share (less than 2% in the UK), and there are plenty of other lenders and investors queuing up to finance or buy into even the murkiest companies.

Furthermore, light-green advocates point out that there's an odd logic to "financially boycotting" sectors which we continue to support as consumers and voters. Does it make sense, for example, to object to our money being invested in oil companies while we continue to drive cars? Or shunning arms firms unless we're committed to the total abolishment of British armed forces?

These are all fair points. But does the pragmatic option actually work? Can investors and bankers really make a difference by "engaging" with companies? Exponents of this approach claim there have been numerous successes. Friends of the Earth point to **McDonald's** phasing out environmentally problematic polystyrene packaging, for example, and **Ford** pulling out of the Global Climate Coalition (a now-defunct pressure group which argued against the Kyoto treaty and other measures to combat climate change). Others point to the role that shareholders played in the fall of apartheid in South Africa. And British ethical fund managers claim to have made big impacts behind the scenes on a whole range of issues – including the introduction of codes of conduct governing labour abuses in overseas garment factories. But, despite all these examples, there are few cases where it can be said definitively that shareholders' ethical concerns have resulted in a company changing significantly for the better.

That's perhaps not too surprising, because the financial "engagers" are only likely to change a company's practices if they can show not just a moral case for improving behaviour, but also a financial one. Sometimes this may be possible, but very often it's simply not true that better corporate behaviour means more profits. As one city analyst told *The Observer* in 2002, "On current share trends it pays to be socially irresponsible all the way."

To really *force* a company to change requires the progressive investors – or "**shareholder activists**", as the more extreme ones are known – to **table a resolution** at the company's AGM (annual general meeting). These are occasionally successful on some issues, such as the 2003 GlaxoSmithKline shareholders' protest against the outrageous pay awarded to the company's CEO. But specifically *ethical* resolutions are rare in the UK (unlike in the US; see www.iccr.org). And when they do happen, they don't generally achieve landslide support. The Greenpeace-led resolution against BP Amaco's Northstar project in Alaska, for example, was considered a major success when it achieved around 13.5% of the vote.

But that doesn't mean the engagement approach is worthless. Such resolutions can force issues not just into the AGM but also into the media. They can also play their part in wider protest. For instance, British construction company Balfour Beatty withdrew from the Ilisu Dam project in Turkey – which would allegedly have displaced thousands of people and have had potentially disastrous environmental consequences – after a wide-ranging campaign against the company. Shareholders were not solely responsible, but they played their part, delivering, in the words of Simon McRae from Friends of the Earth, "a big slap in the face" at the AGM.

The bigger the better

Ultimately, dark green and light green strategies are both valid, and in practice many ethical banks and investment funds favour a **mixed approach**: excluding some industries and giving preference to companies with positive practices; but also taking the engagement path on some issues. Similarly, rather than boycotting a whole industry, an organization may be more selective – the Co-operative Bank policy, for instance, doesn't explicitly rule out all companies involved in manufacturing armaments for defence, but it won't invest in any firm which produces torture devices, or any which exports arms of any kind to countries deemed to have oppressive regimes.

Regardless of the shade of green or the type of approach, the biggest determinant of the impact of ethical finance is simply the size and number of organizations involved. Indeed, when really major investors – such as **CalPERS**, the Californian public pension fund worth nearly £100 billion – start throwing their weight around, even governments start taking notice. According to journalist Jon Entine, when Thailand found itself on the CalPERS investment blacklist, "government officials pleaded for time, saying 'there should be sufficient channels in which we are given appropriate opportunities to show that Thailand has complied with good-practice standards, as we

ETHICAL FINANCE BASICS

THE FTSE4GOOD SERIES

FTSE4Good Index Series

Launched in 2001, the FTSE4Good is the world's first significant series of share indices (statistical tools which list companies and share prices) designed specifically for socially responsible investors. It's essentially a screened version of normal FTSE indices, in which tobacco, nuclear-power and arms industries are excluded. Other companies only qualify if they meet "globally recognised corporate responsibility standards". These standards, set out by FTSE and EIRIS (see p.246), focus on three areas:

▷ Working towards environmental sustainability
▷ Developing positive relationships with stakeholders
▷ Upholding and supporting universal human rights

There are two indices each for UK, US, Europe and Global: a "benchmark" index listing all the companies that qualify, and a "tradeable" index listing the current top 50 or 100 companies. Numerous ethical investors use the index as a reference tool – they pay a fee, which is donated to UNICEF (the UN's children's fund).

There's no doubt that the FTSE4Good has increased public awareness of corporate ethics. For example, when the index was launched, the exclusion of Tesco (for its failure to publish an environmental report) was widely reported in the mainstream press. But not everyone approves of the indices. Some critics see them as yet another tool for promoting corporate social responsibility – which they consider a hopeless substitute for proper regulation (see p.64) – while many in the ethical investment world have criticized the criteria it uses for being too vague or loose. Presumably in response to these concerns, the requirements have been made more rigorous numerous times since the indices first launched. But it's still towards the "light" end of the green spectrum, with oil firms and other controversial companies lurking on the list. For more visit: www.ftse.com/ftse4good

A less-high-profile operation is the Corporate Responsibility Index, maintained by Business in the Community. It's aimed more at managers than investors: anyone can join and the members are ranked each year. For more information or to see how the members compare, visit: www.bitc.org.uk/programmes/key_initiatives

have every intention to do'". So even if ethical finance is not revolutionizing the world right now, its impact gets greater with each person who changes bank on ethical grounds, or signs up for an ethical pension or investment fund.

ETHICAL FINANCE Q&A

Does "going ethical" mean getting less interest?

In the case of banks (see p.248), having an "ethical" account certainly doesn't need to mean you being poorer – quite the opposite. Most of the population get practically no interest on their high-street current account, and pay over the odds for services and overdrafts. Compare that with Smile, the Internet arm of the ethically progressive Co-operative Bank. At the time of writing it offers 3.04% interest and a free £500 overdraft.

Things are a bit more contentious when it comes to investments and pensions, but the evidence suggests that "screened" pension and investment funds are actually just as good a bet as non-ethical ones. Probably the most in-depth assessment of the issue is *Does Ethical Investment Pay?*, produced in 1999 by EIRIS (see p.246). The study examined the performance of fifteen leading ethical funds over a long period, and found that ethical investment generally involves marginally less risk, but offers marginally lower returns than conventional investment. The balance of risks and returns, it concludes, is "not materially different". In other words, you're less likely to see your savings rocket, but also less likely to see them plummet.

EIRIS's study also compared the impact of different "levels" of ethicalness. They defined five "ethical indexes", each of which excluded between one- and two- thirds of the FTSE All-Share Index; all five returned a risk–return balance "broadly similar" to the All-Share. If you're feeling really keen, you can download the 74-page study in pdf format from www.eiris.org

Some studies – such as a recent Australian survey carried out by AMP Henderson – have even suggested that ethical investments funds are actually *more* profitable than average. As SocialFunds.com reported, the survey found that ethical funds "outperformed the most relevant benchmark, the S&P/ASX 200, over the one-, two-, three-, and five-year periods, through September 30, 2003", despite under-performing in 2002.

Who does the research?

Some banks and investment funds have their own research teams, but many ethical investors trust a research service to screen companies on their behalf. The UK's largest service is **EIRIS**, the

Ethical Investment Research Service. Set up in 1983 – with the support of the Church of England, the Joseph Rowntree Trusts, Oxfam and the Society of Friends, among others – EIRIS has both commercial and charity wings, and keeps tabs on companies and oppressive governments for many institutional investors, as well as the FTSE4GOOD share indices (see p.244). The EIRIS website is a valuable resource, whether you want to find out more about responsible investing or locate an ethically minded financial adviser:

EIRIS www.eiris.org

Other organizations that provide screening research are **SIRI Group** (www.sirigroup.com), **Core Ratings** (www.coreratings.co) and **Ethical Screening** (www.ethicalscreening.com).

Who gets the money?

It is sometimes said that "ethical" banks, pension managers and investment funds do invest in corporate bastards – just slightly lesser bastards. It's certainly true that most SRI funds, while they shun arms, tobacco and the like, nonetheless invest in a list of companies that you might not exactly think of as moral trailblazers. As the box below shows, the most popular shares in ethical portfolios include major banks, supermarkets and retailers that are themselves highly criticized from some corners.

This may not bother you, but if it does, bear in mind that not all ethical policies are alike. The Triodos Bank (p.254), for example, only finances schemes and companies "which add social, environmental and cultural value" to the world; and there are investment policies out there ranging from **vegan** (avoiding all forms of animal products and testing) to **Islamic** (ruling out alcohol and money-lending firms), so there's no reason why you shouldn't find one that suits you. Ask a financial adviser for more advice (see p.269).

THE ETHICAL SHARE CHART

The following list, drawn up by EIRIS in 2002, shows the companies invested whose shares crop up in the biggest number of ethical investment funds – starting with the most popular. For more details, visit the "media" section at www.eiris.org

1 Vodafone Group
2 FirstGroup
3 National Express Group
4 Prudential
5 HBOS
6 Abbey National
7 BG Group
8 Centrica
9 ARM Holdings
10 Halma
11 The Royal Bank of Scotland Group
12 Berkeley Group
13 BT Group
14 Reuters Group
15 RPS Group
16 Nestor Healthcare Group
17 Cable and Wireless
18 mmO2
19 Northern Rock
20 CGNU
21 Electrocomponents
22 The Sage Group
23 Pearson
24 Tesco
25 Xansa
26 Reed Elsevier
27 Compass Group
28 Johnson Matthey
29 Debenhams
30 First Technology
31 Marks & Spencer Group
32 The Go-Ahead Group

BANKS & BUILDING SOCIETIES
Your savings, your landmine

The major banks have got a pretty unimpressive ethical track record, and though some have improved to a certain extent, they still leave a lot to be desired. This includes the "Big Four" – HSBC, Lloyds TSB, Barclays and Royal Bank of Scotland/NatWest – who between them account for around two-thirds of the UK current-account market.

The most common criticism they face relates to who they lend to (and offer accounts to). Barclays and HSBC, for example, have been accused by Friends of the Earth of funding illegal deforestation in Indonesia by lending to companies such as Asia Pulp and Paper. But all the Big Four have been attacked at some stage by NGOs focusing on areas such as arms exports to – and natural-resource extraction from – countries with oppressive regimes.

Some progress has been made recently in the area of unethical lending, with three of the Big Four (minus Lloyds TSB at the time of writing) having signed up for the **Equator Principles**, a set of guidelines on socially and environmentally sound financing. However, as with most voluntary schemes, campaigners claim that the "EP" framework hasn't stopped banks making irresponsible loans. For instance, in a report called *Principles, Profits, or Just PR?*, pressure group Bank Track noted that "despite the existence of the Principles, many controversial projects such as the Baku Ceyhan oil pipeline went ahead virtually unaltered while other, similarly disastrous projects, such as Sakhalin II oil project in the Russian Far East and the Nam Theun dam in Laos are lined up for financing by the EP banks". For more info, see:

Equator Principles www.equator-principles.com
Bank Track www.banktrack.org

Another high-profile issue – **third-world debts** held by Western banks – is now less pressing, as most UK banks have bowed to years

Another section of the Amazon is razed to the ground. UK banks have long been criticized for lending money to companies involved in destruction of rainforests, which are home to at least half the world's plant and animal species. Besides the collection of valuable wood, deforestation is driven by gold mining, the claiming of farmland for animal feed and palm oil, urbanization and global warming. If current rates of deforestation continue, there will be no tropical rainforest left by 2100.

of pressure to write off their debts in the poorest countries, or "swap" them for commitments that governments spend the money they would be repaying on reducing poverty in their countries.

But other problems remain. One of these is **currency speculation**, which is linked to the destabilization of developing-world economies (see box below). According to a 2002 report by War on Want, the UK's biggest currency gamblers included HSBC, Barclays and Royal Bank of Scotland/NatWest, with Lloyds TSB not too far behind. Most of the big banks also have offices in **tax havens**, which are associated with high-level tax dodging and money laundering. And, according to EIRIS (see www.eiris.org/pages/PersonalFinance/Bank.htm), most of the big names in banking have yet to make much progress in areas such

CURRENCY SPECULATION

Every day, an estimated $1–2 trillion is traded on the international currency markets. To put this figure in perspective, imagine a couple of hundred pounds for every single person on the planet, or a stack of £50 notes reaching from the earth to the moon. Some of this is related to trade and long-term investment, but the vast majority – probably at least 90% – is the speculative "**hot money**" of banks, investment funds and super-rich individuals aiming to profit from short-term changes in exchange rates. Currency speculation is nothing new, but it has grown out of all proportion in the last decade.

The problem with this potentially lucrative activity is that it can be hugely damaging to economic stability, especially for developing countries whose governments lack the financial weight to protect themselves against the speculators. There isn't space here to go into the details but, in short, when there's a speculation "run" on a particular currency, the economy of that country can be left in tatters, with a devalued currency and a messed-up banking system. It is now widely accepted, for example, that currency speculation played a major role in the recent financial crisis of East Asia, which resulted in massive job losses and increased poverty. To add insult to injury, speculators pay no tax on their winnings, even though the sums involved are massive: according to ATTAC (the Association for the Taxation of Financial Transactions for the Aid of Citizens), NatWest made £432 million from currency trading in 1998, while HSBC made £2.3 million a day from it in 1997.

drawing up regular reports on their own social and environmental standards, let alone developing a serious ethical investment code.

To cap it all, there's also a pretty strong case for saying that the big banks rip off their customers. Even the UK's Competition Commission – not known as the most zealously anti-corporate watchdog – has accused the Big Four of making too much profit, while a report commissioned by the Treasury, published in 2000, described them as holding a "complex monopoly". But then, top-executive salaries of up to £10 million a year have to come from somewhere.

Increasingly, economists and anti-poverty campaigners are calling for the "caging" of speculative money. One suggested means for doing this is the introduction of a minimal tax on all currency transactions, set at perhaps 0.1%: small enough to leave trade unaffected, but big enough to calm speculation, which relies on very marginal changes in exchange rates. According to its proponents, the would-be **Tobin Tax** – named after James Tobin, the Nobel Prize-winning economist who thought up the idea in the 1970s – could stabilize global finances, to everyone's benefit, and simultaneously raise huge sums of money that could be used to tackle global poverty. Even after the shrinking effect it would have on the currency market, it is estimated that a 0.1% tax could raise up to $300 billion each year – roughly six times the combined international aid budget. For more information, visit the War on Want campaign site (www.tobintax.org.uk) or ATTAC (www.attac.org).

Scores of NGOs and MPs have given their support for the Tobin Tax, and Canada and France have taken a lead by committing to implementing it once other countries agree. But even if it never happens – and many commentators see it as unworkable due to the practical problems of implementing any system of global taxation – consumers already have the option of switching to a bank, such as any of those recommended in this chapter, which promise not to take part in harmful speculation activities.

BANKING OPTIONS

Ethical specialists: current & savings accounts

The Co-operative Bank

www.co-operativebank.co.uk ▷ 08457 212 212

Set up in 1872 as the Loan and Deposit Department of the Co-operative Wholesale Society, the Co-operative Bank now has more than three million customer accounts and is the only UK Clearing Bank to publish an ethical investment policy, which it first did in 1992. Available at branches and at their website, the policy is largely determined through regular consultation with their customers, and addresses concerns about human rights, arms, corporate responsibility, genetic modification, social enterprise, ecological impact and animal welfare (see box opposite). A mix of negative and positive screening, it's a medium shade of green: companies that use animal tests are OK, for example, but only in the field of medicine; arms firms that export to oppressive regimes are no-go, but arms firms in general aren't explicitly ruled out. The bank also attempts to support charities and positive business ventures such as fair-trade and research into alternatives to animal testing.

Practicalities 140 branches; 170 Handybanks; pay-in and withdraw at post offices; 30,000 Link cash machines; 24-hour phone and Internet banking. Accounts offered: current, numerous savings, ISAs, business, student.

Smile

www.smile.co.uk ▷ 0870 (THE BANK) 843 2265

The UK's first Internet-only bank, Smile has been a huge success since it was launched by the Co-operative Bank in 1999. It shares the same ethical policy as its parent (see box opposite), but as it has no branches it can offer better interest rates (currently 3% on current accounts; 4% on savings). It regularly scores highest in the country in banking customer-satisfaction surveys.

Practicalities No branches; excellent Internet banking with 24-hour backup phone line; postage-free envelopes provided for cheques; pay-in/withdraw at post offices; 30,000 Link cash machines. Accounts offered: current, instant savings, ISAs, student.

THE CO-OPERATIVE BANK & SMILE ETHICAL POLICY

Following is an edited summary of the ethical policy of the Co-operative Bank and Smile at the time of writing, with crosses for those practices that the banks avoid investing in and ticks for those which they try actively to support. For a full, up-to-date version, see: www.co-operativebank.co.uk/ethics

Human rights
✗ Governments or business which fail to uphold basic human rights within their sphere of influence; businesses with "concerning links" to oppressive regimes

Arms trade
✗ Manufacture or transfer of armaments to oppressive regimes; manufacture of torture equipment or other equipment used to violate human rights

Corporate responsibility
✗ Irresponsible marketing practices in developing countries; tobacco product manufacture; currency speculation
✔ Responsible position on fair-trade; labour rights in their own operations and through their supply chains in developing countries

Genetic modification
✗ Uncontrolled release of GMOs into the environment; "terminator" technologies; patenting of indigenous knowledge; non-medical cloning

Social enterprise
✔ Charities and organisations involved in the "social enterprise" sector, including co-operatives, credit unions and community finance initiatives

Ecological impact
✗ Extraction/production of fossil fuels; environmentally persistent or harmful chemicals; unsustainable harvest of timber, fish and other natural resources
✔ Recycling; renewable energy and energy efficiency; sustainable products and services such as organic produce; the pursuit of ecological sustainability

Animal welfare
✗ Animal testing of cosmetic or household products; intensive farming; blood sports; the fur trade
✔ Development of alternatives to animal experimentation; farming methods which promote animal welfare

The Ecology Building Society

www.ecology.co.uk ▷ 0845 674 5566

Established in 1981, the Ecology is a small mutual building society whose savings accounts are only used to fund mortgages considered to be "green" (renovation projects, energy efficient construction and the like). It's perhaps the world's only financial organization that will enquire if you are a member of a green group before offering you an account. Interest rates depend on the withdrawal period and amount deposited, ranging at the time of writing from 1.5% to 3.5%.

Practicalities No branches; pay-in/withdraw by cheque or transfer. Accounts offered: instant and 60-day-notice savings accounts; Cash Mini ISA.

Ethical specialists: savings only

The Triodos Bank

www.triodos.co.uk ▷ 0500 008 720

Established in Holland in 1980, with a British office opening in 1995, the Triodos Bank is a specialist ethical savings bank with a "causes-based" approach. It only invests in "organisations which create real social, environmental and cultural value" – charities, social businesses, community projects and environmental initiatives – but it still offers good rates of interest. Triodos doesn't offer a current account, but does offer a wide range of savings accounts, from the general Positive Saver account to those focusing on investment in a more specific area: Charity, Just Housing, Earth, Organic, etc. Notice periods are 1, 30 or 90 days (you can use the savings calculator on their website to compare accounts and rates, which go up to 3.8% at the time of going to press). A model of transparency, the bank publishes a full list of all the companies and organizations it invests in.

Practicalities No branches; pay-in/withdraw by cheque or transfer. Accounts offered: ISAs, young saver, regular saver, social investor cheque, and others.

Charity Bank

www.charitybank.org ▷ 01732 520 029

Describing itself as "the world's first not-for-profit bank", Charity Bank was established in 2002 by the long-standing Charities Aid Foundation, an organization that provides credit to charities, who frequently find credit very hard to come by. The bank itself is a registered charity and their notice-period savings accounts (no current accounts are offered) are aimed at people more interested in knowing that their money is doing something useful than they are in earning huge returns. However, over and above the 2% interest on offer, customers can make a substantial savings on their tax bill by investing money for a minimum of five years. For high-rate tax payers, the bank claims, this can work out at a return equivalent to more than 8%.

Practicalities No branches; pay-in/withdraw by post. Accounts offered: various notice-period savings.

Mutual building societies

Though they don't really fit into the ethical specialists category, mutual building societies (ie those which haven't been turned into banks) are often described as a more ethical place to put your cash. After all, they don't invest in anything other than people's mortgages and, since they don't take business accounts, they don't have any dubious multinationals as customers. Most mutuals also make significant policy decisions democratically, with each saver entitled to one vote, regardless of the amount in their account.

Despite all this, mutuals generally offer very **good rates of interest** – perhaps because they're not floated on the stock exchange, so have no shareholder dividends to pay, and perhaps because their focus on service rather than profits allows them to be much more efficient (running costs rise about 35% when mutuals turn into banks, according to the Building Society Association).

Building societies that are no longer mutuals include Abbey National, Alliance and Leicester, Bradford & Bingley and Halifax. For a full list of the remaining mutuals, and for more information, visit:

Building Society Association www.bsa.org.uk

Credit unions

Credit unions are co-operative-style alternatives to the savings accounts offered by standard banks and building societies. The basic idea is that a group of people, who must be connected by a "common bond" – such as sharing a residential area, employer, occupation, trade union or church – join together to form a union. They invest their savings into a pool, from which loans can be made to union members.

Credit unions claim to offer a number of advantages – ethical and financial – over conventional savings options. On the ethical level, the unions can help tackle **financial exclusion**. Banks often refuse finance to the poorest members of society due to their having a credit history tarnished long ago, but credit unions can make a case-by-case decision on who can borrow based on their current ability to repay and savings record with the union. Furthermore, since only members can borrow, there are no loans to dodgy businesses.

On the financial level, savers can expect dividends of up to around 8% on their investment (largely because there are so few overheads to pay), and borrowers receive much better terms on their loans than a bank would offer. For example, under UK law, interest on a loan from a credit union can't be set at more than 1% a month on the reducing balance; all loans are insured, at no cost to the borrower; and there are no fees for the arrangement of a loan, or for paying it off early.

Credit unions are owned by their members and are **run democratically** within a clear legal framework – including the obligatory training of people elected as officers. They've been around since the nineteenth century, but they're becoming increasingly popular: there are now more than 35,000 unions in more than eighty countries, with a collective membership of more than 100 million people, including more than 25% of the population in the US, Canada and Australia. For more information, or to locate a credit union, visit:

British Association of Credit Unions Limited www.abcul.coop

Credit unions have made an enormous impact in the **developing world**, where rural populations live many miles from the nearest bank, and the poor have few possessions to put down as security. To read more about this, see:

World Council of Credit Unions www.woccu.org/development

CREDIT CARDS

None of the major credit card providers – such as Visa and Mastercard – are known for being particularly ethical companies, but there are a wide range of **charity**, or "affinity", credit cards available, which support causes ranging from the RSPCA and NSPCC to your local football team.

Usually, when you sign up for such a card, the bank or other issuing company will make a lump payment (often in the region of £25) to the relevant charity. After that, they'll make a small donation each time you spend a certain amount on the card – for example, 10p donated for each £50 spent.

Most of these cards have no fixed charges and offer competitive rates, so if you use a credit card, there's no reason not to sign up. Many of the high-street banks offer charity-linked cards, though you're free to choose a more ethically minded supplier – such as the **Co-operative Bank**, whose Amnesty International card has already raised more than a million pounds for the human rights organization.

PENSIONS
Responsible retirement?

It's difficult to overestimate the financial weight of pension funds. In the UK they are worth hundreds of billions of pounds and account for a huge chunk of the stock market – around a third of it, according to most estimates. As such, they have the potential to put enormous pressure on companies to improve their ethical standards.

This potential is a very long way from being fully realized, but the last decade has seen a steady rise in the number of specialist ethical pension options. And, perhaps more importantly, the new millennium has seen a huge increase in the number of "standard" pensions taking ethical factors into consideration when investing. This is largely because the Labour government passed a law in July 2000

Nice motor! Patriot missile launcher at 1997's IDEX Arms Show in Abu Dhab, United Arab Emirates. Arms firms are widely invested in, or receive loans from, UK pension funds, retail funds, insurers and banks.

obliging trustees of occupational pensions (including local government schemes) and stakeholder pensions to declare if and how "social, environmental or ethical considerations are taken into account in the selection, retention and realisation of investments". The trustees are not obliged to invest ethically, but they must at least state their position and make it available to all members in a document called a **Statement of Investment Principles** (SIP).

This is all good news, but research shows that there is still a huge gap between what pension-fund members want and what is actually happening. Perhaps there's something about pensions that makes people feel more strongly about ethical issues: according to studies carried out by EIRIS (1999) and SustainAbility (2000), the vast

IT'S THE FINDING OUT THAT COUNTS

So much of ethical consumerism comes down to information provided by the media. A good illustration of this is the pension fund for UK MPs. You might imagine that, of all people, MPs would have an idea about how the world works – including, for example, the fact that pension funds often invest in dubious businesses. However, it was only when *The Observer* newspaper specifically drew their attention to the fact that their retirement pool was being pumped into arms exporters and tobacco giants that the right honourable members took any action. Almost immediately after the article was published in 2001, MPs tabled a motion to establish an ethical pension option.

majority of people think their pension fund should operate an ethical policy, give members input into it and publish a list of companies invested in. Yet, according to surveys carried out by Friends of the Earth (2000) and Just Pensions (2002), only "a handful" display good practice when it comes to ethical investment, despite the fact that most pension managers claim to consider SRI principles.

Campaign Against the Arms Trade highlighted this fact in 2002, when they published lists showing the number of shares in defence companies owned by the major pensions schemes. NHS trusts, trade unions and nearly every local authority were all revealed to have **arms manufacturers** in their investment portfolios. More recent research from Just Pensions suggests some improvement – with 30% of fund managers making some investment decisions on ethical grounds – but there's still a very long way to go.

For more details, see:

Campaign Against the Arms Trade www.caat.org.uk
EIRIS www.eiris.co.uk
Friends of the Earth www.foe.co.uk
Just Pensions www.justpensions.org
SustainAbility www.sustainability.com

PENSION OPTIONS

If you are already pay into an **occupational** or **stakeholder** pension (see box below), you can request the SIP from your fund managers, asking for clarification if the wording is unclear or noncommittal. It may also be worth doing some research online: EIRIS surveyed the UK's top 250 pension funds in 2002/03 (their findings are available at www.eiris.org/Pages/Pensions/Pension.htm) and the studies and sites mentioned above refer to many specific funds.

Once you have the information you need, if you're not satisfied with the stance of the current scheme, **send your views** to the managers – and encourage like-minded colleagues to do the same. You may want to lobby for the introduction of a specific ethical plan, or request that social or environmental considerations are taken into

PENSION BASICS

In the UK, everyone is entitled to the basic state retirement pension. However, this offers no red carpet into retirement, so most people will want to take out a second pension to top it up. There are three main types:

Occupational pensions Offered by employers, including local government, for their employees. These generally offer the best deal, as the employer usually contributes.

Stakeholder pensions Low-charge, flexible pensions available to everyone but designed for people who are not offered an occupational pension. Since 2001, all companies with more than five employees must offer a stakeholder pension, though you can also get them direct from financial services companies, trade unions and other organizations.

Personal pensions These are bought from financial services companies, such as insurance companies, banks, investment companies and building societies. Since the emergence of stakeholder pensions, for most people there is little reason to choose a personal pension.

For more on pension types visit the government website at: www.pensionguide.gov.uk

account on the standard plan. If you want help working out what to ask and say, visit the website of EIRIS (see p.246) and download their latest *Pensions Guide*. You may also want to direct the fund managers' attention towards the research done by Just Pensions, who produce information specifically designed for pension managers and trustees interested in implementing SRI (see www.justpensions.org). If all else fails, you could ditch your employer's scheme and switch to a separate stakeholder or personal pension plan that reflects your ethical criteria. However, this may significantly reduce the amount you are able to save (you'll probably lose any employer contributions) so you'd be well advised to seek advice from a financial adviser before proceeding. See p.269 to find one.

If you have a **personal pension**, your fund isn't actually obliged to inform you of their angle on socially responsible investment. However, it is highly likely that they will be happy to reveal their position and also offer you the option of transferring to a specific ethical plan (though you may have to pay for the privilege).

If you're feeling particularly vigilant, you may also want to contact your **council**. As Martin Hogbin from Campaign Against the Arms Trade points out, council taxpayers also have the right to "question the investment policies of their local authority, as their taxes are used to top up existing pension funds".

Ethical stakeholder providers

If you want to start paying into a stakeholder or personal pension, you can buy one through a pension scheme provider, directly from a pension company, or through an independent financial adviser (IFA). You'll pay for the services of an IFA, of course, but you'll also reduce the risk of making the wrong decision. And many advisers now specialize in ethical investment (for a list turn to p.269).

Stakeholder pensions tend to be a more popular ethical option with financial advisers than personal pensions, so that's what we've listed below (for information purposes only: this is *not* financial advice). Note, however, that many ethical personal pensions are also available and, because the companies selling them are able to charge higher costs than with stakeholder pensions (and therefore can employ more research staff), they may be more suitable if you have unusually specific concerns. The following list of ethical stakeholder pension schemes was provided by the UK Social Investment Forum. For the most up-to-date version, visit www.uksif.co.uk

Clerical Medical www.clericalmedical.co.uk ▷ 0870 602 2244
Friends Provident www.friendsprovident.com ▷ 0870 607 1352
Legal & General www.landg.com/pensions ▷ 0800 027 1818
Norwich Union www.your-pension.com ▷ 0800 056 2326
NPI Stakeholder www.npi.co.uk ▷ 0870 898 6961
Scottish Equitable www.scottishequitable.co.uk ▷ 08456 100 010
Scottish Life www.scottishlife.co.uk ▷ 0131 456 7777
Scottish Widows www.scottishwidows.co.uk ▷ 0131 456 7777
Standard Life www.standardlife.co.uk ▷ 0845 606 0012

INSURANCE
Not the most enlightened of sectors

Like pension companies, insurers have huge assets – it is estimated that at any one time the industry controls roughly 10% of the world's capital flows. Technically speaking this isn't consumers' money, but to all intents and purposes insurance funds are collectively owned by their policyholders – and, since the money is widely invested, that makes taking out insurance a bit like any other form of investing.

You might expect, therefore, that there would be a range of ethical insurance schemes on offer, from companies operating screened investment policies (see p.239). This is true of the side of the industry that deals with life assurance and pensions (see above) but when it comes to the other side – the one that insures homes, contents, travel and the like – the options are surprisingly limited. Some companies claim to be committed at least to an **engagement strategy** (see p.241), but screening is still elusive in the insurance world.

The main reason for this is the interrelated structure of the industry. To be an actual insurer – rather than a small insurance firm selling policies *underwritten* by an insurer – requires an enormous amount of money. Even if you did have the required cash, you'd rely on a **re-insurer** to underwrite you, and there aren't any re-insurers with serious ethical investment policies. Also, according to some insiders in the industry, the culture of the whole sector is inherently at odds with the idea of anything beyond profits – even more so than that of other financial industries.

Quite apart from what your insurance company is investing in, another issue is who and what insurance companies are willing to cover. Indeed, since many environmentally dangerous projects wouldn't be feasible without insurance, the insurance companies collectively wield major influence over what does and doesn't go ahead. As such, they could be a force for good if they imposed industry-wide ethical standards.

In 1995, some in the industry made moves towards recognizing their responsibilities by signing up to the UN's *Statement of Environmental Commitment by the Insurance Industry,* also referred to as **UNEP III**). This focuses on sustainable development and includes the statement "we will seek to include environmental considerations in our asset management". However, as with many non-binding agreements, the document has allegedly been largely ignored by many of its signatories. Friends of the Earth's aptly named report *Capital Punishment* (2000) emphasized this, listing some of the environmentally damaging companies, mainly within the oil industry, that big-name insurers continue to invest in.

Insurance options
Despite the failings of UNEP III, it's better than nothing, so as a first step you may want to ask your insurer if they've signed up. On the

next ethical level up, a few of the big insurance firms claim to have a policy of using their power as institutional shareholders to "engage" with the companies they invest in (see p.241). Among these, the Co-operative Bank's sister organization, **CIS** (Co-operative Insurance Society), has probably the most widely respected policies. Finally, there are two specialist insurance companies committed to ethical practice or charity donations: **Naturesave** and **Animal Friends**.

CIS

www.cis.co.uk ▷ 08457 464 646

CIS have had a "Responsible Shareholder" policy – for shareholder engage-ment – for a few years, and at the time of writing it is in the middle of a massive customer consultation exercise in which policyholders are being invited to give their views about what should be in the more comprehensive ethical policy that's due in early 2005. Though some of CIS's investments have raised eyebrows in the past (for example, it used to hold a stake in Huntingdon Life Sciences, the controversial animal-testing centre), this is as ethical as the big insurers get.

Naturesave Policies

www.naturesave.co.uk ▷ 01803 864 390

This small insurance intermediary covering home, contents, travel and business, sells policies underwritten by Lloyd's of London. It claims to be deeply committed to sustainable development, and 10% of the premium made from each policy sold is put towards the Naturesave Trust, which funds environmental and conservation projects (this is taken from the profits rather than added to the policy price). The company also lobbies the insurance industry to spend money on dealing with environmental risks at their roots instead of paying out compensation once disasters happen.

Animal Friends Insurance

www.animalfriends.org.uk ▷ 0870 403 0300

A small insurance firm offering home, contents, travel, motor, pet and life, which promises to devote its profits to animal welfare charities. It also claims to try and influence the investment policies of underwriters.

MORTGAGES
When eco-warriors become eco-borrowers

Whereas it's quite clear what makes a bank or investment fund ethical (it attempts to exert an influence somewhere by selectively investing or by being an active shareholder) an "ethical mortgage" seems to mean different things to different people.

However, there are two main considerations. The first is the ethical credentials of the lender. After all, during the lifespan of a mortgage you'll potentially be handing over tens of thousands of pounds' worth of profit to whoever lent you the money in the first place. So if, for example, you don't trust the ethical standards of the major banks (see p.248), it would certainly be a logical step to avoid them for mortgages as well as for current accounts.

The second consideration relates to **interest-only** mortgages. With these, instead of paying off part of the loan and part of the interest each month, you only pay back part of the interest – the rest of your payments being used to invest in a package, such as an **endowment** or **ISA**, that at the end of a fixed term will be used to pay off the mortgage (assuming the investment grows enough). This is roughly the same as any other kind of investment, so the same ethical screening processes can be applied. Many companies now offer ethical endowments and the like; speak to a financial adviser for more information (see p.269).

Mortgages options

The standard ethical advice is to favour mutual building societies over demutualized ones and banks, since a mutual is unlikely to do anything more dodgy with your money than lend it out as mortgages. Happily, mutuals very often offer a better deal anyway, so favouring them needn't mean bigger charges or monthly payments.

One exception to the rule is the ethically renowned **Co-operative Bank**. Like those of the **Norwich & Peterborough** (also listed below), their "ethical" mortgages are really just standard mortgage packages in which the free extras are aimed at eco-conscious people. But in taking out a mortgage plan with them, you are at least supporting an ethics-led organization.

For more comprehensive information on mortgages, seek the help of a clued-up financial adviser. One company that specializes in mortgages is the **Ethical Investors Group** (listed below). For others see p.269.

Co-operative Bank

www.co-operativebank.co.uk ▷ 08457 212 212

As well as offering good rates on its CAT-standard mortgages, the Co-operative Bank, for each mortgage sold, will commit to eliminating or absorbing all the CO_2 emissions arising as a result of the average household's electricity and gas consumption. Also, along with each valuation, they'll provide a free Home Energy Rating, detailing a building's energy efficiency and potential energy- and money-savings measures.

The Ecology Building Society

www.ecology.co.uk ▷ 0845 674 5566

This small mutual building society (see p.255) lends on the grounds of the building rather than the individual, giving mortgages to fund energy-efficient housing, renovation of derelict and dilapidated properties, small-scale and ecologically driven enterprise, and "low-impact lifestyles". Many lenders refuse to touch derelict properties, but the Ecology, being small, can work one-to-one with borrowers to make sure their renovation project is financially sound. And if renovation is going well, and the building gaining value, the society may offer further funds for more improvements.

Ethical Investors Group

www.ethicalmortgage.co.uk ▷ 01242 539848

Formed in 1989, this Cheltenham-based company (which donates half of its profits to charity) offers financial advice on ethical borrowing. It has grouped mortgage lenders into five categories according to their ethical positions and promises to help you find "the very best mortgage rate from the lender that you feel most comfortable with".

Norwich & Peterborough Building Society

www.npbs.co.uk ▷ 0845 300 6727

Norwich & Peterborough, another mutual building society, offers two "environmental" mortgages. For each of their Green Mortgages sold, it will plant eight trees a year for five years, enough in theory to absorb the carbon-dioxide produced by the property, while their Brown Mortgage offers a good deal for people intending to convert or restore a building.

STOCKS, SHARES & ADVISERS
Retail funds and IFAs

There are more than fifty SRIFs – socially responsible investment funds – on offer in the UK. They run the whole gamut of ethical investment strategies to products ranging from unit trusts and OEICs to investment trusts and ISAs, and they have an estimated total value of more than £4 billion (up from a just a few hundred million pounds at the beginning of the 1990s). With so many options out there, and new players entering the market all the time, we've decided that a list of funds here would be of little use. Instead we've provided links to resources where you can find information, and a list of independent financial advisers who have experience in the ethical investment field (see p269). For basic information about how ethical investment works, turn to the beginning of this chapter.

INVESTING DIRECTLY

Occasionally, ethically focused organizations issue shares, allowing people an opportunity to invest in them directly. For example, Traidcraft and the Ethical Property Company had share issues in 2000, and CaféDirect in 2003. The only problem is that such offers only come up sporadically and aren't announced anywhere specific, so its very easy to miss the boat.

EIRIS Guide to Ethical Funds

www.eiris.org ▷ 020 7840 5703

Published by the Ethical Investment Research and Information Service (see p.246) *The Guide to Ethical Funds* contains summaries of each fund's policies and gives their top ten holdings. It can be ordered for £7.50 directly from EIRIS. You can download an extract from the guide from the website.

Ethical Investors Group

www.ethicalinvestors.com ▷ 01242 539 848

The Ethical Funds Directory on the website of this IFA group provides detailed information about the policies of UK ethical funds. The site also covers general issues about ethical finance and provides some information on mortgages, pensions and other areas.

SRI World Group

www.sriworld.com

Since the SRI World Group is based in the US, not all the information they provide is relevant to UK readers. However, the four sections of the site constitute such a massive resource – including news on global SRI developments – that it's certainly worth a visit.

Trustnet

www.trustnet.com

This massive, daily updated but free-to-access website contains information about all kinds of investment funds – ethical and otherwise. It maintains two specific ethical lists (Unit Trust & OEICs and Conventional Investment Trusts), and provides full information about each fund's performance, size, charges, etc. The ethical lists can be quite hard to find, but you should be able to go straight to them via: www.trustnet.com/help/focus.asp?ethical

UK Social Investment Forum

www.uksif.org ▷ 020 7405 0040

Established in 1991, the UK Social Investment Forum is a "membership network" for promoting socially responsible investment. Their Member

Directory provides links to nearly all the main companies and organizations involved in ethical investment, and their homepage covers recent news and developments.

INDEPENDENT FINANCIAL ADVISERS (IFAs)

An increasing number of financial advisers, or IFAs, are developing expertise in the ethical sector, so finding advice shouldn't be difficult. The following list includes the ethical specialists who are members of the UK Social Investment Forum (see above). For the most up-to-date list and full addresses, visit their website – you can also locate relevant IFAs through EIRIS. For more information about IFAs in general, contact IFAP, the UK association that promotes the profession. Their website lets you search for advisers in your area, and they can give some information about specialists in ethical matters:

UKSIF www.uksif.org ▷ 020 7405 0040
EIRIS www.eiris.org ▷ 020 7840 5703
IFAP www.ifap.org.uk ▷ 0117 971 1177

Barchester Green Investment (Salisbury)
www.barchestergreen.co.uk ▷ 01722 331 241

Bromige and Partners (East Sussex)
www.bromige.co.uk ▷ 01342 826 703

CCF Financial Services Ltd (Cambridge)
www.ccf-ifa.co.uk ▷ 01223 472 200

Crowe Money Advice (North London)
020 7485 9738

The Ethical Investment Co-operative (Darlington)
www.ethicalmoney.org ▷ 01325 267 228

Ethical Investments (Sheffield)
www.ethicalinvestments.co.uk ▷ 0114 229 5959

Ethical Investors Group (Cheltenham)
www.ethicalinvestors.com ▷ 01242 539 848

Ethical Money (Sheffield)
www.ethicalmoneyonline.com ▷ 01539 823 041

The Ethical Partnership (Eastleigh, Lincoln, Northallerton, Whitchurch and Whyteleafe)
www.the-ethical-partnership.co.uk ▷ 023 8036 1361

Ethical Plus (Surrey)
ep@dwvivian.idps.co.uk ▷ 020 8763 1717

Ethikos Independent Financial Advisers (Reading)
E23571@exchange.uk.com ▷ 0118 958 6998

Falcon Asset Management (Surrey)
www.falconasset.co.uk ▷ 01932 862 414

The GÆIA Partnership-Global & Ethical (Manchester)
www.gaeia.co.uk▷ 0161 434 4681

Helm Godfrey (Bournemouth, Chester, East Sussex, London and Norwich)
www.helmgodfrey.com ▷ 020 7614 1024

Holden Meehan (Bristol)
www.holden-meehan.co.uk ▷ 0117 925 2874

Investing Ethically (Norwich)
www.investing-ethically.co.uk ▷ 01603 661 121

Kingswood Consultants (Oxfordshire)
www.kingswoodconsultants.com ▷ 01869 252 545

Lifestyle Financial Services Ltd (Kingston upon Hull)
www.moneywells.co.uk ▷ 01482 217 234

Ivan Massow (West London)
www.massow.co.uk ▷ 020 7539 7777

Social Investment Advisers Ltd (Wolverhampton)
www.social-investment.com ▷ 01902 711 414

Towers of Taunton Ltd (Somerset)
www.towersoftaunton.co.uk ▷ 01823 423 418

Stephen Walters (Edinburgh)
smvw@onetel.net.uk ▷ 0131 556 4171

HOUSEHOLD 07

From the electricity that powers them to the hardwood furniture that adorns them, our homes involve us in all kinds of environmental and social issues. In terms of global warming (see p.330), the average UK household accounts for an estimated six tonnes of CO_2 every year – far more than the average car. And much of this is avoidable. Meanwhile, our soft furnishings, such as bedlinen, curtains or rugs, are linked to many of the same issues of poor labour conditions as clothes and shoes. This chapter takes a look around the home – and garden – and gives some ethical-shopping pointers.

HOME ENERGY
From greenhouse to green house

When we flick on a "natural light" 100-watt bulb, the first thing that comes to mind is unlikely to be a coal mine, gas field or oil rig. And yet around two-thirds of the UK's electricity – and, of course, all of our gas – is generated from these **fossil fuels**, which pose environmental problems on an altogether different scale from other products we consume.

That's your plug socket, that is. The bellowing smokestack of a fossil-fuel power station.

It's not just that fossil-fuel use is driving **global warming** – arguably the most serious issue facing humanity (see p.43) – but also that burning, extracting and processing these fuels releases a whole range of harmful chemicals. "Flaring" (burning off) waste gases, burning coal and refining oil, for example, generates huge quantities of **pollutants**, many of which – such as benzene – can accumulate in the flesh of animals and humans. Other noxious emissions include volatile organic compounds (VOCs), polycyclic aromatic hydrocarbons (PAHs) and hydrogen sulphide.

Most of the other third of our electricity comes from

"LOCAL" POWER COMPANIES

Ever since the electricity and gas markets were opened to competition in the early 1990s, we've all had the choice of switching suppliers and tariffs. One reason to do this is to save money: if you've never compared your current providers with others, it's almost certain that you're paying more than necessary. Another reason is to choose one of the ethically minded tariffs listed over the next couple of pages.

If you're thinking of switching but reluctant to change on the grounds of loyalty to your current "local" supplier, bear in mind that it's probably not that local at all. Most of the big suppliers are owned by multinationals – at the time of writing, for example, Northern Electricity is part of Mid American Energy, London Electricity is owned by Electricité de France, and Eastern and Midlands Electricity is part of Powergen (itself part of German giant E.ON AG). And, of course, multinational energy corporations aren't known as the most ethically enlightened of organizations.

nuclear power, which poses its own problems. Even though the risk of Chernobyl-style disasters is relatively low, there is still no way to dispose safely of the radioactive waste that nuclear power stations generate. This waste, most of which is currently in "temporary storage" while permanent solutions are researched, looks set to end up buried deep in solid rock, where it will remain highly dangerous for tens of thousands of years. Critics of nuclear power point out that the waste is enormously expensive to manage, poses risks to people and the environment (in the case of an accident occuring), and, in the wrong hands, could be a major security threat.

The UK is planning to phase out coal and nuclear power over the coming decades, and we're soon to exhaust our natural gas reserves, which means that, within twenty years, our electricity supply will rely on gas imports from pipelines passing across a variety of unstable Asian countries.

So what can consumers do about all of this? One option is to buy electricity from renewable sources – or even buy the equipment to generate your own. People argue about whether the UK could be entirely reliant on green sources such as wind, solar, tidal and so on. But no one doubts that the more we generate, the better. Secondly, we can try to simply use less power – something we can do surprisingly effectively with a bit of thought. The following pages reveal all.

GREEN ELECTRICITY SUPPLIERS

As a windy island surrounded by strong waves and tides, the UK has unusually strong potential in terms of renewable energy – it has as much as 40% of Europe's total "wind resource". However, right now only a few percent of our electricity comes from renewable sources, and much of that comes from the incineration of waste, which environmental groups claim is polluting and a disincentive to recycling.

These days, however, there are a wide range of **green electricity tariffs** on offer – both from major electricity suppliers and specialist companies which only deal in renewable energy. Green tariffs offer consumers a way to help support renewable energy, but they work in a few different ways – and some have a far bigger effect that others.

The basic premise of most green, "eco" or other such tariffs is that you pay a little bit more and the company supplies you with energy generated from renewable, environmentally friendly sources. Obviously, the actual flow of electrons arriving in your plug sockets won't come straight from the wind farm, but the supplier will agree to put green-generated electricity into the national grid to match all (or some, depending on the specific scheme) of the energy you buy.

But it's not quite this simple. The complication comes from the fact that recent UK law requires all electricity providers (except those in Northern Ireland) to buy a proportion of their power from renewable sources – 4% in 2004 rising each year to 10% in 2010. This is good news, but, amazingly, the companies can use the green electricity they provide to people who have specifically signed up for it to help them meet this legal obligation. So even when you go out

COMPARING UTILITY PRICES

Various websites make it quick and easy to compare your current electricity and gas charges with other suppliers and tariffs, including the various green options. All the sites are much the same, but use the one at **Switch and Give** and a donation will be made to a charity of your choice if you do decide to change supplier.

Switch and Give www.switchandgive.com

of your way to choose a tariff where the supplier agrees to "put renewable energy into the National Grid to match the amount you use", in many cases you'll simply be helping the company achieve the quota of green energy it was going to have to buy anyway. In which case you probaby wouldn't be having any effect at all on the amount of green energy being produced.

Even if your supplier buys more than the legal minimum from renewable sources, it doesn't necessarily make them more green. For each unit of renewable energy that a company buys, it gets a **certificate**; and if it buys more than the legal requirement, it can sell the extra certificates to other companies, which in turn can use them towards their own legal minimums. So the only green tariffs that directly increase renewable energy generation are those from companies that buy more than the required percentage of green power and then *keep* some of the certificates.

To complicate things further, some tariffs use some of the money from your bill to fund the building of new wind farms or renewable energy research. So, even if they are selling all their extra certificates, they may still be doing some good.

So which tariff?
It's difficult to know which green tariff is the most green. One option is to follow the advice of environmental organization Friends of the

Earth (FoE), which compares green tariffs each year. To qualify for an FoE recommendation, an electricity company must:

▷ Only sell green electricity, or produce green electricity in a large percentage of the power stations they own
▷ Buy or generate one unit of green electricity for every unit you buy, and hold on to at least some of the proof that they have done this

FoE penalizes tariffs, meanwhile, from companies that "own carbon dinosaurs – ancient and inefficient fossil fuel based power stations – or if it isn't clear how their tariff would benefit the environment".

At the time of writing, Friends of the Earth recommends only five tariffs – four in mainland Britain and one in Northern Ireland:

Eco Energy (from Northern Ireland Electricity)

www.nieenergy.co.uk ▷ 08457 643643
The issue of selling on green energy certificates doesn't apply in the case of this tariff, because Northern Ireland has no laws regarding minimum green-electricity purchasing. Annual price for typical household: £315.

Ecotricity "Old Energy Tariff"

www.ecotricity.co.uk ▷ 08000 326100
Holds on to 11% of the certificates of proof. Annual price for typical household: £246.

Good Energy – previously known as unit[e]

www.good-energy.co.uk ▷ 0845 456 1640
Holds on to 7% of the certificates. Annual price for typical household: £277.

Green Energy 100 (from Green Energy UK)

www.greenenergy.uk.com ▷ 0845 456 9550
Re-invests 50% of its profits in "renewable electricity generation projects" and holds on to 6.8% of the certificates of proof from these projects. The

first 100,000 subscribers also get the offer of becoming shareholders. Annual price for typical household: £273.

RSPB Energy (from Scottish and Southern Energy)

www.southern-electric.co.uk ▷ 0845 744 4555
Holds on to 10% of the proof certificates, and, for each customer, £30 in the first year and thereafter £5 per year is spent on environmental schemes. Annual price for average household: £250.

There are many other green tariffs, including **Juice** from NPower (www.npower.com), which is endorsed by Greenpeace and doesn't cost any more than the same company's normal electricity. Such schemes are certainly better than standard options, but judging by Friends of the Earth's criteria of holding on to certificates, the above five should be the first choice.

For more on green electricity, try these websites:

Friends of the Earth www.foe.co.uk
Green Electricity www.greenelectricity.org
Positive Power www.positivepower.co.uk

SOCIALLY EQUITABLE ELECTRICITY?

One completely different option for your power supply is an account with EquiPower, a non-profit organization which focuses on **social equity** rather than the environment. With conventional electricity suppliers, the poorest members of society end up paying the most per unit, since they don't have the means to benefit from direct debit and discount schemes. EquiPower doesn't offer such schemes, making the price consistent across all members of society. Yet because it's non-profit-making – so any money made is put to work keeping prices down rather than benefiting directors and shareholders – the price is still competitive. For more details and to see prices, see:

EquiPower www.ebico.co.uk ▷ 0845 456 0170

GAS VS ELECTRICITY

Natural gas – basically **methane** by the time we get it – is the vapour equivalent of coal and oil, formed underground by decomposing matter over millions of years. Gas extraction, processing and burning is a bit less harmful environmentally than either oil and coal, resulting in slightly less greenhouse gas and fewer poisonous gasses and particles. As such, gas **boilers**, **ovens** and other devices are generally considered more eco-friendly than the electricity-powered equivalents.

However, natural gas is still a much worse polluter and climate-change-inducer than most of the things we buy. So the greenest option is still to use electric devices powered by a green eletricity tariff (see above).

Which gas supplier?

Despite a wide range of brands, there are only a handful of large companies now supplying gas in the UK. These include **Centrica** (British Gas), **Scottish Power** (UK Power), **Electricité de France** (SEEBOARD), **E.ON** (PowerGen) and **RWE** (NPower). The first two are probably the most actively "socially responsible" of the big companies, but the only gas supplier that would make claims to being an overtly "ethical" option is EquiGas.

EquiGas

www.ebico.co.uk ▷ 0845 456 0170

As with EquiPower (see p.277), EquiGas is a non-profit scheme that aims to create a socially just delivery system in which everyone gets a fair price, and in which the economically disadvantaged don't end up paying the most.

GROW YOUR OWN POWER

If you want to put renewable power in your home on a more tangible level, there are a number of options. Most of the renewable energy sources – from wind and solar to hydro and geothermal – can be tapped into on a household level. Some of these make sense not only from an environmental perspective but also from a financial one: you'll probably save money in the long run, and there are numerous grants available to contribute to the price of installation. You may even be able to feed any extra power back into the national grid and get paid for it. For example, Npower and Good Energy (see p.276) will both pay you 5p for each kilowatt hour of electricity you generate.

That said, a system that will make you basically self-sufficient or even an "exporter" of power – such as a **decent sized solar roof** – will require a massive up-front investment and probably won't pay for itself for a good decade. Until prices come down, the most realistic and sensible option for most households interested in going green is a solar hot water system (see box below).

Systems, costs and grants

Now, more than ever, there are many grants available to UK householders who want to buy some kind of renewable energy source. These range from around 10% to 50% of the total cost. Typical prices,

---

SOLAR HOT WATER

With a solar hot water system a "**collector**" panel is placed on your roof, which focuses the sun's energy directly into your hot water system. This is not to be confused with a photovoltaic (PV) system for generating electricity (what most people tend to think of by "solar panel").

The technology is much more efficient today than it used to be, so a few thousand pounds will buy a system capable of providing up to 70% of your hot water, generally reducing your fuel bill by around a third. However, you'll probably need a **south-facing roof** without too many shadow-casting chimneys, and installation costs can rise if your roof is difficult to access.

Many companies offer solar hot water systems, among which the best-known is probably Solar Twin:

Solar Twin www.solartwin.com ▷ 01244 403 407

and the grants available, are detailed below. Note that much bigger grants – 50% of the cost, up to £100,000 – are available for community projects.

To qualify for a grant you have to purchase from a recognized installer. For more details, and lists of installers, contact **Clear Skies**. The Centre for Alternative Technology website is another good source of information about home-grown power.

Clear Skies www.clear-skies.org ▷ 08702 430 930
Centre For Alternative Technology www.cat.org.uk ▷ 01654 705 950

▷ **Solar for hot water** See box on previous page. **Typical cost:** £2000–5000. **Available grant:** £400.

▷ **Solar for electricity** Photovoltaic panels generate electricity without any moving parts or chemical emissions. According to the government, the average south-facing UK house has enough roof space to install a system capable of providing the majority of its power needs (see www.pv-uk.org.uk for more info). **Typical cost:** entirely depends on the number of panels you buy, but around £10,000–15,000 is around average for a 2kWp system, which will provide around half of typical household power consumption. **Available grant:** "fairly automatic" grants of 50% of system cost are available until 2005, as part of the government's three-year PV programme. For more details contact the Energy Saving Trust (www.est.org.uk/solar; 0800 512012).

▷ **Wind** Household wind turbines are these days near silent and also pretty efficient. The electricity can be directed either into batteries on onto the grid. **Typical cost:** £2000–5000 per kWe installed. **Available grant:** £1000 per kWe up to £5000.

▷ **Micro-hydro** systems provide a reliable and highly efficient source of power – if, that is, you happen to have a fast-flowing river at the bottom of your garden. **Costs:** vary widely depending on positioning. **Available grant:** £1000 per kWe up to £5000.

▷ **Ground source** heat pumps concentrate heat from the ground and use it to heat water. **Typical cost:** £4000–6000. **Available grant:** £1200.

▷ **Room heaters and stoves** with automated wood pellet-feed qualify for a grant whether they are used to heat water, a room or a whole house. Non-automated systems such as Agas don't count. **Typical cost:** £2000–3000. **Available grant:** £600.

▷ **Wood fuelled boilers** run on logs, wood chips and wood pellets (again, Agas don't count) qualify for a grant where they're used as the main heating system. **Typical cost:** £4500. **Available grant:** £50 per kWth up to £1500.

REDUCING YOUR HOUSEHOLD ENERGY USE

With the possible exception of those who have spent their life savings going energy self-sufficient, it pays – environmentally and financially – for us to reduce our household power consumption. After all, homes currently account for more than a quarter of the UK's fossil fuel use, and therefore also a huge chunk of our contribution to global warming and pollution.

Reducing energy use doesn't have to mean drastic lifestyle changes (though that might be ideal). After all, at present a large proportion of our household power is simply wasted, frittered away by the likes of energy-inefficient fridges, drafty windows, uninsulated hot water tanks and TVs on standby. Indeed, according to the Energy Saving Trust, the average UK household could reduce its CO_2 emissions by around two tonnes each year – that's around a third of current output – just by becoming a bit more **energy efficient**.

Other than the obvious stuff – such as not overfilling the kettle and turning off electric devices at the wall ("standby" often uses almost as much power as "on") – there are four main ways that consumers can increase their energy efficiency. Not all of these involve "ethical shopping" as such, but they warrant a mention here nonetheless…

SHOPPING FOR ENERGY EFFICIENCY

A number of energy-efficiency labels now appear on electrical goods. The main ones are:

▷ **EU Energy Label** By law, all retailers – whether shops, mail-order or online – must show the EU Energy Label on or alongside all new fridges, freezers, washers, tumble dryers, dishwashers, lamps, ovens, light bulbs and air conditioners. Each item is ranked from A (efficient) to G (inefficient) in terms of its power consumption under standard running conditions.

The label also generally contains other information – such as water usage – and how well the machine actually does what it's supposed to do ("performace"). Washing machines are usually given a three-letter rating, in the form AAB, referring to energy efficiency, wash performance and spin performance, respectively.

The EU label usually includes a measure of energy consumption per cycle or per day, measured in kWh (kilowatt hours). If you're trying to balance cost with efficiency, factor in the future savings you'll make by multiplying this kWh figure by 7 (the average price in pence of one kilowatt hour) to give the cost in pence.

These days all UK washing machines tend to be graded A–D and fridges/freezers A–C, so a "middle" rating is actually relatively low.

#1 Buying energy-efficient appliances

Kitchen appliances are our biggest power eaters. Household **fridges and freezers** alone consume more energy than the total used in running all the offices in the country. Efficient models often use less than half as much power – and the same is true of other electrical goods such as lamps and TVs. So when buying an appliance, make sure it's rated highly for energy efficiency. By law the retailer has to display EU energy-rating info, and there are various other energy labels you may come across (see box above).

▷ **Energy Efficiency Recommended** Administered by the UK's Energy Saving Trust, the Energy Efficiency Recommended Logo (EER) was developed to point customers to the most energy-efficient products on the market. It can be found on light bulbs and appliances as well as boilers, heating controls, insulation and more. The criteria are strict. For example, to bear the logo at the time of writing, fridges must be A+ or A++ (25%–45% more efficient than standard "A" models) and washing machines must be AAA. You can find endorsed products online or by phone:
www.saveenergy.co.uk/appliances/choosing.cfm ▷ 0845 727 7200

▷ **EU Ecolabel** You may occasionally see products bearing the EU Ecolabel flower, usually alongside the main EU Energy Label. This means the product has passed numerous environmental criteria, not just relating to energy efficiency but also to its expected lifespan, ease of disposability and the like. The scheme also covers everything from paints to tissues to computers, but right now very few labelled products are available in the UK. The Ecolabel criteria have been criticized as too lax by some, such as Ecover, who refuse to display the label. For more info and an online product catalogue, see:
www.eco-label.com

#2 Insulating

Almost half of heat-loss in the average home goes via the loft or walls. Most people will save around a fifth of their heating bill just by installing decent **loft insulation**, so it will pay for itself in a few years. Cavity wall insulation, though more expensive and not suitable for all walls, will have an even bigger effect. Bear in mind that some forms of insulation are more environmentally friendly than others. As a rule, those that use minerals as their raw material use more energy and chemicals in their production, and are less likely to be locally sourced, than those that use natural materials like **wool** or **flax**. The latter – though often more expensive – allow for a greater circulation of air and help to avoid the retention of toxins in a building, linked by some to "sick building syndrome" (see p.302). Draught-proofed windows and doors, meanwhile, can have a massive impact for a tiny amount of money.

#3 Choosing low-energy light bulbs

Light bulbs account for around 10–20% of our electricity usage – that's more than £1 billion each year between us – yet around 90% of the energy they use is lost in heat. Energy-efficient ones reduce wasted energy by more than 75% and they last around ten times as long. Decent ones cost £5–8 each (the cheapest ones tend to produce slightly "artificial" light), but will pay for themselves within the year on light fittings used more than around four hours a day – and each will save you some £75 in power and replacement bulbs during their lifetime. According to the BBC, if each UK household installed three of these bulbs, it would save enough electricity to power the entire country's street lights.

#4 Tweaking your heating

There are many ways to make your heating more efficient and in the process you may save a couple of hundred pounds each year. Make sure you have an **insulation jacket** on your hot water tank (if you have one); reduce the temperature of your **hot water**; make sure the heating only comes on when you want it on and are there to enjoy it; consider fitting **thermostats** so you actually get around to changing the temperature; and use thermostat **radiator valves** to control each room's temperature independently. Finally, if you're fitting a new

boiler, be sure to get a condensing model – they're usually a bit more expensive but will save you around £1000 over ten years. For more info, see: www.green-boilers.com

Grants and further information

There are various **grants** available to help pay for insulation, a more efficient boiler and even energy-efficient light bulbs, especially for people over the age of sixty. For more on these, or any other issue relating to saving energy in the home, contact the Energy Saving Trust. Or if you want advice about your home in particular, organize a home energy audit from your local Energy Efficiency Advice Centre:

Energy Saving Trust www.saveenergy.co.uk ▷ 0845 727 7200
Energy Efficiency Advice Centre 0800 512 012

CLEANING & LAUNDRY PRODUCTS
A green clean?

When it comes to cleaning and laundry, one thing worth thinking about is the energy efficiency of your machines – as discussed above. Some washers and dryers use significantly more power than others to do the same job – in the process creating unecessary greenhouse gas – and dishwashers in general use far more energy and water than good old-fashioned washing-up.

But what about the cleaning and laundry products themselves? Partly because of the ubiquity of "green" alternatives, most people already have a suspicion that there may be something slightly dodgy about conventional surface cleaners, washing-up liquids, washing powder, polishes and the like. The main issues are what's in them and who makes them – including, of course, whether or not the company in question carries out tests on animals.

The chemical question

Different categories of cleaning and laundry products are based on differents types of chemicals. Many of these chemicals are uncontroversial, but some, if environmental and consumer groups are to be believed, pose serious risks both to human health and to the environment.

The detergents that form the basis of products such as washing-up liquids are chemicals known as surfactants ("surface active agents"), which do their work by dissolving partly in water and partly in organic substances such as food and grime. Some surfactants – especially those derived from **petrochemicals** – are toxic and relatively slow to biodegrade, and the plant-derived alternatives used by the "eco" companies are less harmful. However, surfactants rarely feature on the list of the most potentially risky chemicals: at the levels used, they're not widely believed to be a serious health hazard to humans, and with water quality in the UK rivers improving all the time, not everyone is convinced they do that much damage to aquatic life.

More worrying, according to campaigners such as Greenpeace, are the additive substances used, some of which were recently classified as "chemicals of high concern" by the EU. Some of these substances, such as the **phthalates** found in certain multi-surface cleaners, are thought to pose a threat to our hormone systems, while others are known to be **carcinogenic** (cancer causing) in animals. Furthermore, some of the chemicals in question, such as the **artificial musks** widely used as fragrances in laundry powders and other cleaning products, are **bioaccumulative**, meaning they can build up in the body tissue of humans and other organisms, and be passed on through the food chain or by birth.

"Babies are born with toxic chemicals already contaminating their bodies", according to Greenpeace, while wildlife groups have raised concerns that bioaccuulative chemicals are even starting to turn up in the livers of arctic animals such as polar bears, presumably having been passed from plug holes and factories via water treatment systems to plankton, and then up the food chain via crustaceans, fishes and seals, increasing in concentration at each level. They may also pass back to other humans via the consumption of fish.

But how serious are these environmental and health risks? In most cases, we're not exactly sure. In part this is because causal links between specific chemicals and specific effects are almost impossible to prove. Whether you're talking about cancer in humans, or endocrine disruption in arctic birds, there's no simple way to isolate the effect of any single chemical.

But it's also because not a great deal of research has been done. According to *Chemicals in Products*, a recent government report from the Royal Commission on Environmental Pollution, "Society might reasonably expect that adequate assessments have been carried out on chemicals that are on the market, and that appropriate risk management strategies are in place for potentially harmful substances. This is not the case..." Hence the government has only recently set

HOUSEHOLD TOXINS: BEYOND CLEANING PRODUCTS

The debate about whether or not the chemicals found in our homes pose genuine risks to people and planet tends to focus almost exclusively on household cleaning products, paints (see p.302), and cosmetics and toiletries (see p.223). However, many of the same chemicals, and numerous others besides, are found in all kinds of household items – from carpets and computers (which may contain substances such as brominated flame retardants) to PVC shower curtains (which may contain phthalates).

Again, there's no pressing evidence to say that, in the quantities we're exposed to them, the chemicals are really that risky. But many people take the view that ethically minded shoppers should avoid any company using bioaccumulative, dangerous and poorly understood chemicals – even if just to reduce the environmental risks of producing them. If you take that view, or you simply want to minimize your exposure to the "chemicals of high concern", visit the Greenpeace Toxic Home website for a list of "green" and "red" products:

Toxic Home www.greenpeace.org.uk/Products/Toxics

out to discover the effects on people and the environment of many of the chemicals already widely used – an initiative called **REACH**. This idea is very popular with anti-chemical campaigners, but not popular with animal rights groups, since it is due to involve a huge number of animal experiments.

It's worth keeping all this in perspective. Even if the health risks of these chemicals are proven, they are almost certainly many orders of magnitude lower than the risks posed by, say, smoking – or the likelihood of having a car accident while driving. And the environmental impacts of our cleaning products are minute compared with the output of similar chemicals from the oil, gas and coal industries that power our plug sockets, cookers and cars, or the plastics industries that produce everything from our plant pots to our computer monitors.

Still, with greener alternatives to most of the potentially risky cleaners available, there is certainly a decent case for adopting the "precautionary principle" and favouring companies that have promised not to use the most worrying chemicals. This basically means favouring the **green specialists** (see below), who usually also shun animal-based products, as well as chemicals that aren't risky to humans but pose other environmental problems (one example being **phosphates**, which can encourage excessively fast plant growth and clog up water systems).

Animal testing

New ingredients for washing and cleaning products are widely tested on animals, both in the UK and elsewhere. Often this is for such useful ingredients as "optical brighteners" – chemicals added to big-brand detergents to make our whites appear more luminously white than white can be. However, unless there is a recognized alternative test, the law requires *all* relevant chemicals to be tested on animals, including those ingredients produced specifically with the aim of reducing environmental impact and toxicity. This sometimes creates a tension between "eco" product manufacturers, who are constantly looking for greener ingredients, and animal welfare groups, who think that no new ingredients should be used if they necessitate animal testing.

What to buy

The vast majority of cleaning and laundry product sales are accounted for by a handful of large companies. Here are the biggest players, and some of their most popular brands:

Colgate-Palmolive Ajax
Procter & Gamble Ariel ▷ Bold ▷ Daz ▷ Fairy ▷ Flash
Reckitt Benckiser Dettox ▷ Finish ▷ Harpic ▷ Haze ▷ Mr Sheen ▷ Vanish
SC Johnson Pledge ▷ Toilet Duck ▷ Mr Muscle
Unilever Comfort ▷ Domestos ▷ Cif ▷ Persil ▷ Radion ▷ Surf

Perhaps unsurprisingly, none of these multinationals get a clean bill of health on the grounds of chemicals, animal testing or various other measures. So how do the alternatives compare?

The best-known and most widely available "green" cleaning range is **Ecover**, which now includes scores of products, from floor cleaner to fabric softener (for the full list, see www.ecover.com). Ecover claim that "environmentally friendly detergents do not exist", but theirs are about as close as you can get, being almost entirely plant-based and excluding all the "high concern" chemicals discussed above. In 2002, the company even released their own detergent's chemical formula, so that other producers could "improve their impact on the environment". Ecover is widely available in both supermarkets and health-food shops, and often comes top in user tests of green household products.

DO GREEN CLEANERS ACTUALLY WORK?

They may be kind to baby polar bears, but are "ethical" cleaning products as mean as they are green? It depends on the individual company and product, of course, but these days the eco options are generally very good. Ecover washing-up liquids and surface cleaners, for example, work almost indistiguishably as well as the big brands, despite the washing-up liquid being forty times less toxic to aquatic life than the market leader (if Ecover's PR material is to be believed).

As for laundry, you probably *will* notice a difference in performance between the green detergents and the big brands for clothes that have oily or greasy soiling. But for day-to-day freshening up they work absolutely fine. So consider mixing and matching.

In truth, however, you can almost get by with no washing powder at all, since sweat and much other dirt is water soluble and removed perfectly well by the warm water and rotating action of a washing machine. Hence the success of products with names such as **eco-balls**, **eco-discs** or **aquaballs** (see www.aquaball.com) that claim to remove the need for detergent by "ionizing" or "magnetizing" the water. Many people swear by them, but few have tried comparing the result to using nothing at all.

Still, Ecover does have its critics. For years, the company was even on boycott lists, due to the fact that they were part-owned by **Group 4**, the private security firm criticized for violence against anti-road protestors and for its involvement in the controversial Campsfield immigration detention centre. Today that link is no longer direct – the two companies just share a significant individual investor – but Ecover continues to be unpopular with the animal-rights lobby. The company claims to be actively "against" animal experiments, and they won't use an ingredient animal-tested in the last five years. However, this kind of **"rolling cut-off date"** policy – as opposed to picking a fixed cut-off year and sticking to it – leaves open the option of Ecover using ingredients being tested on animals now or in the future. Granted, they don't necessarily make use of this option, but their quest for green-ness means they don't want to rule out a future eco-friendly ingredient just because the law means it has to be tested on animals. The same is true of **ACDO** – another popular eco-cleaner company.

If you'd rather buy products from companies with stricter animal-testing policies then look for the **Humane Household Products Standard** (HHPS) jumping rabbit logo. Like the longer-established Human Cosmetics Standard, the HHPS scheme is managed by the British Union for the Abolition of
Vivisection and can only be displayed on products made by companies that shun all products tested on animals after a *fixed* cut-off date, and which are audited to prove it.

Since the HHPS scheme is quite new, only a few companies are certified at the time of writing. These include the **Co-op** – for its own-brand cleaners and detergents – and the following two specialists. These three companies all shun the "chemicals of high concern" in their products. For a full list of certified companies, see www.buav.org

Astonish (by the Oil Refining Company)

www.astonishcleaners.com ▷ 0113 236 0036
The Astonish range includes basics such as washing-up liquid as well as cleaning products for everything from tiles and glass to upholstery and cars. Available online, via mail order, or by retailers such as Sainsbury's, Morrisons and John Lewis.

Clear Spring (by Faith Products)

www.faithinnature.co.uk ▷ 0161 764 2555
Dishwasher products, washing-up liquids, window cleaner, liquid detergent and polishes. Available in health stores, via mail order and online.

Another popular green-products company with a fixed cut-off date policy is **Bio-D** (www.biodegradable.biz ▷ 01482 229 950). At the time of going to press, it's in the process of applying for Humane Household Product Certification. Bio-D and other green.cleaners are available in many health-food stores and from green websites, such as:

Ecozone www.ecozone.co.uk
Green Shop www.greenshop.co.uk
Natural Collection www.naturalcollection.com

Back to basics

Trading in your Ajax for baking soda will be uncomfortably close to green extremism for most punters, but this kind of good old-fashioned, eco-friendly alternative works surprisingly well. As does **lemon juice** as a bleach substitute and **white-wine-vinegar solution** as a descaler and glass cleaner (though it does smell a bit). The more adventurous among the eco-minded community even swear by **tomato ketchup** (organic, of course) as a pot scrubber.

FURNITURE & DIY
Home improvements

FURNITURE, TIMBER & OTHER WOODEN THINGS

Wood is a natural, renewable, recyclable, biodegradable and non-toxic material. It's more energy efficient to produce than metal and most other materials and, in theory, if trees are planted in greater numbers than they're cut down, the timber industry can even help reduce global warming by soaking up CO_2. But, unfortunately, some of the wood we buy – whether it's used for beds, floorboards or candlesticks – comes with serious environmental and social costs. Britain still imports large amounts of wood from irreplaceable

ancient forests – which continue to be chopped down at the astonishing rate of a football-pitch-sized area every two seconds. And most
of the rest comes from quick-growth plantation forests that are also
associated with certain environmental problems.

Sumatra in your sitting room?

Next time you admire the rich, dark grain of a mahogany sleigh bed
or eye up a teak table, bear in mind that the Western demand for
tropical woods such as these has been a consistent driving force of the
clearance of the world's **rainforests**. Though this isn't the headline

Sumatran tigers, such as this cub, are the last of the Indonesian tiger subspecies.
They are now critically endangered, partly due to habitat loss caused by logging
and partly due to hunting. Only a few hundred remain alive in the wild, and many
conservationists expect them to become extinct within ten years.

issue it once was, it is still just as massive a problem, with millions of acres being cleared every year. In fact, recent surveying by the National Institute for Space Research found that forest clearance in the Amazon was actually speeding up. This isn't only due to logging – the creation of farmland for cattle feed and palm oil is another major factor, just as urbanization is causing massive deforestation in South East Asia – but logging remains a key contributor.

Such destruction is an environmental disaster. As well as exacerbating global warming and contributing to soil erosion and water pollution (since forests help purify groundwater), it threatens as much as half of the world's biodiversity. A recent peer-reviewed study led by Barry Brook of the Northern Territory University in Darwin, Australia, suggested that deforestation in South East Asia alone looks set to make one-fifth of the world's plant and animal species extinct within the next hundred years. In Indonesia, especially, species are already being lost on a daily basis, with remarkable creatures such as the **orangutan** and **Sumatran tiger** likely to be gone within the next decade or so. According to the Global Trees Campaign, eight thousand species of tree are also currently threatened with extinction.

But deforestation is not only an environmental issue, of course. It's also a human rights one. Many forest-based people have contracted diseases from loggers, and have been forced off the lands where they have always lived, but to which they don't necessarily have any formally recognized rights. From Asia to Latin America, forest-based indigenous people have even been murdered when they've refused to leave. And the wider population can also be affected if the logging – as in the recent case in Liberia – is funding a military conflict. You don't have to take the green groups' word for it either: a recent European Commission statement reported that "In some forest-rich countries, the corruption fuelled by profits from illegal logging has grown to such an extent that it is undermining the rule of law, principles of democratic governance and respect for human rights."

The UK imports around four-fifths of its wood, and when it comes

OF CUES, CASKETS AND CLARINETS

Furniture and timber are the products most widely associated with eco-friendly (and eco-unfriendly) wood. But, naturally, the same issues apply to tree-based products of all shapes, sizes and functions. For instance, Andrew Wasley recently reported in *Red Pepper* magazine that the UK imports nearly 300,000 budget **snooker cues** made "from the timber of the ramin tree – a rare species listed under the Convention on International Trade in Endangered Species (CITES) – chopped down and exported illegally from Indonesia's dwindling tropical forests".

Of the 200 trees estimated to be used in **musical instruments**, meanwhile, more than 70 are included in the World Conservation Union 2000 Red List of globally threatened trees, according to Fauna & Flora International's SoundWood programme (www.soundwood.org). Some of these so-called "tone woods" are critically endangered, including species of ebony used in several string and wind instruments (but not any longer on pianos, Stevie Wonder songs notwithstanding).

Even as we leave the earth we may not be treading lightly upon its forests, since some **coffins** are veneered or made out of tropical hardwood such as mahogany. Also widely used are chipboard and plywood, both of which commonly contain illegally sourced wood.

It's currently difficult to imagine the FSC logo (see overleaf) becoming a common sight in music shops, sports stores and funeral homes. But pressure from ethically minded consumers – even if it's only asking questions – will at least encourage importers and manufacturers to consider the issues.

As for eco-alternatives, you're unlikely to come across green cues or clarinets. But with the first generation of eco-warriors getting on a bit, there's a growing number of "alternative" coffins on the markets. These avoid not only avoid hardwood, but also MDF sides made with formaldehyde-containing glues, plastic handles and linings which give off pollution when cremated, and other such green anathemas. This will be taking things a bit too far in most people's eyes. But if you're really keen to ethically shop till you drop, so to speak, you could look into the recycled cardboard, bamboo or wicker options from companies such as:

Eco Coffins www.eco-coffin.co.uk ▷ 01162 333566
Greenfield Coffins www.greenfieldcoffins.com ▷ 01376 327074
Peace Funerals www.peacefunerals.co.uk ▷ 0800 093 0505

to rainforest varieties such as mahogany and teak, a great deal of it has been illegally sourced – that is, cut down or exported in a way that breaks the laws of the country it came from. There are no definitive figures, but Friends of the Earth estimates that 60% of the UK's tropical wood has been illegally sourced, with much of the rest being legal but not from sustainably managed forests. The timber industry disputes such claims, yet cases keep popping up which suggest that even wood specialists with ethical policies and big budgets are failing to keep their noses clean – as the Royal Family found out in 2002 when the Queen's Gallery was refurbished with wood from endangered forests in Cameroon. None of this is helped by the fact that illegally sourced wood isn't actually illegal to import and sell in the UK.

Illegally sourced wood from the West is much less common, though from the US to Scandinavia campaigners are still having to battle to save the tiny remaining areas of ancient forest. Such forests are under threat of being cleared not only for their hardwoods, but also so that their land can be used for fast-growing softwoods such as pine, from which most of our flatpack furniture and paper is made. Replacing old forests with pine forest is certainly better than slashing and burning for pastureland, but the process of uprooting the old trees gives off more CO_2, according to *The Ecologist*, than will be absorbed by the new trees in their first ten years. Furthermore, herbicides as unpleasant as napalm are often used to get the new trees to grow, and the biodiversity of the new forests is severely limited by the fact that they consist of only one or two types of tree. So "one tree planted for every one cut down" isn't necessarily as good as it sounds.

Good wood

Whether you're buying a salad bowl, a bed or a set of shelves, the only way to be sure that your wood has come from sustainably managed forests is to choose products bearing the logo of the **Forest Stewardship Council** (**FSC**). There are various sustainable wood labelling schemes out there. But many of them – such as the American Sustainable Forestry Initiative – are highly noncommittal efforts of the timber industry, and the FSC remains the only one to take seriously.

An international, independent, non-profit-making organization, the FSC was founded in 1993 after extensive consultation between "timber users, traders and representatives of environmental and human-rights organizations". It only accredits wood when it can vouch for the entire supply chain – or "**chain of custody**" – from forest to sawmill to processor. The scheme isn't without its critics: in late 2002 the Rainforest Foundation (www.rainforestfoundationuk.org) released a report entitled *Trading in Credibility*, accusing the FSC of being "seriously flawed" and "knowingly misleading the public" in terms of the gap between its image and the reality of its operations. But even if these accusations are true – and they're not widely supported – it's still by far the best scheme currently around and the only one recognized by the major environmental groups.

FSC-approved wooden objects – ranging from beds and breadbins to firewood and floorboards – isn't too difficult to come by. For a list of products and suppliers go to:

FSC Product List www.fsc-uk.info/products.asp ▷ 01686 413 916

Reclaimed wood

FSC certified wood is a good choice, but most environmentalists agree that the ideal solution is to avoid new wood whenever possible and opt instead for **reclaimed (recycled) timber**. After all, for all its recycleable credentials, wood accounts for a significant proportion of our waste: Friends of the Earth reckon that 3000 tonnes of perfectly good wood is thrown away or burnt each day just from buildings being demolished in the UK. And yet reclaimed wood is usually much better quality, as it contains less water, is less likely to contract and was usually "harvested" before the advent of super-quick-growth forests,

FURNITURE SHOPS & SUPPLIERS

The furniture market is increasingly dominated by **IKEA** (www.ikea.co.uk). A true giant, this chain has almost 200 superstores in 37 countries, and its founder, Ingvar Kamprad, recently dethroned Microsoft's Bill Gates as the world's richest person. This, along with its global-domination-style expansion policies, has earned IKEA the usual criticism from anti-corporate groups but, for a business of its size, the company has also received quite a lot of praise. Friends of the Earth have lauded its phasing out of hazardous chemicals, and WWF its commitment to eco-friendly wood sourcing. On the latter issue, IKEA has a long-term plan to only sell wood from certified forests (FSC is currently the only certifier it recognizes). But for now, it only buys some FSC wood and, annoyingly, the label is not displayed on products, since the managers "want the IKEA brand itself to stand as a guarantee of genuine concern for the environment and social responsibility". Still, the company claims to ensure that even its non-FSC-approved woods don't come from intact natural forests, and its code of conduct also covers human and worker rights in supplier factories. Recent research by SOMO (www.somo.nl) suggests that, as usual, breaches to this code are not uncommon. But compared with other companies of its size, IKEA doesn't fare too badly.

The big household/DIY centres such as **B&Q** (www.diy.com) and **Homebase** (www.homebase.co.uk) also both sell FSC-certified furniture. B&Q, especially, is one of the most progressive big firms in the UK. It has a near-faultless timber sourcing policy as well as codes of conduct on everything from employment practices to the selling of environmentally problematic peat (see p.312). It has even worked with fair-trade groups in India.

At the other end of the scale, under the large "Code of Conduct" heading at the website of that other household/furniture giant, **Argos**, the only thing on offer at the time of writing is the assurance that the company subscribes "to the British Retail Consortium Best Practice Code on Extended Warranties on Electrical Goods". So forget the Sumatran tiger, or migrant Chinese labourers losing limbs in factory machines: you can sleep soundly knowing you'll be ethically treated when it comes to selling you a three-year TV warranty!

If you'd rather support a small, independent furniture company than risk your sanity and/or marriage in a Greenland-sized out-of-town warehouse, you could investigate some of the numerous "eco-furniture" specialists around. They generally produce very high quality, though not inexpensive, pieces. A few are **accredited by the FSC**, such as:

Anna Childs and John Thatcher Furniture, Yorkshire
0114 249 8222

Avad, Yorkshire
0114 249 3695

High Weald Furniture, East Sussex
www.the-green-oak.co.uk ▷ 01435 810 402

Minety, Swindon
01793 486 762

Pendlewood, Salford
www.pendlewood.com ▷ 0161 789 4441

Others aren't actually FSC-approved but claim to be eco-minded:

Eco Furniture, Devon
www.ecofurniture.co.uk ▷ 01237 431 849

Trannon, Wiltshire
www.trannon.com ▷ 01722 744 577

Wood School, Scottish Borders
www.woodschool.ltd.uk ▷ 01835 830 740

And, though they're fewer and further between, there are some furniture makers who only work with **reclaimed wood**. Browse the list at the WasteBook (www.recycle.mcmail.com/furnrec.htm) or try:

Arbor Vetum, Gloucestershire
www.arborvetum.co.uk ▷ 01386 840 438

Reclaimed-Pine-Online, Dorset
www.reclaimed-pine-online.co.uk ▷ 01202 573 676

Reel Furniture, Norwich
www.reelfurniture.co.uk ▷ 01603 629 396

which are better at growing fast than delivering really fine woods.

The **Reclaimed Building Supply** will help you find local suppliers of reclaimed timber and other products. Also check out the amazing **Salvo** website – which has classifieds for everything from reclaimed floorboards to staircases and cinema seats – and the relevant page of the **WasteBook** site.

Reclaimed Building Supply www.reclaimbuildingsupply.com ▷ 01883 346 432
Salvo www.salvo.co.uk
The WasteBook www.recycle.mcmail.com/furnrec.htm

Or for in-depth information about reclaimed timber, try:

Timber Recycling Centre www.recycle-it.org

Or if buying new, uncertified wood...

If buying FSC-certified or reclaimed wood isn't an option, at the very least avoid tropical hardwood such as **mahogany**, **teak**, **redwood**, **rosewood** and **ebony** wherever possible. Such products won't *necessarily* have been logged from virgin rainforests, but it's not unlikely. Also try to avoid suppliers that can't tell you about the origins of their woods.

For more information about the specific woods and the issues they raise, see the **Friends of the Earth website**, or order their book, *The Good Wood Guide*.

Friends of the Earth www.foe.co.uk ▷ 020 7490 1555

To read more about "chainsaw criminals" visit Forests Monitor, or, for the industry's perspective, see the site of the Timber Trade Federation. Good rainforest primers and more links can be found at RainforestWeb or Forest Conservation Portal.

Forests Monitor www.forestsmonitor.org
Timber Trade Federation www.ttf.co.uk
RainforestWeb www.rainforestweb.org
Forest Conservation Portal www.forests.org

BAMBOO

Bamboo is something of a wonder crop. The central building material of East Asia since time immemorial, it has also served as everything from a foodstuff to jewellery. And today it is hailed by some as the future green alternative to hardwood. It's very strong, and yet doesn't contract as much as wood, and with modern processing it can even be used for "wooden" flooring. It grows incredibly fast – some species can manage two feet in their first day – making it completely sustainable to grow in large quantities, unlike many hardwoods.

Significantly, the way that bamboo grows means that when the plant is harvested it isn't killed: it simply grows back up from where you cut it, so the roots remain in place and the soil isn't damaged or washed away. Furthermore, bamboo doesn't require lots of pesticides, can grow nearly anywhere and is even thought to be capable of sucking pollutants *out* of the water cycle. So, while there's no reason to believe that bamboo furniture and other products have been ethically sourced or made in decent working conditions, the material itself would clearly be a contender for the world's most sustainable hardwood. Were it not for the fact, of course, that it's actually a type of grass.

PAINTS & DIY OTHER PRODUCTS

Many people dutifully buy their eco washing-up liquid, but don't consider environmental issues when shopping for DIY products such as **paint** and **paint stripper, brush cleaner, wood stains** and **preservatives, glues** and **varnishes**. This is a touch ironic, since many of these products, which are mostly derived from non-degradable petrochemicals, are on a different level of eco-unfriendliness from washing-up liquids and laundry detergents.

One issue is that many paints, varnishes and solvents – both in their manufacture and application – release **volatile organic compounds** (VOCs) into the air, leading to the creation of polluting ground-level ozone, among other things. The EU is currently in the process of tightening up the laws about VOCs, and most big paint manufacturers now specify the VOC level on their tins. This development has been widely welcomed, but it doesn't deal with the heavy metals, solvents and other controversial chemicals used in many paints and their DIY products. From dyes to plasticizers, many of these ingredients are fat-soluble, and therefore prone to accumulating in our bodies (and those of animals, being passed up the food chain from low-level aquatic life to fish, birds and mammals). Not all of these are known to be harmful, but some are toxic or carcinogenic.

As with all household chemicals, the direct **health risks** to humans of occasional exposure to DIY products are mostly unproven – and likely to be extremely small. But longer-term use does seem to be harmful. In 1989, for example, the International Agency for Research on Cancer concluded that "occupational exposure as a painter is carcinogenic". Furthermore, paints and varnishes can continue to emit fumes once they're on the door frame or table, and this is thought to be a contributor to sick building syndrome (SBS) – headaches and other health effects which seem to be brought on by a specific building. Though this all sounds a bit New Agey, SBS is an all too real malaise, and has been formally recognized by the World Health Organization since 1982.

As for the effect on the **wider environment**, the amount of VOCs, bioaccumulative toxins and otherwise problematic chemicals released into the atmosphere at the time of application is relatively small with most DIY products. That is, as long as you don't pour any down the sink (instead, give any unwanted half-full paint tins to charity via www.communityrepaint.org.uk). But the manufacture of a litre of paint can create ten or more litres of toxic waste – which, considering that the UK gets through a few hundred million litres of paint each year, adds up to pretty staggering total. And paint factories emit a whole range of noxious fumes into the air.

Still, as ever, it's worth keeping this in perspective: most of us account for the release of far greater quantities of problematic chemicals through our cars than we do through our DIY.

Greener DIY products

Due to a gradually increasing awareness of all these issues, an ever-growing range of greener DIY products is available, including a wide selection of paints and some varnishes, strippers, waxes, stains and other related products. The main producers are:

Auro Organic www.auroorganic.co.uk ▷ 01799 543 077
ECOS www.ecospaints.com ▷ 01539 732 866
Ecotec Paints www.natural-building.co.uk ▷ 01491 638 911
Livos www.livos.demon.co.uk ▷ 01952 883 288
Nutshell Natural Paints www.nutshellpaints.com ▷ 01364 73801
OSMO www.osmouk.com ▷ 01296 481 220

Alternative paints tend to impose a slightly smaller ecological burden on the world. They also give you a chance to avoid the major paint firms, whose parent companies includes such controversial über-polluters as ICI (which owns **Dulux**). However, "eco" paints themselves vary widely, from those which include synthetic chemicals but no solvents – such as **ECOS** – to more comprehensively "natural" products such as **Auro Organic**. In general, the greener the product, the more expensive it is and the smaller the colour choice (especially for bright colours).

You can get prices, order colour charts and buy online from most of the above suppliers, but for advice you might be better contacting a specialist store, such as:

Construction Resources, London
www.ecoconstruct.com ▷ 020 450 2211

Eco Merchant, Kent
www.ecomerchant.co.uk ▷ 01795 530 130

Green Building Store, West Yorkshire
www.greenbuildingstore.co.uk ▷ 01484 854 898

The Green Shop, Gloucestershire
www.greenshop.co.uk ▷ 01452 770 629

Natural Building Technology, Buckinghamshire
www.natural-building.co.uk ▷ 01491 638 911

GREEN CONSTRUCTION

If you're planning a serious green building project, three of the top firms in eco-friendly building design are:

BBM Sustainable Design, East Sussex
www.bbm-architects.co.uk ▷ 01273 480 533

Gaia Architects, Scotland
www.gaiagroup.org ▷ 0131 557 9191

Bill Dunster Architects, Surrey
www.zedfactory.com ▷ 020 8484 1380

For more info, as well as inspiration, tips, links and books, visit:

Environmental Building News www.buildinggreen.com
The Centre for Alternative Technology www.cat.org.uk
Association for Environment-Conscious Building www.aecb.net

If you'd rather stick to your home-town DIY centre, then try to favour **B&Q**, which, as already mentioned (see p.298), is exceptionally progressive for its size.

For some products, though, there's no particularly green equivalent. For example, the Association for Environment-Conscious Building recommends avoiding wood preservative altogether. If it must be used, they claim, **boron** is the best option (it's available from Auro and Livos, both listed above).

SOFT FURNISHINGS & HOMEWARE
Ethical decor

RUGS & CARPETS

Most of the rugs and carpets we buy are machine-made in the West. About the only ethical problem that anyone has with these is that some of them contain benzene-based flame retardants and other "chemicals of high concern", despite the fact that less potentially harmful alternatives are available. At the time of writing, Greenpeace recommends avoiding carpets by **Axminster** and **Stoddard** on chemical grounds, and recommends **Cavalier** and **Ulster**.

More contentious are the high-quality "exotic" rugs that we traditionally associate with the Middle East, but which are just as commonly made in the Indian Subcontinent. These are usually **hand-knotted** and, with as many as 250,000 knots per square metre, each rug is the result of months of painstaking work.

Carpet making is a venerable tradition that employs millions of poor workers from South Asia to North Africa. However, the sector has become increasingly tarnished by allegations of widespread child labour – including "forced" or "bonded" child labour, with kids being used to pay off debts in conditions roughly equivalent to imprisonment or slavery.

Child workers (sometimes said to be favoured for their small fingers) are found throughout much of the rug-producing world, but there are no accurate figures of exactly how many they are in each country, and how many of them are in forced-labour positions (as opposed to supporting their families, perhaps even in between schooling hours). It seems, though, that the problem is particularly acute in **South Asia**, which saw a boom in carpet production from the 1970s, after a crackdown on child labour in Iran. Figures vary widely but it is thought that as many as one million children may be working in the carpet industry in India, Pakistan and Nepal alone.

RUGMARK and fair-trade carpets

As is always the case with child labour, the question of how to solve the problems of the South Asian carpet industry is a thorny one. It goes without saying that a complete solution is going to require the political will of the governments in each country. But what can consumers do?

One option is only to buy rugs bearing the **RUGMARK** label, which identifies carpets made without the use of child labour. Set up in 1994 by a collection of human rights organizations, exporting companies, UNICEF and other bodies, the scheme also guarantees that a proportion of the price for a rug goes towards providing an education

for former child weavers that its inspectors have discovered. RUG-MARK currently only covers India, Pakistan and Nepal, but there are plans to extend it to other countries, such as Afghanistan, Turkey and Morocco, if and when funding permits it.

To put the label on their carpets a company has to agree to anti-child-labour policies and allow random inspection of their premises, both by RUGMARK inspectors and other non-profit child-welfare organizations. And to protect against counterfeit, each carpet is individually numbered, allowing it to be traced back to the specific loom on which it was made. RUGMARK accredits around fifteen percent of registered Indian looms and its inspectors have "rescued" more than 2500 children, nearly all of whom have received education at RUGMARK schools.

Some RUGMARK lines can be found in most of the major carpet retailers in the UK, but **B&Q** and **Co-op Homemaker** have committed to stocking RUGMARK exclusively. Full a list of retailers and more information about the scheme, see:

RUGMARK www.rugmark.org

Not everyone approves of RUGMARK, however. Some carpet producers and exporters have claimed that the labelling organization has exaggerated the extent of bonded child labour, and that by publicizing child labour it has reduced the demand for all South Asian rugs, hence hurting the industry's millions of workers, most of whom already live in extreme poverty. Such critics also point out that no labelling system can genuinely ensure "child-labour free", and that it's irresponsible to make such claims. For more on the resentment felt towards RUGMARK by some in the Indian carpet industry, see Mark Tully's recent book, *India In Slow Motion* (Penguin).

On the other hand, RUGMARK has also been criticized for not going far enough – or at least getting its priorities mixed up – since it focuses on illegal child labour rather than the wider social issues that create it. To be fair, RUGMARK does work alongside ethical trade organizations and their inspectors try to keep an eye on wages and health and safety. But it's true that it doesn't claim to be labelling "fair-trade" rugs, as such. For a more comprehensive fair-trade approach, check out the following:

SOFT FURNISHINGS & HOMEWARE

Mala Carpets

www.malacarpets.co.uk ▷ 01904 786 880 ▷ 64–68 Low Petergate, York

Mala Carpets is a BAFTS fair-trade shop (see p.349) that sells classic, high-quality Indian carpets produced by Mela Handicrafts. This non-profit project aims to create a pragmatic solution to child labour, seeking out working children in remote Indian villages and giving them "a three-year non-formal education course, designed adopting Gandhian principles", without restricting their use of non-school time "to relieve their poverty" (ie working).

The organization really knows its product. The rugs, which range in price from around £100 to £3000, come with a lifetime guarantee and you can rest assured that "60- to 100-count wool" is used "where higher definition is needed", and that "the warps will mostly be strong cotton with two wefts". Phew! Shop online, at the store in York, or through the Third World Craft Centre (01202 849898 ▷ 8 Crown Mead, Wimborne, Dorset) and Adam Flude Rugs (01243 786333 ▷ 28 North Street, Chichester).

One Village

www.onevillage.co.uk ▷ 0845 4584 7070 ▷ On the A44 in Woodstock, nr Oxford

If you're after something less expensive, check out the rugs and other floor coverings from "alternative trading organisation" One Village (another member of the British Associate For Fair Trade Shops). Instead of expensive hand-knotted carpets, they offer a range that includes soft, unbleached cotton rugs from the Ganges region and tough coir mats from a village co-operative society in Kerala.

OTHER HOMEWARE – FROM BEDDING TO BOWLS

We increasingly buy our homeware, such as linen, cushions, kitchen-ware and ornaments, from a few giant companies such as IKEA and Argos (see p.298). But there are now quite a few "ethical specialists" in this field. As with clothes, these companies fall into two categories: the **fair-traders**, who buy direct from marginalized small-scale producer groups in the developing world; and the **greens**, who attempt to be "non-exploitative" but focus primarily on organic fabrics and other eco-friendly materials.

The following all sell online and/or mail order, but you could also check out your nearest Fairtrade shop – see the list on p.352. And if you have a penchant for fairly traded homeware, ornaments and the like, consider subscribing to *New Consumer* magazine (see p.362).

Fair-trade

Earth Squared

www.earthsquared.com ▷ 0131 556 0987 ▷ 1st floor, Ocean Terminal, Ocean Drive, Leith, Edinburgh

Earth Squared, who describe themselves as a fair-trade outfit, offer a small but chic and pricey range of household items on their website. This includes Indonesian Bamboo-resin mirrors (£80–130), the very plush "Chocolate Brown Velvet Quilt with cappuchino coloured silk backing" from Vietnam (£160) and silk taffeta cushions (£24).

Ganesha

www.ganesha.co.uk ▷ 020 7928 3444 ▷ 3 Gabriel's Wharf, 56 Upper Ground, London

A member of BAFTS (see p.349), Ganesha have a range of nicely designed homeware. Transform your sofa with a cotton handloom throw (£35 from a weavers' co-operative in West Bengal) and a couple of "retro chintz printed" silk cushion covers (£20 from an IFAT member in South India). They also stock drapes, placemats, beautiful bamboo bowls and more.

One Village

www.onevillage.co.uk ▷ 0845 4584 7070 ▷ On the A44 in Woodstock, nr Oxford

One Village (another BAFTS member; see p.349) offers a massive selection of good-value "functional interior products". Once you get used to the website's intimidatingly big and confusing pages, you'll find everything from hand-thrown *ökopots* (glazed terracotta tableware) and salad bowls made of mango wood (not-FSC certified but apparently from sustainably managed orchards) to Filipino bamboo lampshades and Xmas decorations.

Eco/organic

Green Fibres

www.greenfibres.com ▷ 01803 868001 ▷ 99 High Street, Totnes, Devon

Bedroom and bathroom linen, as well as duvets and mattresses, in organic and eco-friendly textiles. The range is impressive but prices aren't low. Organic bed sheets, for example, come in cotton classic, cotton poplin, cotton/organic or cotton flannel, ranging from £25 to £45. Organic mattresses are for serious green shoppers only, starting at around £500.

Natural Collection

www.naturalcollection.com ▷ 0870 331 3335

Selling online or via a catalogue, the Natural Collection offer a wide range of eco-friendly goods (or, in their rather wordy terms, "eclectic, unusual, useful and interesting products carefully chosen to inspire ideas towards a sustainable future"). The household selection includes everything from organic bedding and towels to FSC-approved wooden furnishings and a log maker (£30), which will turn yesterday's newspaper into brick-shaped "pulp log" capable of burning for an hour.

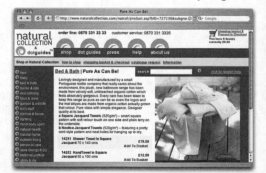

CUT FLOWERS

The overwhelming majority of our cut flowers are imported. Some come from **Holland**, but we also import massive quantities from further afield, in particular from **Kenya**, **Israel** and **Colombia**. This raises a whole mix of environmental and social concerns. On the environmental side, there's the fact that flowers (due to their short shelf life) are usually **air-freighted** into the UK, with the global-warming impact that implies. Furthermore, the demand for cosmetic perfection of the blooms means that huge quantities of **pesticides** are used in their production. This is not only an environmental issue but also a labour one, since these chemicals can be dangerous to workers when not carefully regulated. According to the US-based International Labour Rights Fund (www.laborrights.org), flower workers in Colombia and Ecuador are exposed to up to some hundred different agrochemicals (some of them extremely toxic, and banned elsewhere in the world), and one in five suffers from work-related health problems – from nausea to congenital malformations in their offspring.

In Kenya, meanwhile, the industry has provided much needed jobs and most of the suppliers are governed by codes of conduct (such as those demanded by the UK supermarkets which are members of the **Ethical Trading Initiative** – see p.68). However, according to the Kenya Human Rights Commission, many of the workers earn less than one dollar per day, have poor health and safety conditions, little collective bargaining power and no job security. The industry is also accused of seriously burdening **local water sources**. As for Israel, that's another can of worms, of course, since the country's activities in the Occupied Territories put it near the top of most lists of oppressive regimes.

A few specialist food shops and box schemes now offer "ecologically sound" – even organic – UK-grown flowers. These have environmental advantages, but, as ever, boycotting those from the poor world is likely to cause more harm than good for those people who rely on the sector for work. In the future, we may start to see a decent range of flowers bearing the **Fairtrade Mark**. The first – roses from Kenya – were introduced by Tesco in time for Valentine's Day 2004. And a new Dutch labelling scheme called **FFP** (Fair Flowers & Plants) may reach the UK in 2005.

In the mean time, about all that shoppers can do is to raise questions of labour and environmental standards with retailers. This can only serve to encourage improvements on every link of the supply chain.

GARDENING PRODUCTS
Even greener fingers

With so much agricultural land being given over to mono-crop industrial farming, some commentators hope that gardeners could be the saviours of British **biodiversity**. But certain garden products can have the opposite effect, causing harm to the environment either through their toxic contents or their extraction from the earth. Following is a quick look at the most pressing issues.

Pests and weeds

As the abundant health warnings on the packets attest, many garden **insecticides** and **herbicides** contain some seriously nasty substances. Many of these hit not only the target species, but also poison birds and other wildlife, and pollute local water systems. As with many household chemicals, they're also likely to be the result of polluting manufacturing.

Just as with farming, however, pest and weed killers can easily be avoided with a bit of effort. For weeds, this generally means getting down and dirty and pulling them out by hand. But with pests, there are all sorts of techniques, from encouraging **predators** such as birds and ladybirds to **companion planting** (strategically using one plant to attract – or repel – the pests of another). For more information on chemical-free gardening, see the website of the HDRA (Henry Doubleday Research Association), or, for supplies, go straight to their catalogue/online store.

HDRA www.hdra.org.uk
Organic Catalogue www.organiccatalog.com ▷ 01932 253 6660

Compost: the peat problem

Of the various garden products collected at cost to the environment, the worst is **peat**, which is the basis of much of the compost on sale in garden centres and elsewhere. The problem is that harvesting peat means draining and digging up irreplaceable **peatland bogs**, which are home to a wide range of increasingly rare plant and animal species (and which also serve a valuable role in stabilizing ground-water levels). According to a 2003 report from two environmental groups – the World Wildlife Fund and Traffic (www.traffic.org) – around 2000 hectares of peatland bogs are dug up in Ireland each year, mainly to supply British gardeners.

The advice of all the green groups is to only buy compost specifically labelled as peat-free (which is just as good, and makes use of sustainable alternatives such as **coir peat**, a biodegradable by-product of the coconut industry). Peat-free compost isn't difficult to find in the big home-improvement centres such as B&Q and Homebase, both of which have decent peat-sourcing policies. However, it might be trickier in specialist garden centres, which came bottom of the list in a recent survey, conducted by the RSPB, of how successfully peat is being phased out.

Alternatively, **make your own compost**. Waste food now makes up around a quarter of what we throw out. A standard or **worm** composter will let you turn much of this into something usable, rather than just bagging it up and having it stuck in a landfill. They're available in all big garden centres, as well as via the Organic Catalogue (see opposite).

More garden tips:

▷ Look out for the Forest Stewardship Council logo (see p.297) when buying **wooden garden furniture**.

▷ Avoid "water-worn", "Irish" or "weathered" **limestone**. Limestone "pavements" – outcrops of rocks that have been weathered into "paving blocks" – support rare plants and wildlife, but most of those in the UK have been removed, carved up and made into rockeries and water features.

▷ Favour garden centres which either cultivate their own plants and flowers or are sure where their stocks came from. Legal records suggest that the **illegal collection of bulbs** from British woodlands is a growing problem, Traffic and the WWF recently reported. This problem relates primarily to bluebells and snowdrops.

▷ For low-carbon outdoor lighting, check out the sun-powered options, such as the **Nautical Solar Garden Light**, available for £55 from Natural Collection (www.naturalcollection.com ▷ 0870 331 3333).

▷ For lounging around in your eco-friendly garden, bag yourself a **fair-trade hammock**. Tumi (www.tumi.co.uk ▷ 01225 446 025) sell a selection of colourful numbers from Mexico, or for £74 you could invest in a South Indian canvas hammock (pictured) from One Village (www.onevillage.co.uk ▷ 0845 4584 7070). Apparently it's "the Rolls-Royce of hammocks", no less, and "the best you can buy, for extreme comfort and delight".

The fabulous
fabric hammock™
from One Village

08
TRANSPORT & TRAVEL

Both at home and abroad, we travel further today than ever before. According to the Department for Transport, every year we manage on average 7000 miles each within Great Britain, most of them by car. And, as the price of air travel drops, we also leave the country with growing frequency: Brits take foreign holidays around 250% more often than we did just twenty years ago. The main ethical issues surrounding all this extra movement are the environmental impacts – global warming, most pressingly – and the effects of our tourism on the countries we visit. This chapter takes a brief looks at these and other topics that relate to our cars, fuels, air travel and holidays, examining the ethical options in each case.

CARS & FUEL
What are you driving?

You might wonder why cars and their fuel are even in this book, assuming them to be a lost cause. Our motors account for around a fifth of the UK's greenhouse gases, contributing to the **climate change** which is already causing massive environmental and human problems (p.43). On average, each car produces its own weight in CO_2 for every 6000 miles driven. And their emissions also include a cocktail of carcinogens and otherwise **noxious fumes** which, according to the government, are largely responsible for the airborne pollution that causes around 25,000 premature deaths and as many hospitalizations each year in the UK alone.

Road accidents, of course, are responsible for thousands more deaths and hundreds of thousands of injuries annually, as well as costing the economy tens of billions of pounds. More Brits have died on roads since 1945 than were killed in World War II – and many of the victims have been children, pedestrians, cyclists and other non-drivers. You can, alarmingly, watch the human and financial costs increasing in real time at:

Accident Count www.uk-roadsafety.co.uk/Rs_Documents/accident_count.htm

And that's not all. New roads eat ever further into the countryside and consume huge amounts of resources; buying petrol supports the famously ruthless activities of oil companies and **countless oppressive** governments; and many of the big car manufacturers have highly questionable records on everything from political donations to workers' rights.

But despite all this, for as long as we continue to use cars, writing them off entirely as an ethical no-go zone may be counterproductive. All cars consume energy, but some are far more efficient than others. All petrol will cause climate change, but a more ethical oil industry could have an enormous impact on the human rights and wealth of millions of people. This section takes a quick look at moral and not-so-moral choices you may come across when shopping for petrol, cars and breakdown organizations.

PETROL & DIESEL

Oil is responsible for much of the West's present-day wealth, powering not only our transport system but also the machines behind modern agriculture and countless other production processes. But its benefits have often not come cheap. Black gold, as it's known, has been responsible for the suffering of millions who have been evicted from their land to make way for drilling, or forced to live under murderous oil-funded regimes. As Christian Aid has observed, oil-dependent poor countries have an unusually high incidence of poverty, corruption, war and unrepresentative government.

Oil has also hit the environment hard, not just in terms of climate change (to which it is the single most important contributor) but also via spills, deforestation for drilling and other types of destruction. And, of course, oil continues to be the driving force behind international **conflict**, both figuratively and literally (at the height of the 2003 Iraq war, Western troops were estimated to be using more oil each day than the entire Indian population of more than one billion).

While it would be absurd to suggest that the giant petroleum firms are solely responsible for these problems – corrupt governments and unconcerned Western consumers deserve large slices of the blame – the big firms do have a pretty shocking history of ignoring human rights, supporting oppressive regimes, damaging the environment, denying climate change and funding pro-oil politicians. For a worrying insight into the politics of the present-day oil industry, see:

Centre for Public Integrity www.public-i.org/oil

Recently, however, some of the major oil firms have tried to clean up their image, and while their ethical claims should not be taken at face value, there is a strong case for shopping selectively.

The Esso Boycott

At the time of writing, **Esso**, as part of the Texan-based energy giant **ExxonMobil**, is the subject of a major consumer boycott, supported by mainstream groups such as Greenpeace and Friends of the Earth. The company's record on human rights and oil spills is certainly not pretty, but the impetus behind the boycott is global warming.

Exxon's detractors claim that while most of its competitors have made at least some efforts to address the issue, the world's biggest oil company has done everything possible to persuade people in power that human-induced climate change isn't worth worrying about. This has involved, according to the StopEsso campaign, a "multimillion-dollar, ten-year campaign of dirty tricks" that has had a real influence

Body artist Rick Mills (right) taking a stand against "E$$o" in Trowbridge, Wiltshire, May 2002

on US, and even Russian, global-warming policy. These "tricks" have included massive political donations – Exxon employees donated more than $1 million to Bush's Republicans for the 2000 election campaign, according to their own figures – and the funding of various ultra-conservative climate-change-sceptic **think-tanks** and **lobby groups**.

It would certainly be an exaggeration to say that Exxon was solely responsible for the US abandoning the Kyoto treaty – which at the time faced widespread cross-party opposition among American politicians. But it seems undeniable that Exxon has aided the Republican government in its playing down of global warming. For instance, in the autumn of 2003 (within days of World Health Organization scientists suggesting that 160,000 people already die each year from climate change), leaked emails and documents showed that the Bush administration had sought the help of an Exxon-funded thinktank – the **Competitive Enterprise Institute** – to try and undermine and dilute the predictions of its own government scientists.

While it is still openly anti-Kyoto, Exxon now officially recognizes the climate-change issue and has made some investment in alternative energy. But critics claim that it continues to spend millions on lobbying via a whole range of groups to ensure that no restrictions are placed on the market for fossil fuels, whatever the human and environmental costs. For both sides of the debate, see:

Esso www.esso.co.uk
StopEsso www.stopesso.com

PETROL FROM SUPERMARKETS

The supermarkets now account for a very large chunk of UK petrol sales, but, as you probably guessed, they're not in the business of oil extraction and refining. Instead, they buy from a range of oil companies. All the major supermarkets have claimed they're not supplied by Esso, according to the StopEsso campaign.

BP & Shell – greener or greenwashed?

Unlike Esso, who have until recently seemed relatively unconcerned about being seen as a global villain, other Big Oil companies have spent millions trying to redefine themselves as trailblazers of corporate social responsibility. **BP** (part of BP Amoco) has very much led this trend – swapping its shield logo for a green and yellow flower/sun and deciding that its initials now stand for "Beyond Petroleum". **Shell** (of Royal Dutch/Shell) has followed close behind with numerous CSR initiatives, keen to bury associations with Ken Saro-Wiwa and other anti-Shell campaigners who were executed in Nigeria in the mid-1990s.

Both companies still spend much of their time involved in highly controversial projects. Since "going green", for example, BP has been condemned by leading groups such as Amnesty International for trying to create a "human-rights-free corridor" as part of its **Baku–Tbilisi–Ceyhan** pipeline. It's also been slammed by the World Wildlife Fund in relation to drilling in **Alaska**, and even named as an offender in the UK in the government's *Spotlight on Business and Environment Performance 2002*. Shell, meanwhile, has been widely accused of failing to deal with problems faced by local people near its facilities worldwide (for example, in Friends of the Earth's *Other Shell Report 2002*). Furthermore, while Shell and BP have been better than Exxon in admitting the role that oil plays in climate change, they're both members, along with practically every oil company selling in the UK, of industry groups which lobby against the Kyoto treaty.

Clearly, then, there is still an enormous gap between the rhetoric and reality of these companies. If you're not convinced compare the the rhetoric at BP's own website with the press articles catalogued at the BP Without the PR site:

BP www.bp.com
BP Without the PR www.bpamoco.org.uk

But despite the high-budget greenwashing, there are signs of some improvement. Both companies have started to be more transparent in their payments to third-world governments (though BP is accused of secrecy in its Baku project). Alongside all the criticism, both have both gained occasional and previously unimaginable praise from groups ranging from Human Rights Watch to Greenpeace. They have drawn up codes of conduct relating to human rights and the environment, which, even if they are not always put into practice, at the very least makes them much easier targets when they misbehave. BP has also pledged to end donations to any "political activity or party" (it previously gave millions to US presidential candidates), reduced its operational greenhouse-gas emissions to pre-1990 levels (something which many thought would be impossible), and expanded its solar power business (still a tiny part of the company, but a big boost to solar power's credibility nonetheless).

Due to all this, there may be a case for favouring BP and Shell while being aware that they're still a bunch of bastards, so to speak. After all, other than Esso, most of the other companies – such as **Total** (on the "dirty list" at www.burmacampaign.org.uk), **Q8** (owned by the oppressive government of Kuwait) and **Texaco** – are just as bad, but not as good.

SHOPPING FOR CARS

Buying a credible car is a complex business. For one thing, you have to balance up the social and environmental record of the company you're supporting with the environmental performance of the specific model. Then there's the fact that many smaller car firms are completely or partly owned by bigger corporations such as **Ford** (Aston Martin, Jaguar, Land Rover, Mazda and Volvo), **General Motors** (Saab and Vauxhall), **DaimlerChrysler** (Jeep, Mercedes and Smart) and **Volkswagen** (Audi, Seat and Skoda).

Added to this is the fact that any single car is likely to be the result of many different factories in as many different countries – seat covers from Indonesia, say, body panels from Italy and wheel nuts from Mexico.

BIODIESEL AND VEG OIL – SERIOUS ALTERNATIVES?

The term **diesel**, by definition, simply means a fuel for powering a diesel engine. Today it generally refers to a type of petroleum, but when Rudolph Diesel invented his super-efficient combustion engine at the end of the nineteenth century, he envisaged the fuel of the future coming from plants; he famously ran his prototypes on peanut oil. Today, with climate-change kicking in, so-called **biodiesel** – essentially vegetable oil treated with ethanol – is making a comeback, contributing power to everything from US bus fleets to the Indian railway.

Though biodiesel churns out plenty of CO_2, just like normal oil, most of this will be soaked up from the atmosphere by the plants grown to produce the next bath of fuel, and so on. This elegant cycle isn't entirely "carbon neutral", since energy (usually from fossil fuels) goes into preparing and moving the stuff, but it does reduce greenhouse emissions by around half compared with standard diesel. And it also cuts down on various other exhaust-pipe particulates and **poisonous gases**. It's not really a big-scale, long-term substitute for oil, since it will encourage more mono-crop industrial farming and eventually compete with food production for land: even if half of Britain's farms produced nothing but crops for biodiesel fuel conversion, they probably wouldn't be able to provide enough fuel to match the UK's current car use. That said, most of what's currently available in the UK is recycled from oils used in chip-shops, schools and food factories, so this doesn't require any new growing.

Biodiesel can be used in many recent diesel cars without any modification and, when purchased from a legitimate vendor, of which there are hundreds around the country, it's completely legal. Indeed, in 2002 the government finally starting encouraging its use with a 20p-per-litre **tax reduction**, meaning it's now usually cheaper to buy than its "mineral" equivalent (though still far more expensive than in much of Europe, where it's completely tax-free). It's usually available either neat or in a mix with 95% normal diesel, which is obviously nowhere near as good from a carbon perspective but still reduces certain harmful emissions (and makes an engine run more efficiently). Before filling up, check with the manufacturer of your car whether they approve the use of neat or mixed biodiesel, otherwise you could invalidate your engine warranty. And only buy fuel that conforms to government standards EN14214/EN590. For a list of filling stations that meet these criteria, try:

Powershift www.powershift.org.uk ▷ 0845 602 1425

More stations can be found at www.biodieselfillingstations.co.uk

So that's biodiesel. But what about all those stories in the press about people filling up with plain old **vegetable oil** in supermarket car parks (such as Welshman Daniel Blackburn, who made the headlines in 2003 by using veg oil to motor all the way from John O'Groats to Land's End)? Well, it's true that, after a conversion that will cost between £500 and £1000, many diesel engines will run perfectly well on standard cooking oil. And the result may be even greener than biodiesel, since veg oil requires less energy-intensive processing. As long as you do the courtesy of declaring and paying the relevant

© Daniel Blackburn

Yum yum. Daniel Blackburn just couldn't get enough of that eco-friendly veg oil on his way from John O'Groats to Land's End

tax to Her Majesty's Customs and Excise, it's perfectly legal, too. At the time of writing, you can expect to pay around 70p per litre – including 25p in tax – making it cheaper than normal petrol and diesel. Still, be aware that many car manufacturers claim it can be bad for the engine. For more information about using cooking oil to save the planet from frying, including conversion quotes and a list of which cars are suitable, see Daniel Blackburn's site:

Veg Oil Motoring www.vegoilmotoring.com

Car companies

Of the various car manufacturers, the three US giants **Ford**, **GM** and **DaimlerChrysler** – the first two of which are among the biggest five corporations in the world – have arguably the worst ethical records. For one thing, they're big political donors: all three ranked among George Bush's top benefactors in 2000. And they have a pretty appalling record on climate change, not just in terms of promoting gas-guzzling sports utility vehicles (SUVs), but also through seeking to undermine the scientific evidence on human-induced global warming. For example, the detractors point to underhand tactics such as their funding of the **Coalition for Vehicle Choice**, a significant anti-Kyoto pressure group in the 1990s, which took out ads in the US national press. It claimed it represented the American people and that it was financed by "public support", but allegedly more than 95% of this support actually came from Ford, GM or DaimlerChrysler.

Though none are squeaky clean, the European and East Asian firms have typically courted less controversy. Two exceptions are **Suzuki** and **Daewoo**, both accused at the time of writing of being involved in projects with direct financial links to the Burmese military government. It is beyond the scope of this book to do a full comparison of every brand available in the UK, but the most recent in-depth report in *Ethical Consumer* put **Peugeot**, **Citroen**, **Rover**, **MG** and the various **VW** companies at the top of their list (see p.362 for subscription and back-issue details for the magazine).

How to buy a greener car

Cars are getting better environmentally, and **fuel efficiency, CO₂ output** and other environmental factors are now usually very easy to come by – in car showrooms, online and in magazines. One question is whether to go for a petrol or diesel engine. **Diesel engines** are much worse in terms of poisonous emissions – so perhaps not the most ethical choice for city use – but they're more fuel-efficient and hence better in terms of global warming. Likewise, diesels leave you the option of using **biodiesel** (see p.322), but petrol engines are cheaper and easier to convert to **LPG** (see p.327).

Another question is whether to opt for a fuel-efficient, low-emission "normal" car or for one of the various "alternative" fuels or engine types. The latter are generally more expensive to buy but they're more environmentally friendly and cheaper to run (due to their efficiency and the low tax on their fuels). Also, the government will usually pay a percentage of the cost of buying a new "green" car or converting a used car to a greener fuel. For details on the grants available, try:

Powershift www.powershift.org.uk ▷ 0845 602 1425

Besides **biodiesel** and **vegetable oil** (discussed on pp.322–323), the main alternative fuels and engine types include the following.

Electric cars

Recharged via a standard **mains socket**, electric cars are the greenest option available. Like most battery-powered devices, they have literally no emissions, and, if charged up with electricity from renewable sources (see p.274), their use creates practically no carbon dioxide. Even if charged up with "standard electricity", they're still much more eco-friendly than petrol cars, due to their high levels of energy efficiency. The only problems are that most electric cars don't go very fast, that they need to be recharged after a certain number of miles (usually between 30 and 100, depending on the model), and that you need a parking space near a plug socket.

A truly carbon-neutral vehicle? G-wiz!

At the time of writing, the only electric car widely available in the UK is the recently launched **G-Wiz**. Designed for two adults plus either two children *or* shopping, and capable of 40 mph, the G-Wiz will do roughly 40 miles before requiring a recharge (which takes a few hours). At the time of writing, they cost around £6000, but by the manufacturers' calculations you stand to save more than that every year in fuel, tax and congestion charges (as eco-friendly cars are exempt). You'll also save money on maintenance, since electric cars have very few moving parts. For more information, see:

G-Wiz www.goingreen.co.uk

There are also various electric cars that have more room, a longer range and a faster top speed, from SUVs to genuine racing cars (see www.acpropulsion.com). However, none of them are available in the UK at the time of writing. Still, the family-sized **Renault Kangoo Electric**, capable of around 70 mph, is already on sale in France, and likely to find its way to Britain soon. Other models to look out for are the **Th!nk** and **Gem**.

For for more information on electric cars, try:

Electric Vehicles UK www.evuk.co.uk

Electric hybrids

Electric "hybrid" cars, such as the **Honda Prius**, **Toyota Insight** and **Lexus Hybrid Synergy Drive**, look and drive just like normal cars, yet their semi-electric engines are around twice as efficient as their straight petrol equivalents. Unlike "proper" electric cars (see above), hybrids never need to be plugged in and charged up. Instead, the car charges its own battery when the brakes are applied (converting the car's kinetic energy into electrical energy) and also when the petrol-powered part of the engine is powering the car along at high speeds. The battery's energy is then automatically used when lower speeds are required. The result is that hybrid cars can achieve up to around 80 miles per gallon – and with exceptionally low levels of harmful emissions. The only problem is that they're currently quite expensive. If buying new, you can expect to pay around £3000 more than you would for an equivalent non-hybrid model.

The Honda Insight's hybrid petrol–electric engine makes it one of the greenest "normal" cars on the market

LPG

LPG (**Liquid Petroleum Gas**) is basically **propane**, as used in camping stoves and standalone gas heaters. A by-product of oil refining and natural gas extraction, it's a fossil fuel but it does have slightly lower greenhouse emissions than petrol and diesel and much lower poisonous-fume output. Most cars can be converted to run either solely on LPG or on both LPG and petrol; conversion costs a few thousand pounds, but you'll then get very cheap fuel and, in London, exemption from congestion changing.

Fuel cells

Instead of being "charged up", **fuel-cell cars** generate electrical energy on board, using a "**catalytic**" process – generally the combination of **hydrogen** and **oxygen**. The hydrogen can be made on the fly from petrol or methanol, or – more commonly – generated elsewhere using electricity and then stored on board in replaceable canisters.

Like other electric cars, fuel-cell vehicles help reduce air-borne pollution in towns and cities – water vapour is often the only emission. But, in terms of climate change, they're only as good as the fuels or electricity used to generate the hydrogen. So it's questionable whether the creation of a hydrogen infrastructure – production plants, distribution channels and re-filling stations – would be beneficial in terms of global warming without a concurrent growth in renewable energy.

CUTTING BACK ON CARS

If you want to help reduce the number of cars being produced, and the distance they're driven, but you don't want to rely solely on public transport, consider looking into **car sharing** and **car clubs**. This will not only be environmentally sound, but it will also make sense financially: it is said that if you factor in the time it takes to earn the money to buy, run, insure, tax and maintain your own vehicle, drivers achieve an average speed roughly equivalent to walking.

Car sharing – either for a regular commute or a one-off drive – is based on the very sensible rationale that one car carrying four people is four times less polluting, congesting and expensive than four cars carrying one person each. Although the UK has been much slower to grasp this fact than much of continental Europe, the movement is taking off, as a growing number of Brits realize that contributing to climate change (and its death toll) and wasting money are more frightening prospects than talking to strangers. The Internet has also helped, providing the ideal way for people to find and organize sharing. See:

Freewheelers www.freewheelers.co.uk
Liftshare www.liftshare.com
National Car Share www.nationalcarshare.co.uk

"Car clubs" or "car pools" are something else entirely. You don't actually own a car but have access to a communal one situated within 10 minutes' walk from your house. Beside a joining fee and/or small monthly fee charge, you only pay for the hours or mileage you use. Smart moves, for example, currently costs £12 per month plus £26 for each 24 hours' use of the car. See:

Car Plus www.carclubs.org.uk ▷ 0113 234 9299
Smart Moves www.smartmoves.co.uk ▷ 01484 483061

Trials using taxis and buses have already successfully demonstrated that the fuel cell can work well, however, and commercial models – such as the **Necar,** designed by DaimlerChrysler, Ford and Ballard – may be available within the next few years.

More info

For an compete environmental comparison of practically all the cars currently available, call the **Ethical Transport Association** (see overleaf) and order their *Car Buyer's Guide*, which comes out each year. You can also find some information online, though the most in-depth services, such as the US-based **GreenerCars**, are pay-to-view.

GreenerCars www.greenercars.com

For more on alternative fuels in general, the UK and US governments both have informative sites:

PowerShift www.powershift.org.uk
US Department of Energy www.afdc.doe.gov

BREAKDOWN ORGANIZATIONS

You might use a car but still have some issues with the wider automobile world. For instance, you might be dead against expansion of the road network, for environmental reasons. Or you might feel that, in general, public transport should be prioritized over the needs of drivers. If so, then you should seriously consider which company you use for roadside rescue. The **AA** (part of energy group Centrica) and the **RAC** (part of the RAC Group, which also includes Hyundai cars and a giant vehicle leasing firm) may not be the most disagreeable companies in the world, but they do have a long history of lobbying for road expansion and the prioritization of cars over public transport, through groups like the **British Road Federation**. So you might prefer to check out the ETA:

Environmental Transport Association

www.eta.co.uk ▷ 0800 212 810

Set up specifically as an environmentally sound alternative to the big road-side rescue companies, the ETA offers a similar service at a similar cost. It boasts a 35-minute average callout time, 80% success rate in fixing cars by the roadside, and very high customer satisfaction. While it's not anti-car as such, it "conducts and commissions research into environmental transport issues and lobbies the government to encourage its support of alternatives to the car". It even organizes Green Transport Week and National Car Free Day, and also offers roadside rescue for cyclists.

AIR TRAVEL
How bad is it?

An ethical flight is, so to speak, something of a castle in the air. Apart from the little-discussed fact that most passenger aircrafts are produced by arms manufacturers (see box opposite), there's the obvious issue of their environmental impact. An accurate comparison would have to consider individual vehicle types and occupancy levels but, on average, planes – per person, per mile – generate about 25% more CO_2 (the main cause of global warming) than cars. So when you take a return flight from London to California, you're generating the same amount of carbon dioxide as driving 12,000 miles. That's more than the average UK motorist manages in a year.

Furthermore, the real impact on global warming is actually worse – around three times worse – than such comparisons would suggest, since aircraft emit not only CO_2 but also **water vapour** and **oxides of nitrogen and sulphur**. In the upper troposphere and lower stratosphere where planes fly, these gases compound the greenhouse effect (and also damage the ozone layer).

Despite the relatively tiny number of commercial aircraft in existence, they already account for 3–4% of the total human impact on the

BOEING, BOEING ... BOMB!

A growing number of consumers are opting for ethical banks, very often specifically because they want to be sure that their savings aren't invested in arms companies. But, for anyone who travels by air, it's not so easy to completely separate your wallet from the budget sheets of "defence" firms. Next time you fly, instead of ignoring the plane's information and safety sheet, have a look to see who produced your airborne home for the next few hours. With very few exceptions, it will either be **Boeing** or **Airbus**.

Boeing is one of the world's largest arms companies, whose annual turnover of around $50 billion is in no small part generated from selling military equipment to all kinds of governments, including those with very poor human rights records. According to a recent report in the US investigative magazine *Mother Jones* (www.motherjones.com), recent Boeing sales include warplanes to Indonesia, Israel, Kuwait and Saudi Arabia; attack helicopters to Egypt; and missiles to Turkey.

Boeing is even "unethical" according to the low moral codes of the arms industry: in late 2003, its chairman, Phil Condit, resigned after, as the Associated Press put it, "months of ethical controversies over the aggressive methods it used to obtain lucrative defense contracts". And it's also a major political donor in the US. According to figures from Open Secrets (www.opensecrets.org), it guaranteed itself a sympathetic president in 2000 by giving nearly a million dollars to both the main parties.

Airbus, meanwhile, is owned by British Aerospace and other major European arms manufacturers. All in all, the tie between commercial aircraft and military equipment is so entrenched that – as Noam Chomsky has written – many passenger planes are actually modified bombers. There's not much that consumers can do about this link, but if you feel particularly strongly about the arms industry it may tip the balance and make you decide to choose another form of transport whenever possible.

climate, according to the Intergovernmental Panel on Climate Change. That's around the same as the whole of Africa. And this number is set to rise year on year, for while planes are gradually becoming slightly more fuel-efficient, the gain is more than offset by the ever-growing

It's now just how far they fly – it's how high they fly. At the altitude reached by a modern passenger plane, the effect on climate change is three times worse than the CO_2 output would suggest.

number of flights. The number of air passengers flying into and from the UK is expected to nearly treble by 2030 – to around 500 million. Future **supersonic aircraft**, which could fly even higher, could also further worsen the environmental impact of air travel.

Fuel-cell and other less harmful planes will probably emerge eventually. But they won't replace current fleets any time soon, since passenger planes stay in use for decades. Until they do, the only real possibility for reducing air travel's impact is simply to reduce passenger numbers by making the price of a ticket reflect the true environmental costs. A good start would be to make airlines pay tax on their **aviation fuel**, which is currently duty-free. If the fuel was taxed at the same rate as petrol, a long-haul flight would cost each passenger around £500 more.

As for what individuals can do, there are really only two choices: reduce the amount you travel by air, or make your journeys "carbon neutral" via an **offset scheme** (see below). If you do choose to fly, you may also want to consider which airline you choose. Apart from the fact that they all, inevitably, lobby for fewer rather than more restrictions on air travel, none really stand out as particularly malevolent or benevolent companies, though some of the big US firms – including **American Airlines** and **United Airlines** (UAL Corp) – are bigger political donors than the rest, according to www.opensecrets.org. And **Japan** and **Austrian Airlines** are on boycott lists at the time of writing for continuing to operate in Burma (see p.339).

Finally, you might want to consider buying flights via **North South Travel** (see p.345), who will donate the profits to charitable projects in Africa, Asia and Latin America.

Carbon offset schemes

Anyone who wants to neutralize their effect on climate change will be interested in the various schemes that allow you to "offset" your carbon output. Whether you want to cancel out a single long-haul flight, a year of car journeys or your entire existence (in carbon-use terms), you can use a "carbon calculator" to work out the global-warming contribution and then contribute an appropriate amount of money to fund offsetting measures, such as the planting of trees to soak up CO_2. Flying usually clocks in at around **one tree every thousand miles**.

These schemes have proved popular, not least with celebrities: Pink Floyd, Pulp, The Pet Shop Boys, Coldplay and Atomic Kitten all put on "carbon-neutral" tours. But the schemes have also been slightly contentious. The most pressing issue is whether or not "carbon sink" forests – planted and managed specifically to absorb carbon dioxide

actually work as well as they're said to. The new-planted trees certainly soak up CO_2 but critics claim they release much of it when they eventually die. In a few extreme cases, "sinks" have even been accused of harming food security in poor countries, by taking up fertile land which could have been used to produce crops.

Such complaints are slightly unfair. The offset-scheme companies often have respected conservation groups on their boards – such as the World Wildlife Fund in the case of Climate Care. Furthermore, if you don't trust carbon sinks, you can choose instead to offset your carbon contribution with a less-controversial carbon-zapping project. These include initiatives to reduce the future demand for fossil fuels, such as distributing low-energy long-life light bulbs in developing countries.

In the UK, the more popular carbon offset schemes are:

Climate Care www.climatecare.org ▷ 01932 828 882
Future Forests www.futureforests.com ▷ 0870 241 1932

TRAVEL & TOURISM
Happy holidays

Regularly described as the **world's biggest employer**, even the world's biggest industry, the tourism sector provides more than 200 million jobs and accounts for more than 10% of global GDP. And, despite a brief downturn after the September 11 terrorist attacks in 2001, the industry just keeps on growing. According to the World Travel and Tourism Council, the number of international trips made each year now exceeds 700 million; by 2010 that's expected to be a billion; by 2020 a billion and a half. The range of popular destinations also continues to broaden, with journeys to **developing countries** – from Bhutan to Botswana to Bolivia – accounting for an increasing chunk of the total. However, while the growth of the travel industry and its economic importance are not in dispute, its overall costs and benefits are hotly contested.

Tourism has the potential to be good for all parties. Tourists get to enjoy themselves and/or increase their knowledge of the world and its people. And the residents of host countries get jobs and money. This can be especially important in the developing countries, where tourists are often the main source of foreign currency – or even, in cases such as the Maldives, the majority of national income.

The very poorest countries sometimes stand to benefit the most. A 2001 report from the United Nations Conference on Trade and Development pointed out that "International tourism is one of the few economic sectors through which LDCs [Least Developed Countries] have managed to increase their participation in the global economy. It can be an engine of employment creation, poverty eradication, ensuring gender equality, and protection of the natural and cultural heritage."

Few, however, would claim this ideal exchange of benefits is an accurate characterization of the whole of the modern tourism industry. Tourists, holiday-makers, travellers and trekkers can all unwittingly have damaging social and environmental effects.

Most obviously, while tourism may have the potential to facilitate mutual understanding, in many cases the visitors are unwelcome, imposing or simply **in the way** – unaware of local customs and manners, unable to speak the language and taking up in-demand places on public transport. In poor countries, furthermore, tourists can create resentment by flaunting a degree of leisure time and wealth completely out of reach for most of their hosts.

But more serious still are the issues discussed below: the control of land and resources, environmental damage and the possibility that tourists may be propping up oppressive governments. To make things more complicated, all these problems tend to be more acute in precisely the poor regions which have the most to benefit from tourist money.

Land and water

From the Peru to the Philippines, there have been many cases of marginalized people being forced – legally, physically or practically – off their **land** to make way for tourist development. Sometimes this has happened to make way for modern beach complexes and other resort-style developments. Tourism Concern, which campaigns for a more ethical travel sector, have reported many such incidents including, a few years ago, that of "a British-controlled company, which was planning a £2.8 billion tourist enclave on the Nungwi peninsular of Zanzibar". Apparently, "the development was to be the biggest in East Africa, with luxury hotels, golf courses and an airport. Shockingly, the plan failed to mention the peninsula's 20,000 residents. Local people hadn't had a say…"

But, arguably, this kind of flagrant disregard for the rights of local people has been an even bigger problem in the areas popular with **"nature" travellers**, since areas set aside for conservation and wildlife purposes have often been linked to the displacement of indigenous groups. The famous conservationist Bernhard Grzimek once commented that a national park will be effective only if "no men, not even native ones, should live inside its borders", and such views have been responsible for the eviction or even murder of indigenous groups in parks ranging from the California's Yosemite and Tanzania's Serengeti to, more recently, Botswana's Kalahari and Tanzania's Mkomazi. Critics of nature travel claim that common tourist expectations – that locals should live a visually exciting "tribal" existence or not be there at all – are a major factor in initiating or maintaining such human clearances.

Just as serious is the appropriation of resources such as water, which is scarce in many of the hot destinations beloved by Western tourists. A single inefficient hotel – especially one with a swimming pool – can require more water than a whole town. And **golf courses** can require up to a million litres a day in some climates (as well as more agrochemicals than even the most intensive farmland). Yet they're now relatively common resort features in even the driest countries.

In poor countries, it's possible that the water demands of rich travllers can speed up the development of reliable water infrastructures that will benefit residents. But it's also possible that hotels can buy a monopoly over, or unsustainable access to, the water, emptying groundwater aquifers and causing serious long-term damage. In fact, this is also an issue in relatively wealthy countries. As *Ergo* magazine recently reported, Mallorca's water table has plunged 90 metres in just 20 years.

Environmental damage

Travel can provide the perfect incentive for countries to look after their environments. If tourists are coming to see beautiful landscapes of wildlife, these very "features" become valuable assets worth protecting. And in countries where few other employment opportunities exist, the travel sector can simultaneously create jobs that offer an alternative to ecologically damaging work such as small-scale mining or tree-felling.

In many cases, however, short-term financial gain wins over long-term ecological protection. From coastal Spain to Goa, whole areas have had their biodiversity decimated by large-scale tourist development. Cruise ships dump sewage straight into the ocean (see www.stopcruisepollution.com). And in countries that lack decent waste disposal, tourist waste – from sun-lotion bottles and food wrappers to toilet paper – may end up in rivers that both people and wildlife depend on for their survival.

Even where tourism does encourage conservation – such as in game reserves – it needs to be carefully managed. If not, the tourists and their guides may cause harm to the very animals they have come to see. As Philip Seddon of New Zealand's University of Otago in Dunedin recently told *New Scientist*: "Transmission of disease to wildlife, or subtle changes to wildlife health through disturbance of daily routines or increased stress levels, while not apparent to a casual observer, may translate to lowered survival and breeding."

Who gets the money?

It goes without saying that real or potential problems described above have to be balanced both with the enjoyment of the tourists and the economic benefits gained by the people in the visited countries – both of which can be enormous. However, in many cases, the cash tourists spend exits the country as soon as it leaves their pockets, heading straight into the bank accounts of foreign travel firms.

With package holidays, this economic "leakage" is often as high as four-fifths of the total money spent during a holiday, or even more for **all-inclusive pay-up-front deals**, where tourists get to consume as much as they like as long as they stay in the hotel complex (and hence give their custom to no one else). In both these cases, the main economic beneficiaries are not the residents but a surprisingly small number of multinational companies. As with every other area of

The preservation of local culture or a patronizing "human zoo"? A Kikuyu dressed as a Masai selling trinkets to tourists on the east coast of Kenya.

THE BURMA TRAVEL BOYCOTT

The Asian state of Myanmar, still more widely known as Burma, has been living under a brutal military regime since the early 1960s. This junta has murdered and tortured tens of thousands of innocent people, imposed slave labour on countless children and adults, spent vast sums on arms while the population live in poverty, and imprisoned political opponents such as Nobel-laureate Aung San Suu Kyi, who won free elections in 1990 by a landslide, but was never allowed to take office. Despite all this, Burma – which, like neighbouring Thailand, is a place of remarkable ancient history and natural beauty – still has an active tourism industry. The human rights abuses are mostly hidden from travellers since the government has a direct financial interest in maintaining the flow of visitors: it owns most of the tourism infrastructure and obliges each person who enters to buy more than £100 of local currency, providing valuable foreign reserves.

Unsurprisingly, Aung San Suu Kyi and others have called on foreigners to stop visiting the country, and the British government has appealed to UK travel companies to remove Burma from their list of destinations. Some have refused and, accordingly, groups such as the Burma Campaign UK are encouraging us not just to boycott Burma itself but also these companies, along with all the others still on their "Dirty List". At the time of writing, travel-related firms listed include Japan and Austrian Airlines; tour operators such as Andrew Brock Travel, EastTravel, Explorers Tours, Mekong Travel and Visit Vietnam; and publishers Lonely Planet, Insight Guides, Frommer's and Let's Go (Pan Macmillan).

Some of these firms seem simply uninterested in the ethical implications of working in Burma, ignoring the political situation in their literature or even using it as a kind of selling point: "decades of social and economic isolation have preserved many traditional features which have been lost in other Asian countries" boasts the EastTravel website. Others acknowledge the issues but claim that tourism may help rather that worsen the problem. Lonely Planet, for example, haven't stopped publishing their Burma guide since it would mean "betraying the very principle upon which our company is based: namely that travel CAN make a difference". Burma campaigners describe this view as naïve, anti-democratic and irresponsible.

For more information, see:

Burma Campaign UK www.burmacampaign.org.uk

business, tourism has undergone massive "consolidation" in the last decade, with big firms snapping each other up across Europe. In the UK, just a handful of companies now account for nearly all the "air-inclusive" (package) holidays. These includes German giants such as **World of TUI** – whose fleet of businesses include Thomson Holidays, Lunn Poly, Travel House and Britannia Airways – and **Thomas Cook AG**, which owns, among other things, JMC, Thomas Cook Holidays and Club 18–30. Other big players are First Choice and My Travel Group.

The money spent by **independent travellers** is less likely to disappear overseas. In India, for example, where non-package travel is the most popular type, around half of total tourist spending is thought to stay in the country. Independent travellers can also choose to favour small businesses, from where money is more likely to trickle down through the local economy – and which also tend to pose smaller environmental burdens. However, there's no escaping the fact that the independent traveller is very often the harbinger of the foreign-owned resort. As tourism academic Brian Wheeller has written, "In the rush to escape the mass tourist [the] individual traveller is forever seeking the new, the exotic, the unspoilt – the vulnerable. Inevitably, however, they are inexorably paving the way … The sensitive traveller is the perpetrator of the global spread, the vanguard of the package tour".

Perhaps more of a concern than money not benefiting the country in which we spend it is the possibility that it may stay in the country and line the pockets of an oppressive, corrupt or otherwise harmful government. After all, governments nearly always benefit financially from tourism. And an oppressive administration can impose tourist development on a population for its own advantage. The most obvious and extreme example of this is Burma, where the military regime has been partly funded by tourism (see p.339).

But while Burma is an unusually clear case, with a boycott call coming from recognized elected leaders within the country, many other countries are less so. Should we avoid travel to China on the grounds of its government's appalling human rights record and its occupation of Tibet (where, incidentally, it is endeavouring to replace Tibetan tourist guides with Chinese ones, in order to keep visitors from getting too many answers about the regime)? What about **Russia** for its activities in Chechnya, or **Indonesia** for its actions in Papua?

Browse recent news reports by country at Amnesty International (www.amnesty.org/library) and you might wonder exactly how many countries you *can* visit with a clear conscience. Human rights abuses abound in many favourite destinations, from **Cuba** ("hasty and unfair trials" of dissident leaders) to the **Maldives** ("systematic repression of peaceful political activists").

Whether visiting countries with oppressive governments will exacerbate or lessen human rights abuses is debatable. If a government is keen to promote tourism, it may be less likely to commit day-to-day abuses with foreigners around, or it may be sensitive to complaints from tourists who have witnessed any mistreatment. Foreign visitors may also provide income for people who otherwise would be at the financial mercy of the state, and they may also raise awareness of issues back at home. According to George Monbiot, travelling can even be a disincentive to war: "the people of powerful nations might be reluctant to permit their leaders to destroy the countries they have visited".

As with choosing whether to buy or boycott products from specific foreign countries – discussed on p.27 – there are no easy thumbs-up or thumbs-down lists of where and how it's "ethical" to travel. You have to do your own research and make your own rules. You might, for example, decide to avoid big travel companies when travelling in countries whose governments you consider to be problematic, since the bigger firms are more likely to have links to those in power. Or you might decide only to travel to countries with participatory democracies since, with any other system, the people you're imposing yourself upon might not have had the opportunity to vote for a government that will reduce tourism development.

THE MIXED BLESSINGS OF ECOTOURISM

The most widely known area of travel to claim to have a socially responsible edge is "ecotourism", which in the last decade or so has grown from a niche market into a major sector, embraced both by tourism industry bodies and the UN, who named 2002 the International Year of Ecotourism, complete with a World Ecotourism Summit in Quebec. But what exactly *is* ecotourism?

According to the International Ecotourism Society, the term refers to "responsible travel to natural areas that conserves the environment and sustains the well-being of local people". Or, as the World Conservation Union put it, ecotourism describes "environmentally responsible travel ... to relatively undisturbed natural areas ... that promotes conservation, has low negative visitor impact [and] provides for beneficially active socioeconomic involvement of local populations".

Advocates of ecotourism claim that the sector has contributed a great deal both to conservation and economic empowerment of people in remote regions. However, the term has been tarnished by criticism from a range of commentators.

One issue is that ecotourism has no legally binding definition, which means there's nothing to stop an unscrupulous travel agent from slapping the label on any nature-focused holiday, regardless of the damage it may cause. As EcoTravel.com puts it: "an 'eco-lodge' may dump untreated sewage in a river, and still call itself 'eco' simply because it is located in a natural setting." This in itself isn't a reason to avoid travel companies selling "ecotourism" trips, but it is a reason to quiz them carefully on their ethical standards.

However, the vagueness of the term isn't the only problem that critics of ecotourism raise. In all tourism sectors, what starts as a trickle of travellers can often end up as an influx – there's a risk that adventurous ecotourists will inevitably be opening up the world's most fragile environments to unsustainable tourism. According to a recent report by Conservation International and the environmental wing of the UN, in the 1990s alone, leisure travel to the world's "biodiversity hotspots" (those areas with richly diverse but delicate ecologies) more than doubled, with rises of more than 300% in Brazil, Nicaragua and El Salvador, 500% in South Africa and 2000% in Laos and Cambodia.

Some NGOs, such as Malaysia's Third World Network and Thailand's Tourism Information Monitoring, have gone so far as to say that ecotourism's viability is "another myth that needs to be exploded", and that it "will destroy more biodiversity and harm even more local communities". They raise wide-ranging issues such as the low pay of tourism workers and the patronizing phenomenon of "tribe tourism", in which people are encouraged by tour firms to act out a way of life for the cameras that is often long-gone in reality. They even worry about bio-piracy: the patenting of traditional natural remedies by multinational drugs companies. "What does it mean", they ask, "when Thailand's National Centre for Genetic Engineering and Biotechnology, which is collaborating with giant biotechnology firms such as Monsanto, gives financial support to eco-tourism research projects", such as a university research project entitled "The Exploration of the Different Species of the Birds in Mae Hong Son province and the Promotion of Eco-tourism"? Surely legal protections should be in place, they argue, before we "indiscriminately promote tourism forms that facilitate the stealing and smuggling of local biological resources and traditional knowledge".

Hard-line greens also point out that there's something slightly ironic about flying halfway around the world to look at sensitive environments. And there is an obvious logic to this. For instance, a recent report by the University of Queensland's Centre for Marine Studies suggested that Australia's Great Barrier Reef will lose 95% of its living coral by 2050 – the cause is global warming, driven by carbon-intensive activities such as, say, flying from London to Sydney. And that's not to mention the fact – discussed on p.337 – that some conservation beloved by ecotourism firms may be the result of land appropriation, or may harm the very animals they're designed to protect.

Some of these accusations are a bit unfair. But what is clear is that the term "ecotourism" does not in itself guarantee any particular ethical standards. The tips for finding an ethical travel operator detailed overleaf apply to this sector of tourism just like every other.

For more on ecotourism, see:

The International Ecotourism Society www.ecotourism.org

"ETHICAL TOURISM"

The issues raised above – and the global-warming impact of our flights – shouldn't necessarily make us stay at home. After all, a recent ILO report states that, in the post-9/11 tourism downturn, around 6.5 million jobs are likely to have been lost, mostly in poor countries. But such issues should feature in our decisions of where to go, what we do when we get there and, in the case of non-independent travel, what kind of tourism companies we support.

Certain volunteering projects aside, there's no point in deluding ourselves that we're saving the world by going on holiday; but if tourists and travel companies act and operate with an eye on social justice and environmental sustainability, there's no reason the destination countries can't reap more of the benefits and bear fewer of the costs. This is the rationale behind the various "ethical", "responsible" and – more recently – "fair-trade" initiatives which are growing in the travel industry. You can now even do an MSc in "Responsible Tourism Management" (find out more at this magnificently long Web address: www.theinternationalcentreforresponsibletourism.org).

Self-declared ethical travel took off primarily with **ecotourism** – a loose term for nature travel with a responsible edge (see p.342). But all areas of the travel sector are increasingly being asked to consider their social and environmental impact. This has been in part due to pressure from groups such as **Tourism Concern** (www.tourismconcern.org.uk), though a number of surveys suggest that it also reflects the fact that the travelling public are concerned, though certainly not preoccupied, with the problems.

Research by anti-poverty group Tearfund, for example, found that more than half of holidaymakers would prefer to book a holiday with a company that has a written code covering working conditions, the environment and the support of local charities. But only when people start asking these kinds of questions in travel agents will pressure for a truly ethical tourism industry be felt.

Finding an ethical holiday

As in any sector, a travel company genuinely committed to acting ethically is very likely to tell you about it. If the promotional literature or website doesn't touch on things discussed above, you can have a pretty good bet that they haven't been considered at a very high level. However, that doesn't mean that every company claiming ethical credentials is for real, so read their claims carefully and ask questions.

Here are a few pointers of where you can go to find ethically minded travel companies, and some of the various award schemes and initiatives that you may come across when shopping around for a trip.

Flights and travel companies

North South Travel

www.northsouthtravel.co.uk ▷ 01245 608 291

Like many other agents, North South travel offers discount airfares to destinations around the world. Uniquely, however, when you buy a flight from this company the profits are ploughed into a charity – the NST Development Trust – which contributes to "grassroots projects" in developing countries. These range from poverty relief and healthcare projects to recycling and shipping bicycles to poor countries. North South has been running since 1981.

ResponsibleTravel.com

www.responsibletravel.com

Backed by the Body Shop's Anita Roddick, ResponsibleTravel.com is a website selling trips and tours from around 200 separate travel firms, covering everything from European skiing and tropical beach holidays to Asian jungle treks. But, unlike other travel agents, it selects its partner firms not just in terms of their service but also by their moral credentials. In order to have its holidays sold on the site, a travel operator needs to fulfil a series of criteria relating to codes of conduct, use of local suppliers, the provision of advice on the social and political situations in each destination, and advice to staff and customers on reducing the negative impacts they make. This scrutiny can't be exhaustive, of course, but ResponsibleTravel.com turn away five companies for each one admitted, so they're clearly no slackers.

AITO

www.aito.co.uk ▷ 0870 751 8080

AITO – the Association of Independent Tour Operators – is the industry body for small, specialist travel agents. It has been an advocate of more ethical tourism for at least a decade and a half, and all members are required to sign up to its Responsible Tourism Guidelines. Recently it has also implemented its own Responsible Tourism Awards and developed a scheme in which members can qualify for two stars by carrying out an environmental review and establishing a comprehensive responsible tourism policy, and then three stars by "engaging in specific RT initiatives or projects". You can browse the members, or go straight to those with two and three stars, on their website; alternatively, call the above number for a brochure.

EcoTravel.com

www.ecotravel.com

This searchable directory lists "tour operators, lodges, private guides, non-profit organizations and ancillary travel services" with a progressive outlook. There's no "screening" as such, but each listing includes the company's response to an "EcoResponsibility Survey", which asks them to detail their policies, philosophy, and the way in which their practices preserve the environment and benefit the local community.

Fair Trade in Tourism South Africa

www.fairtourismsa.org.za ▷ 00 27 12 342 8307/8

The concept of "fair trade" tourism is a relatively new one, and there are no global standards to define exactly what it means. Still, this ground-breaking South African initiative could be the start of something much bigger. The idea is to ensure that "the people whose land, natural resources, labour, knowledge and culture are used for tourism activities, actually benefit from tourism". This is done by certifying travel establishments that fulfil criteria relating to six areas: democracy, respect, reliability, transparency, sustainability, and, most importantly, "fair share", which means that "all participants involved in a tourism activity should get their fair share of the income, in direct proportion to their contribution to the activity". The Sabi Sabi Game Reserve and the Stormsriver Adventures Co are among the seven establishments certified at the time of writing. You'll find links to each at the above website.

Responsible tourism awards

BA Tourism for Tomorrow

www.ba.com ▷ 0870 850 9850

British Airways have been running the Tourism for Tomorrow Awards, to "recognise and encourage sustainable tourism initiatives across the globe", since 1992. BA admit that they can't run a complete "health check" on the entrants – who include tour and hotel companies of any type and size – so the awards recognise "better" rather than "best" practice. Still, they've been welcomed by the likes of Tourism Concern. You can find information about past winners on the BA website.

World Legacy Awards

www.wlaward.org

This award scheme – which so far has only been run in 2002 and 2004 – is overseen by *National Geographic Traveler* magazine and Conservation International, with the aim of promoting "environmentally, culturally, and socially responsible tourism practices across a wider spectrum of the tourism industry". You can find details of, and links to, winners and finalists on their website. The 2004 top prizes went to AL Maha Desert Resort in Dubai, Gunung Rinjani region of Indonesia, Anangu Tours in Australia, and the Casuarina Beach Club in Barbados.

Green travel labels

EU Eco-label

www.eco-label-tourism.com

You may recognize the European Union's little flower logo from energy-efficient washing machines and the like (see box on p.283). Recently the scheme has been extended to take in tourism accommodation. Anyone "from a large hotel chain to a small farmhouse" can apply, and the flower is awarded to those who meet criteria such as the use of renewable energy sources and measures to reduce waste to less obvious things such as offering organic food and using low-emissions paints and cleaning chemicals. Since the scheme is very young, you're unlikely to come across many accredited hotels for at least a year or two.

The Green Globe 21

www.greenglobe21.com ▷ 020 7838 9400

The Green Globe 21 environmental certification standard (the number refers to the Agenda 21 Sustainable Development Principles from the 1992 Rio Earth Summit) was established by the World Travel and Tourism Council, a coalition largely made up of CEOs from major hotel chains, large travel companies and airlines. As such, while it's undoubtedly raising the profile of the environmental and social impact of tourism, it's sometimes been accused of having more to do with advertising and greenwash than achieving real results. But it's certainly worth knowing about their three-tier membership policy – an "ABC Pathway" referring to Affiliation, Benchmarking and finally Certification. Only level "C" companies that have been externally audited can use the logo with a tick on it; "A" and "B" companies, who have had no external assessment, can use the logo, just without the tick.

Confused?

The above mixture of issues, schemes, logos, claims and groups can make the world of ethical travel seem pretty impenetrable. For this reason, and to encourage global good standards, some groups have called for the establishment of a **Sustainable Tourism Stewardship Council** – much like the Forest Stewardship Council for wood (see p.296) or the Marine Stewardship Council for fish (see p.147). An extensive 2003 report by the Rainforest Alliance concluded that this was a realistic goal, and although the scheme is still in its conceptual stages, it may emerge in the next few years. For more information see: www.rainforestalliance.org

09

GENERAL FAIR-
TRADE SHOPS

The previous chapters have listed "ethical" suppliers focusing on a specific product area. But the UK also has a number of shops, online stores and catalogues that sell a wide range of fair-trade items. The non-food products they stock are of the uncertified fair-trade variety (see chapter two), but that's not to say everything is entirely based on trust. Stores and websites which are members of the **British Association for Fair Trade Shops** (BAFTS) must also fulfil a number of criteria in order to become members, including sourcing the majority of their goods from a directory of respected fair-trade importers.

A few BAFTS members only sell clothes or rugs, say, and as such are listed in the previous chapters. But most of the rest – which are listed

BAFTS: CRITERIA FOR FAIR-TRADE SHOPS

▷ Buying a majority of goods from importers who comply with the FINE criteria and are listed in the BAFTS' Importers' Directory

▷ Showing good reason for selling other goods, and explaining this on the membership application form.

▷ Buying from importers and selling to the public at fair prices, reflecting the value of the products

▷ Promoting and encouraging product quality either through the importers or directly to the producers

▷ Showing concern for social and environmental aspects of products, including child labour, tropical hardwood use and animal testing

▷ Paying invoices in credit time

▷ Ensuring equal opportunities for all shop staff, whether voluntary or paid, and actively opposing discrimination

▷ Showing openness to customers, by having information available on suppliers, BAFTS, aims and working practices

▷ Having an educational/campaigning aspect to the work in the shop

For more info, see: www.bafts.org.uk

in the following directory – sell a roughly consistent range of **gifts, cards, foods, jewellery, clothes, hand-made papers, ornaments, quilts, toys** and **musical instruments**. Many of these items tend towards slightly hippyish styles, and goods include all the clichés of ethical shopping such as rainbow textiles and even the dreaded rain-stick. But some shops, such as London's **Ganesha**, are *plus chic*.

All the shops and sites in the following list are members of BAFTS.

ONLINE & MAIL ORDER

See also the fair-trade listings in clothes (see p.214) and household (see p.308).

Concepts of Peru (online)
www.alpacaonline.co.uk
Peruvian crafts, including Alpaca knitwear, painted ceramics and a slightly scary real-fur teddy bear (made, of course, from "animals that have died from natural causes on the alti plano").

Fair's Fayre (mail order)
01264 771112
Standard fair-trade-shop range of foods, crafts, paper products, etc.

Ganesha (online)
www.ganesha.co.uk
Stylish homeware, gifts, clothing and crafts. The selection ranges from beautiful bambooware bowls to leaf-print cushions.

Paper High (online)
www.paperhigh.com
Classy hand-made paper products ranging from Indian leather-bound ledgers to the legedary Elephant Dung paper of Sri Lanka (strange but true).

Shared Earth (online & mail order)
www.sharedearth.co.uk
Hand-made cards, Balinese notebooks, wooden toys and more.

Siesta (online & mail order)
www.siestacrafts.co.uk
Wide range of ethnic musical instruments – from voodoo guitars to aura chimes – as well as "Buddhist items", masks, crafts and clothes.

Traidcraft (online and mail order)
www.traidcraft.co.uk ▷ 0191 491 0591
Wide range of handicrafts, cards household goods, clothes and more from the UK's leading fair-trade organization.

Tumi (online)
www.tumi.co.uk
Latin American jewellery, clothes, accessories, musical instruments and homeware (including some very colourful hammocks).

SHOPS BY REGION

SOUTH EAST & LONDON

Andover

Fair's Fayre
01264 771 112 ▷ Workshop 8,
Fairground Craft & Design Centre,
Weyhill

Canterbury

Siesta
www.siestacrafts.co.uk ▷ 01227 464
614 ▷ 1 Palace St

Isle of Wight

Traidcraft Shop
01983 752451 ▷ 119 School Green Rd,
Freshwater

London

Baglady
www.gurushop.co.uk ▷ 020 7223 6800
▷ 29 Webbs Road

Concepts of Peru
www.conceptsofperu.co.uk ▷ 020 8855
3282 ▷ 7 Genesta Road

Fair Enough
020 8688 9213 ▷ 136 Church Street,
Croydon

FAIR-TRADE EVENTS

As well as permanent fair-trade shops, you may come across the
occasional fair-trade event. For example, London has for years had a
Fair Trade Fair each December, with scores of stalls offering fairly
traded Xmas gifts. The screening of suppliers is mainly based on trust,
but you're still likely to get a more ethical Xmas sack (and have a less
hellish experience) than you would if shopping
on the high street. For more information about
the main London fair, see:

Fair Trade Fair www.fairtradefair.org

Or to find a fair-trade Xmas event in your
own area, try:

Fairtrade Fair www.fairtradefair.com

Ganesha
www.ganesha.co.uk ▷ 020 7928 3444 ▷
3 Gabriel's Wharf, 56 Upper Ground

One World Shop
020 7401 8909 ▷ St John's Church,
Waterloo Road

Oxford

Tumi
www.tumicrafts.com ▷ 1–2 Little
Clarendon St

Reading

The World Shop
www.risc.org.uk ▷ 0118 958 6692 ▷
RISC, 35–39 London St

Woodstock

One Village
www.onevillage.co.uk ▷ 0845 458
47020 ▷ On the A44

EAST ANGLIA

Colchester

Traders Fair World Shop
01206 763 380 ▷ Portal Precinct, Sir
Isaac's Walk

Ipswich

The Fair Trade Shop
01473 288 225 ▷ 15 Orwell Place

Norwich

The World Shop
www.nead.org.uk ▷ 01603 610 993 ▷
NEAD, 38 Exchange St

St Ives

Just Sharing
www.stivesfreechurch.org ▷ 01480 496
570 ▷ The Free Church, Market Hill

SOUTH WEST

Bath

Tumi
www.tumicrafts.co.uk ▷ 01225 446 025
▷ 8–9 New Bond St Place

Nailsworth, Stroud

Fair Oasis
01453 833 002 ▷ 9 Fountain Street,
Nailsworth

Just Traiding
01453 833 002 ▷ 7 Fountain St

Wimborne

Third World Crafts
01202 849 898 ▷ 8 Crown Mead, Wimborne

MIDLANDS

Birmingham

Shared Earth
www.sharedearth.co.uk ▷ 0121 633 0151 ▷ 87 New St

Leicester

Just
www.justfairtrade.com ▷ 0116 255 9123 ▷ 10 Bishop Street, Town Hall Square

Rugby

World of Difference
01788 579 191 ▷ 20 High St

Wirksworth

Traid Links
www.traid-links.co.uk ▷ 01629 824 393 ▷ 20 Market Place

NORTH WEST

Bolton

Justicia
01204 363 308 ▷ 81 Knowsley St

Carlisle

Carlisle World Shop
01228 550 385 ▷ 1 Lowthian's Lane, English Street

Chester

Chester Fair Trading
01829 770 847 ▷ Wesley Methodist Church, St John's Street

Liverpool

Liverpool World Shop
www.liverpoolworldshop.co.uk ▷ 0151 708 7328 ▷ 71 Bold St

Manchester

Shared Earth
www.sharedearth.co.uk ▷ 0161 236 1014 ▷ 51 Piccadilly

NORTH EAST

Alnwick

A World of Difference
www.aworldofdifference.co.uk ▷ 01665
606 005 ▷ 13 Narrowgate

Berwick Upon Tweed

The Green Shop
01289 305 566 ▷ 30 Bridge St

Blackburn

Fairground
01254 682 210 ▷ Wesley Hall
Methodist Church, Paradise Lane

Durham

Gateway World Shop
www.gatewayworldshop.co.uk ▷ 0191
384 7173 ▷ Market Place

Haworth

Sonia's Smile
www.soniassmile.com ▷ 01535 647
776 ▷ 85 Main Street

Hull

Hull One World Shop
www.oneworldhull.co.uk ▷ 01482 327

727 ▷ c/o Central Methodist Hall,
Waltham Street, King Edward St

Leeds

Shared Earth
www.sharedearth.co.uk ▷ 0113 242
6424 ▷ 86 The Merrion Centre

Sheffield

Traidcraft Shop
0114 272 6455 ▷ 142 Devonshire St

Stockton on Tees

North-South Trading
01740 630 475 ▷ Greystone, Carlton
(ring for directions)

York

Fairer World
01904 655116 ▷ 84 Gillygate

Shared Earth
www.sharedearth.co.uk ▷ 01904 632
896 ▷ 1 Minister Gates

Warrington

Fair 4 All
01925 415121 ▷ Stall 38–39, Retail
Market, Academy Way

WALES

Cardiff

Fair Do's/Siopa Teg
www.fairdos.com ▷ 029 2022 2066 ▷ 10 Llandaff Rd, Canton

Shared Earth
www.sharedearth.co.uk ▷ 029 2039 6900 ▷ 14–16 Royal Arcade

Conwy

Just Shopping
www.justshopping.co.uk ▷ 07720 894 023 ▷ 13 Bangor Rd

SCOTLAND

Aberdeen

Third World Centre
01224 645 650 ▷ St Mary's Chapel, Church of St Nicholas Uniting, Correction Wynd

Balmore

The Coach House
01360 620 742 ▷ Balmore, nr Torrance

Edinburgh

Hadeel
www.hadeel.org ▷ 0131 225 1922 ▷ 1 St George's West Church Centre, 58 Shandwick Place

One World Shop
www.oneworldshop.co.uk ▷ 0131 229 4541 ▷ St John's Church, Princes St

Fife

Fair Shares
07952 161 305 ▷ 128 High Street, Burntisland

Glasgow

One World Shop
www.oneworldshop.co.uk ▷ 0141 357 1567 ▷ 100 Byres Road

North Berwick

Earth Matters
www.earthmatters.co.uk ▷ 01620 895 401 ▷ 67 High Street

Paisley

Rainbow Turtle
0141 887 1881 ▷ 7 Gauze Street

PART III

FIND OUT MORE

HOW TO RESEARCH A COMPANY
MAGAZINES
BOOKS
WEBSITES

10

FIND OUT MORE

Throughout the text of this book, we've included Web addresses and phone numbers that will help you find out more about specific issues and products, from political donations to fairly traded rugs. But there are also scores of publications – on the Net and on paper – that will lead you to info that's either more general (such as news and views about ethical consumerism) or more specific (such as in-depth profiles of the behaviour of individual companies). What follows is a short selection of the best sites, magazines and books in both these categories, starting with resources for getting the low-down on whether a specific shop or brand is a member of the mean mainstream or the moral minority.

HOW TO RESEARCH A COMPANY

If you want to find out about the ethical standards of a particular company, there are a number of excellent online sources that might be able to tell you what you want to know. The following is a list of the best. Alternatively, for a detailed, though possibly slightly out-of-date comparison of the various companies within a specific sector, order the relevant back-issue of *Ethical Consumer* (see p.362) – their website includes an index specifying which products were covered in which issues.

Business & Human Rights Resource Centre

www.business-humanrights.org

A truly amazing resource, this website – run "in partnership with Amnesty International Business Groups and leading academic establishments" – is an index of practically everything on the Web that relates to the effect of companies upon human rights (including environmental damage). Updated hourly, it points to articles and stories published by newspapers, companies, NGOs and academics alike, and the clear, easy-to-navigate structure makes it simple to view all the links that relate to any one of 1600 individual companies (or to specific industries or issues). All in all, a fantastic free service.

Corporate Critic

www.ethicalconsumer.org/research/ecis.htm

"Corporate Critic" is the corporate ethics database maintained by ECRA – the research association behind *Ethical Consumer* magazine (see p.362). It contains thousands of references to good and bad corporate behaviour, categorised under environmental, animal and human rights headings. It's not really designed for individual users, but if you want to find out about a specific company, you could use the free trial (which lets you access ten "records"). After that, it's around £70 subscription, plus 75p per record, or £420 for a year's unlimited access. Alternatively, for £35, ECRA will write you a report about the ethics of an individual company.

IdealsWork

www.idealswork.com

"What companies do. What to do about it" is the strapline of this American site that rates companies up to five stars on everything from labour issues and nuclear energy to women's issues and addictive products. Simply choose a product category and your ethical criteria, and a set of comparative ratings will appear, including the option to send the companies a message (and, for US browsers, to buy products online).

ResponsibleShopper

www.responsibleshopper.com

Run by Co-op America, this site includes hundreds of companies along with a list of their brands and advice on what they've been "praised for" and "criticised for", along with links to the original sources. It's not comprehensive, and it has a US-focus, but it's still a very useful site.

For a more comprehensive guide to examining the dark underbelly of corporate behaviour, visit the **CorporateWatch** website and, with the Resources section, you'll find a few pages titled "DIY Guide: How to Research Companies". This gives tips on everything from finding out about corporate structure to digging the dirt on a firm's financial analysts and shareholders. The same site also provides profiles on a range of big companies. These tend towards the harshly, and occasionally fanatically, anti-corporate, but they're well researched and well written. For more tips and reports from across the Atlantic, see **CorpWatch** and **PR Watch**.

CorporateWatch www.corporatewatch.org.uk
CorpWatch www.corpwatch.org
PR Watch www.prwatch.org

MAGAZINES

Specialist ethical consumerism magazines

Ethical Consumer

www.ethicalconsumer.org ▷ 0161 226 2929 ▷
Published every two months ▷ £3.50
per issue or £19 annual subscription

Ethical Consumer describes itself
as the "the UK's leading alternative
consumer magazine". What it lacks
in the design department it makes
up for with serious research and content. Alongside features and regulars
such as Boycott Updates and Money
News (which keeps tabs on ethical
investment funds), each issue features a
number of in-depth "buyers' guides", which focus on particular product areas – anything from TVs to fruit juice. The various brands are
compared on a *Which*-style table, with columns for oppressive regimes, factory farming, political donations, and so on. Subscription is "risk free" – if
you don't like the first issue you're sent, simply cancel your order and your
money will be refunded.

Ergo

www.ergo-living.com ▷ 020 7405 5633 ▷ Published quarterly ▷ £6
per issue or £22 annual subscription (£20 via
direct debit)

Far and away the funkiest ethical
consumerism mag, *Ergo* is a well-
designed publication aimed at
readers who are sustainably minded
but also style-conscious. Each issue
has a few main features – some
based on specific products, some on
more lifestyle-related issues – as well
as regulars that include (in their words)

"new ideas, sustainable style … celebrity interviews, good food guides, readers' views and actions you can take right now for a better world". Ergo is part of the environmental group Global Action Plan, who also run www.greenscore.org.uk – a website that allows you to measure "how green you really are".

New Consumer

www.new-consumer.co.uk ▷ 0141 335 9050 ▷
Published every two months ▷ £2 per
issue or £10 annual subscription

Edited by *Big Issue* co-founder Mel Young, *New Consumer* is "Britain's only fair trade magazine". Published six times a year, it's as much a shopping catalogue as it is a magazine, with full-colour pages crammed with photos of the latest and greatest fairly traded clothes, gifts, toys, ornaments and more, along with prices and where-to-buy information – a better way to shop than browsing the often second-rate websites of fair-trade suppliers. Elsewhere there are features, news and light-hearted columns on gardening, finance, shopping and more.

Other magazines

A few other magazines relevant to the subjects discussed in this book, many of which publish online as well as in print…

Environmental issues
Ecologist www.theecologist.org
Green Futures www.greenfutures.org.uk
Resurgence www.resurgence.org

Sustainable living
Clean Slate www.cat.org.uk
Pure www.greenguideonline.com
The Green Parent
www.thegreenparent.co.uk

Politics & companies
Economist www.economist.com
Ethical Corporation
www.ethicalcorp.com
New Internationalist
www.newint.org
RedPepper www.redpepper.org.uk
Mother Jones www.motherjones.com
Multinational Monitor
www.multinationalmonitor.org

BOOKS

There isn't space here for a complete bibliography – and anyhow many of the subjects touched on in this book are better covered in magazines, journals and websites than in books. But here are a few particularly relevant recent titles, many of which have been referred to in the text.

Ethical consumerism

The Good Shopping Guide Ethical Marketing Group ▷ ISBN: 0-954-25291-8 (2004 ed) ▷ £12

Published annually since 2003, this colourful, user-friendly guide covers everything from batteries to breakfast cereal to banks. Each product area gets a discussion of the issues and then a table comparing the main brands, each of which are ranked in three categories: good, evil and those in-between. The research is provided by *Ethical Consumer* magazine (see p.362).

William Young & Richard Welford: Ethical Shopping Fusion Press, 2002 ▷ ISBN: 1-904-13208-1 ▷ £7.99

Ranks many high-street shops and brands according to the existence and quality of their codes of conduct. However, the research is now out of date, and the fact that the book grew out of an academic project shows both in the content and presentation.

Go M-A-D Think, 2001 ▷ ISBN: 0-954-136306 ▷ £3.99

Offers "365 Daily Ways to Save the Planet", mostly of the brick-in-your-toilet-cistern school.

Environmental issues

The Good Wood Guide FoE, 2002 ▷ ISBN 1857503422 ▷ £7.50

A complete guide to buying ethical wood, with a directory of timber types and background issues.

John McNeill: Something New Under the Sun Penguin, 2004 ▷ ISBN: 0-140-29509-7 ▷ £10.99

A scholarly yet readable "environmental history" of the last century.

Mayer Hillman: How We Can Save the Planet Penguin, 2004 ▷ ISBN: 0-141-01692-2 ▷ £7.99

A accessible assessment of climate change theory and proposed solutions, including individual action.

James Bruges: The Little Earth Book Alastair Sawday, 2004 ▷ ISBN: 1-901-97052-3 ▷ £6.99

Pithy, fact-filled mini-essays on everything from water to soil.

Globalization and trade

Naomi Klein: No Logo Flamingo, 2001 ▷ ISBN: 0-006-53040-0 ▷ £8.99

The book that put branding, world trade, globalization and sweatshops into the public eye.

Michael Woodin & Caroline Lucas: Green Alternatives to Globalisation Pluto, 2004 ▷ ISBN: 0-745-31932-7 ▷ £11.99

The most recent localization manifesto, co-authored by a Green MEP.

Philippe Legrain: Open World Abacus, 2002 ▷ ISBN: 0-349-11529-X ▷ £7.99

A readable defence of globalization, covering poverty, sweatshops, trade rules and brands, and big business.

Food

Bernadette Clarke: The Good Fish Guide Marine Conservation Society, 2002 ▷ ISBN: 0-948-15031-9 ▷ £10

A scarily comprehensive guide to eating water-borne species ethically. Get it from www.mcsuk.org

Colin Tudge: So Shall We Reap Penguin, 2004 ▷ ISBN 0-141-00950-0 ▷ £8.99

An intelligent plea for sustainable agriculture, including the potential limitations of organic farming.

Craig Sams: Little Food Book Alastair Sawday, 2003 ▷ ISBN: 1-901-97032-9 ▷ £6.99

Small but juicy look at our food, taking in subsidies, sugar, obesity, organics and more.

Joanna Blythman: Shopped Fourth Estate, 2004 ▷ ISBN: 0-007-15803-3 ▷ £12.99

Joanna Blythman: The Food We Eat Penguin, 1998 ▷ ISBN: 0-14027-366-2 ▷ £6.99

A gourmand takes a stand against supermarkets, factory farming and the UK's dying food culture.

Felicity Lawrence: Not On The Label Penguin, 2004 ▷ ISBN: 0-141-01566-7 ▷ £7.99

An investigative tour of the food industry, from gangmasters and pesticides to the coffee crisis.

Travel & Tourism

Mark Mann/Tourism Concern: The Good Alternative Travel Guide Earthscan, 2002 ▷ ISBN: 1-853-83837-3 ▷ £9.99

Greg Neale: The Green Travel Guide Earthscan, 1999 ▷ ISDN 1-853 83596-X ▷ £12.99

Both books discuss the issues and then list hundreds of "alternative", "eco" and "green" holidays.

Ethical Tourism: Who Benefits Hodder Arnold, 2002 ▷ ISBN: 0-340-85734-X ▷ £5.99

Four essays on the the pros and cons of "eco" and "responsible" travel

WEBSITES

Finally, a few miscellaneous websites that aren't covered elsewhere in this book. Also see the sites listed on pp.360–361.

Eco-Labels
www.eco-labels.org
A good site that examines ethical product labels and descriptions. Though aimed at US consumers, much of it's also relevant to the UK.

Ethical Junction
www.ethical-junction.org
An ethical consumerism portal pointing to useful websites and conscientious companies.

Ethical Shopping Online
www.thegoodshoppingguide.co.uk
By the time you read this, it should be possible to shop for products from ethically screened companies via the site of the folks at the *Good Shopping Guide* (see p.384). As well as all the obvious stuff, the site promises to point us to ethical wine, toys and electronics gear such as CD and DVD players, computers, video games and mobile phones.

Good Stuff?
www.worldwatch.org/pubs/goodstuff
Articles and links compiled by the Worldwatch Institute, looking at the human and environmental costs behind cellphones, CDs and scores of other everyday products.

Green Choices
www.greenchoices.org
Large archive of advice and links on ethical and eco-friendly living and shopping.

Green Directory
www.greendirectory.net
The online version of the annual book, this site lists everything green – from courses to shops.

OpenOffice
www.openoffice.org
A superb, completely free alternative to Microsoft Office Suite (Word, Excel, etc). It's compatible with pretty much everything and saves you giving your money to Microsoft, who are, among other things, major donors to George W Bush. If you're technologically literate, and want to avoid Microsoft altogether, buy a computer without Windows pre-installed and get hold of Linux, a highly powerful free alternative. See: www.linux.org

INDEX